Introduction to Race Relations

Introduction to Race Relations
Second Edition

Ellis Cashmore
and Barry Troyna

 The Falmer Press
(A member of the Taylor & Francis Group)
London • New York • Philadelphia

UK   The Falmer Press, Rankine Road, Basingstoke, Hants RG24 0PR

USA   The Falmer Press, Taylor & Francis Inc., 1900 Frost Road, Suite 101, Bristol, PA 19007

This edition first published 1990

British Library Cataloguing in Publication Data and Library of Congress Cataloging-in-Publication Data available on request

Jacket design by Caroline Archer

Typeset in 11/13 Bembo by
Chapterhouse, The Cloisters, Formby L37 3PX

Printed and bound in Great Britain by
Redwood Burn Limited, Trowbridge, Wiltshire.

Contents

1
Introduction to second edition

- Are race and nation inseparable?
- Why are ethnic minorities damned, whatever they do?
- What 'core values' are allegedly threatened by ethnic minorities?
- Is racism disappearing, or changing shape?

Nation of aliens

'Newcomers', or 'slags' as they are known in the racist argot of the Los Angeles Police Department, are extraterrestrials with human-looking bodies but bulbous piebald heads which make them instantly recognizable. Genetically engineered for hard labour, the newcomers descend on California in the early twenty-first century and are allowed to stay by an untypically generous immigration department. At first they make a useful contribution to the workforce, specializing in the manual work for which they were made. But, within a few decades, calumny arrives. Newcomers become equated with all that is frightening and unpleasant: they get drunk and aggressive after tippling sour milk; their females are prone to prostitution; the 'second generation' engage in habitual street crime.

Sounds familiar? It's meant to: British director Graham Baker's film *Alien Nation* (1989) was a cop thriller-cum-race relations fable. It's main message was: that no matter where you come from, what you look like or what you do, if the situation demands it, others will slap a 'them' label on you and make sure 'us' keep as much distance as possible. In the movie, black and white humans are united in their prejudices against the newcomers. They are part of the 'us' that despises the newcomers, a few of whom have sneaked into positions of authority, but the majority of whom either toil or roam the streets, their unusual appearance seeming to radiate menace to humans.

ETHNICITY
A number of people who perceive themselves to be in some way united because of their sharing either a common background, present position or future — or a combination of these. The ethnic group is subjectively defined in that it is what the group members themselves feel to be important in defining them as a united people that marks them off, and not what others consider them to be. There is frequently a coincidence between what others feel to be a racial group and what the members themselves think of themselves. For example, whites may think of Asians as a racial group; Asians may think of themselves as united and therefore an ethnic group.

A second message seemed to be that, when faced with a problem that affects both humans and newcomers alike, differences that were once deemed unalterably large disappear and common interests transcend everything. In the story, a highly addictive and debilitating drug that affects only newcomers is synthesized and marketed on the LA streets. Human and newcomer cops become 'buddies' in their efforts to crush the underground operation.

Many observers of relations between various ethnic groups in modern society would argue that the two themes are basically accurate. Put groups with physically recognizable or even inferred differences together and create conditions in which they all seek similar, limited resources (money, prestige, authority, etc.) and you raise conflict. But when a new threat strikes at all groups indiscriminately, differences that were once unmistakeably important become invisible and irrelevant.

A good idea in theory and in speculative fiction; but does it stand up to reality? This is one of the key questions that has been thrown up in the six years since the original publication of *Introduction to Race Relations*. Is the conflict we described and analyzed in a process of dissolution as different ethnic groups combine to resist greater threats than the ones they pose for each other? Or, are nerves still so raw that the conflict and tension sustained by racism persists?

The *Alien Nation* subtext gets some of it right: divisions between groups are arbitrary and changeable. A hundred years ago, white Protestants in the UK and the USA were calling Irish Catholics a 'race apart' and attributing all manner of evil to them. Charles Kingsley described them as 'white chimpanzees'; an American historian yearned: 'If only every Irishman would kill a negro, and be hanged for it' (quoted in McLaughlin, 1988, p. 154). As anti-catholicism subsided and the Irish ceased to be recognized in racist terms, their position came to be occupied by blacks, as whites saw a new rising threat. Locked in slave chains, 'negroes' were controllable; out of them, they were a possible problem. The *Plessy v Ferguson* case of 1896 established the principle of segregation of blacks and whites in the USA. It wasn't removed until 1954

BROWN v. BOARD OF EDUCATION, TOPEKA

Until 1954 many blacks in the USA believed that the struggle for equality rested largely on the issue of integrated schooling. In the 1950s, the National Association for the Advancement of Coloured People (NAACP) had vigorously pursued this theme. In Topeka, Kansas, the NAACP argued the case of Oliver Brown whose daughter had been forced to travel by bus to an all-black school even though she lived in close proximity to an all-white school. The NAACP insisted that school segregation was unconstitutional and on Monday, 17 May 1954 the case reached the US Supreme Court where Chief Justice Warren resided. What needed answering, according to Warren, was this: 'Does segregation of children in public schools solely on the basis of race, even though the physical facilities and other "tangible" factors may be equal, deprive the children of the minority group of equal educational opportunites?' His verdict? 'We believe that it does . . . in the field of public education the doctrine of "separate but equal" has no place.' According to Harvard Sitkoff, the decision meant that: 'Nothing in American race relations would be the same again.'

when *Brown v Board of Education, Topeka* declared such arrangements unconstitutional. The case set in motion a coruscating civil rights movement that in turn sparked reactionary violence from racist whites. In the UK, racist violence erupted in 1948, when white seamen in Liverpool rioted in protest at the rising number of 'coloured' workers on ships; and again in 1958 when Notting Hill, London, and Nottingham, in the East Midlands, were scenes of largescale attacks on blacks and their property.

While there are no exact parallels, there is a suggestive similarity between these events and affairs elsewhere in the modern world. Indians have felt the weight of racist attentions in Fiji; African students in China have been systematically attacked; Chinese themselves have been victimized in Malaysia. In Soviet Central Asia, Uzbecks have turned violently against the Turkish Meskhetian minority to trigger bloody rioting. In Sri Lanka, it has been the minority Tamils who have responded violently to their exclusion from positions of influence, drawing severe reactions from the majority Sinhalese. In all cases, a certain portion of a population have been identified as in some way troublesome by another portion. Give it time and it's possible that those portions will come together and identify another portion — or even a portion of a portion, the process is so arbitrary and capricious.

Of course racism isn't quite as random as we suggest. Unlike a game of Russian roulette in which the fate of the player is decided by sheer chance, the victim of racism is selected and designated according to specific requirements. Why that selection takes place and how the designation gets done are questions

MINORITY GROUPS
People who live in society where they are singled out for unequal treatment and are victims of a form of discrimination. Nearly always, but not necessarily, a numerical minority, the groups may be singled out because they are thought of as belonging to an inferior race and of possessing undesirable attributes of that race, though there are other criteria such as religion, politics, language, etc. that can be used to distinguish the minority group.

that we confront in this book. The point is that there are no natural or self-evident answers. Groups aren't targetted as 'races' and treated accordingly because they *are*. Alleged biological differences are either pretexts or justifications for other, often sinister reasons. Racial bullets can be fired at white groups as well as blacks.

Migrants are, quite literally, newcomers and this virtually guarantees some suspicion and anxiety. Often the threats they seem to present are illusory. There's an entire history of migrant groups all over the world which have been recognized as problems. After a while, this status may dissolve. Sometimes, it endures for several generations. Our second question is whether we have witnessed any significant dissolution in the West over the past six years. Have old divisions lost their meaning as new problems have emerged that supersede old antagonisms and exert a unifying force? This is an altogether more difficult question and one we will answer by examining events from 1981.

Our people

For Marxists, the so-called 'new' problems are not new at all. The capitalist state is a virtual fixture and one which prospers greatly from racialist conflict, as we will discover in Chapter 2. But, in Britain especially, the state has assumed a new power in the past eight or so years. New legislation affecting police powers in England, Scotland and Wales has accompanied substantial increases in the police budget and a quite deliberate attempt to reorganize the police force into a paramilitary unit with riot control a priority. New technologies, including the Police National Computer, have been used to store information on protesters, such as the women at Greenham Common. Official secrets and the 'national interest' have been invoked to quash the apparent threats offered by the likes of Sarah Tisdell, who sent xeroxes of official documents to a national newspaper, Peter Wright, who wrote the book *Spycatcher*, and the employees of the Government Communications Headquarters (GCHQ), who have been denied the right to belong to trade unions. There are other changes that reflect the state's preoccupation with controlling the 'enemies within'.

A strong-armed state would seem to hold enough fear for everyone to make them put prejudices and racist beliefs on hold and jolt them into worrying about fundamental civil liberties, individual freedoms and the like. Core values seem to be under siege as the state pounds home its plans for restoring law and order. According to one scenario, this should have led to a widespread concern that overrides the comparatively petty disputes about race and ethnicity. People of all backgrounds and beliefs forget their differences and weld themselves together to form a stern resistance to the emergent threat of an authoritarian state. We would expect camaraderie to replace racialism, sociability to crush prejudice, unity to overcome divisions. But things haven't materialized in this way. Instead, we have witnessed a very different series of developments. Racism and racial discrimination in the forms they were witnessed in the postwar period may look to have disappeared. In fact, they have *transmuted*: like baser metals turned to gold, racism and discrimination have become nationalism and cultural inviolability. We can still talk in terms of racism, but we need to stay alert to other warning signs: 'our' nation; 'this' culture. When these flash, we realize racist messages may not be far away. Issues involving nation and culture have peppered the 1980s, spicing debates about racism and ethnic responses to it.

In Britain, the appointment of Margaret Thatcher to Prime Minister in 1979 brought with it what Martin Barker has called 'the new racism', meaning that the subsequent political rhetoric and action of Conservative governments were keyed to the notion of 'a way of life' that was threatened by 'outsiders'. This concept acted as a supporting structure for both political philosophies and actions and homespun day-to-day beliefs and practices. Conservative politician William (now Lord) Whitelaw had publicly introduced the notion and Barker quotes him: 'We all know that the principles of the fair and tolerant society which we seek to uphold will be undermined if individual fears are allowed to grow' (1981, p. 13). No reference to race or ethnic groups in this; but a masked warning about limits. 'Many people, entirely free from any racial prejudice, want reassurance', Whitelaw continued.

Barker's thesis is that the idea that there were 'genuine' unprejudiced fears about losing a British way of life acted as a bridge between apparently neutral descriptions about what was happening and a vague theory of race. For example, possessing a way of life, seeing it as under attack, wanting to defend it; these sentiments contain no reference to racism, nor do they have anything to do with disliking foreigners, or ethnic minorities, or discriminating against them. The argument sounds so reasonable that its racism is obscured by a cloud of logic and plausibility. And what are its policy implications? Imposing boundaries around 'us', the insiders, which also serve to keep out 'them', the outsiders, or at least

COLONIALISM
The policy of subjecting territories or nations to another more powerful state and maintaining those areas and their inhabitants through the exploitation of land and labour.

those outsiders who are not prepared to sacrifice their own 'way of life' and adopt 'ours'.

Barker's account was written before the Falklands war of 1982, which was an occasion for expounding the 'way of life' notion into a much grander affirmation of nationalism. 'The people of the Falkland Islands, like the people of the United Kingdom, are an island race', Thatcher insisted. 'Their way of life is British'. Whereas Barker would see this as further proof of the new racism (though he never defines the 'old racism') another writer, Robert Miles, prefers to see it as an extension of something altogether more continuous. Racism existed before the onset of the 'New Right' (that loosely-structured band of ultra-conservative politicians, journalists and academics, as described by Ruth Levitas, 1986); since the 1960s in fact 'when expressions of British nationalism have increasingly come to contain a form of racism, although without explicit use of the idea of "race" in the case of the main political parties' (Miles, 1987, p. 206).

Although Miles doesn't cite him, Reginald Horsman provides an historical analysis of the complex, jumbled 'hodgepodge of rampant, racial nationalism' and shows how biological notions have underpinned nationalist tendencies that have no obvious connections with biology. Horsman quotes from the *Edinburgh Review* of January 1844: 'Of the great influence of Race in the production of National Character, no reasonable enquirer can now doubt' (1981, p. 60). Nationalism emerged as a coherent ideological package at around the same time as 'scientific' racism, as it was known: mid-nineteenth century.

Miles believes one has covered the other virtually ever since. 'Racism is in the lining of nationalism', he writes (1987). Three episodes in the early 1980s seem to illustrate this; they also created a context for a whole series of events in the remainder of the decade. The first was the Falklands conflict itself, an occasion for buffing up anachronistic images of Britain as 'the nation that had built an empire and ruled a quarter of the world,' as Thatcher described it in her successful attempt to revive a belligerent patriotism (quoted in Barnett, 1982, p. 150). She recalled British colonial history as an august unfolding of predestined greatness. In contrast, this book presents it as a repugnant farce scripted according to the dictates of greed and idealism, in which 15 million Africans were enslaved, many million more South Asians indentured and dominated and populations of Australasia decimated. Such was the cost of ruling a 'quarter of the world'. Yet, it was conveniently forgotten as the 'Falklands factor' exerted an influence on Thatcher's re-election to office in 1983.

Twenty-five years after the Suez crisis and 45 years after the end of the Second World War, the 'Falklands factor' suggested to Anthony Sampson that 'older British values and attitudes were still lurking close to the surface, as if the war and empire had happened only yesterday' (1982, p. 431). This observation connects with the ones we make later in this book, particularly those relating to the colonial mentality, a mental outlook that, in many ways, resists rational argument and measured debate. The Falklands war abroad added fresh substance to the colonial mentality at home and, ultimately, the British sense of superiority was enhanced by a famous victory.

The year before the Falklands conflict saw the passing of the British Nationality Act, amidst protest from groups who envisaged the distress it would cause many families. We cover the clauses of the legislation in Chapter 3, but for now, merely wish to note that British citizenship rights, including the right of abode, fell to those with parents or grandparents born, adopted, naturalized and registered as citizens. A clear intention of the Act was to curb secondary migration to the UK; one implication was a breakup of families because some members could not fulfil citizenship requirements. Many spouses and fiances wishing to travel to Britain to reunite were denied citizenship rights. These two key events of the early 1980s are joined in Martin Stellman's film *For Queen and Country* (1988) in which an Afro-Caribbean returns to London after military service in the Falklands (and, before that, Northern Ireland) to find that the Nationality Act has rendered him a British citizen no longer.

Not surprisingly, the Act lost the government a good deal of confidence among ethnic minorities with relations in New Commonwealth countries. As the ethnic vote was becoming increasingly important, the government mounted an advertising campaign in the run-up to the 1983 election which featured a poster depicting a young black man, arms folded, dressed in a business suit. The copy line read: 'Labour says he's black. Tories say he's British'. Much the same message as in the 1981 Act was being driven home: national identity was all important; ethnic background, skin colour, culture, beliefs were no longer relevant. Zig Layton-Henry believed the import of the campaign to be that immigration from the New Commonwealth was now at an end, so the crucial issues concerned 'the integration of the second and third generations and the need to forge new bases of loyalty and legitimacy to integrate black Britons' (1984, p. xv).

Our disagreement with this is with the choice of terms. 'Integration' could perhaps be replaced more appropriately with assimilation since the underlying theme of the campaign was that ethnic minorities should discard their ethnic character, forget the culture of their parents and become an indistinguishable, upwardly mobile part of an homogeneous British nation. Being British, in this version, is instead of, not as well as, being an ethnic minority group member. It's also one-way: acquisition involves loss. In reply to the campaign's assertion that there are 'no "blacks", no "whites", just people', it could be argued that there manifestly are blacks and whites, who want to regard themselves and be regarded by others in those terms without necessarily inviting conflict.

These three moments in the early years of the 1980s were occasions to elevate a strong and robust conception of British nationalism. Nowhere was there a hint of diversity: nationalism was the force and all other interests were subordinate. Thatcher's administration was finished with the endless debates over ethnic relations. What was the point? Sixteen years after the first British anti-discrimination legislation, there were uprisings by young blacks in many of the country's inner cities. Liberal thinking had amounted to nothing, so the alternative was to lay down the hard assimilationist line. 'Our people, our race' were under threat from Argentinians, from the descendants of populations over which Britain once ruled, from those who saw blacks as 'blacks' and not people and from any number of other factions who disturbed law and order: the miners, women at Greenham Common, trade unionists at GCHQ and so on. Almost every issue, not only those concerning ethnic relations, was geared to the concept of a nation gradually but inexorably restoring itself to its (illusory) former glory and not prepared to tolerate internal disunity or diversity. The Nationality Act had given, according to the government's advertisements, 'full and equal citizenship to everyone permanently settled in Britain.' They were all expected to play their parts in merging into the 'island race'.

With the ascendancy of reactionary approaches, concepts such as integration and cultural diversity — which had previously been bandied about at political levels — were shelved. The favoured goal became to absorb all groups within the single, homogeneous nation. Similar goals have guided policies elsewhere in the world: Bulgaria's 900,000 Turks (1 per cent of the total population) risked police beatings, fines, arrest or even expulsion if caught speaking their native language. The aboriginal population of Australia has been neglected to the point where they either become 'Australianized' and discard their own cultures, or remain excluded from mainstream society. Both groups face assimilation by force.

There is a relationship, however, unclear, between government policy and race relations as they are experienced by members of society. Policy since the war has been marred by an unwillingness to accept the desirability of New Commonwealth migrants and their offspring. The refusal to relax entry requirements to accommodate 3.25 million passport holders from Hong Kong following the Beijing massacre of 1989 supported this policy. Then Foreign Secretary, Geoffrey Howe, listed among the government's main reasons for refusing automatic entry the problems posed by a fresh influx of ethnic minorities. Immigration control has sent a resounding message both to ethnic minorities and the white majority: no more. Social policy has sent another message to ethnic minority residents: blend in. Easier said than done.

Core values

It's this failure, or to be more precise, stubborn resistance, to blend in and respect the cultural mores associated with the 'British way of life' which right-wing analysts invoked to explain what triggered off the disturbances in Handsworth and Tottenham, North London, in 1985. Deploying the language of 'commonsense racism' which as Errol Lawrence (1982) has recognised, was used so creatively in populist interpretations of the 1980 and 1981 disorders, journalists such as Keith Waterhouse, then of the *Daily Mirror*, told his readers that the 'youth of Handsworth' rioted because 'they haven't any values' (12 September 1985). Now, this short, terse assertion is resonant of two critical and interlocking themes. To begin with, it shifts blame for the disturbances fairly and squarely onto the shoulders of the young Afro-Caribbean residents of Handsworth (and Tottenham). And, it makes the corollary point: namely, the exoneration of the police, as an institutional order, from responsibility for what took place. Of course, this still allows for what Julian Henriques calls the 'rotten apple theory of racism' (1984). That is to say, it permits the view that there are likely to be one or two officers who hold racist views and act accordingly. But the argument is firmly made: the views and actions of 'prejudiced' officers are the exception rather than the norm. They are aberrations and racism, as an institutionalized and routine feature of the police force cannot, therefore, be legitimately considered as contributing to the outbreak of violence. This proposition loses all credibility when set alongside the body of empirical research into British policing. According to the authors of the PSI report into policing in London in the mid-1980s, for instance, racism amongst officers was habitual, normal, almost automatic (Smith and Gray, 1985).

Secondly, the insistence that the young Afro-Caribbean residents of Handsworth lack the values that effectively prohibit the use of physical violence in all but extreme circumstances fits in with commonsense assumptions about Afro-Caribbean families and lifestyles, which writers such as Hazel Carby (1982), Lawrence (1982) and Ann Pheonix (1988) have shown bear no resemblance to empirical reality. Again, the corollary of the view that they don't have any values is: we do and our values are threatened by the unwelcome presence of those who refuse to respect them. It seems, then, that we're back to the ominous policy which, for many, stems logically from this formulation:

FUNDAMENTALIST MUSLIMS

Since 1980, religious fervour has erupted in the Islamic world in general and in the Middle East in particular. It has led to a revolution in Iran, the assassination of President Sadat of Egypt, and the fierce resistance to the Soviet invasion of Afghanistan. In Britain, it has prompted outrage at the publication of *The Satanic Verses* and encouraged the move towards the development of Muslim schools. The fervour has been inspired by fundamentalism, an adherence to the traditional basics of religious doctrine as inferred from the Holy Koran. Like other fundamentalist religions, it insists that individual lives are governed by narrowly prescribed rules and rituals. Fundamentalism seems to arise as a reaction to liberal social changes.

blend in or .... Similar sentiments welled-up for four years after the 1985 disturbances, bursting forth in reaction to the Muslim protest against the allegedly blasphemous novel, *The Satanic Verses*, by Salman Rushdie. In their ritual burnings of the book and Rushdie effigies, Britain's fundamentalist Muslims unveiled a staunch and virulent streak of ethnicity, previously unsuspected. Angry young Afro-Caribbeans were one thing; but followers of Islam carrying the *jihad*, or holy war, to the streets of Bradford and London were another. The *News of the World's* 'Voice of Reason', Woodrow Wyatt, could almost have been parodying *Alien Nation* when he wrote: 'Newcomers here are welcome. But only if they become genuine Britishers' (5 March 1989). The *Daily Mail's* 'voice of common sense', George Gale, expressed similar views: ' . . . they must seek to be assimilated', he wrote in March 1989. 'They have chosen to dwell amongst us. In Rome, do as the Romans do.'

But, what are these values which are said to differentiate 'us' from 'them'? Well, like the terms 'Englishness' or 'British culture' they're pretty elusive, subject to change and therefore difficult to define with any precision, continuity or general agreement, according to Robert Colls and Philip Dodd (1987). It could be argued that such notions are largely mythical in character. For some New Right activists and writers, however, such considerations are of little significance, as articles in publications such as *The Salisbury Review*, 'a quarterly magazine of conservative thought', will testify. According to one contributor, John Casey, 'our' deference to authority figures prominently amongst these core values. In contrast, 'There is an extraordinary resentment [amongst the West Indian community] towards authority — police, teachers, Underground guards — *all* authority' (1982). Writing in the same magazine a couple of years later Raymond Honeyford, then Headteacher of Drummond Middle School in Bradford, asserted that a reluctance to accept the word of authority also pervaded the Asian communities. But more than this: in his view, indolence, intolerance, deceit, even a penchant for violence seemed to be amongst the prevailing values in the homes of the Asian pupils who constituted over 90 per cent of his school's population. Consider, for instance, Honeyford's report of a meeting held at the school to discuss the issue of Asian parents wanting their children to accompany them on trips to the subcontinent during term time:

> Against all normal expectations the meeting was packed. There had obviously been a 'three line whip' from the Pakistani leadership. It quickly became evident that what had been proposed as an act of reconciliation, based on the school's concern for the child, was to descend into a noisy and unseemly demonstration of sectarian bitterness. The hysterical political temperament of the Indian subcontinent became evident — an extraordinary sight in an English School Hall. There was much shouting and fist waving.

Consider the lexicon: 'descend'; 'hysterical political temperament'; 'extraordinary'. The idea seems to be that it's a propensity of Indians to reduce the rational discussion of the English to something unfamiliar, undesirable and out-of-place. The report goes on:

> The local authority was accused of 'racism'; the chairman, insulted. One Anglicised Asian stood near the door and, at regular intervals, shouted 'bullshit' at the door. The disorder was orchestrated. Questions were always preceded by a nod from a Muslim leader. A half-educated and volatile Sikh usurped the privileges of the chair by deciding who was to speak. The confusion was made worse by the delays occasioned by the need for interpreting — many of the audience had no English, though there have been freely-available English classes in the area for at least a decade (1984, p. 311).

To talk of 'our' culture, 'our' values, 'our' traditions, then, and juxtapose them against 'theirs', allows the speaker to disown classical conceptions of racism. At the same time, however, it facilitates the spread of racist sentiment, almost with impunity. Frank Reeves has theorised this covert, or vicarious deployment of racial categories as 'discursive deracialisation': it takes place when 'persons speak purposely to their audiences about racial matters, while avoiding the overt deployment of racial descriptions, evaluations and prescriptions' (1983, p. 4). The sleight of hand implied by this process is crucial to the compelling and seductive tenor of New Right rhetoric and the ideology of 'the new racism' which it embraces. In simple terms, it provides a smokescreen for racism. For example, the reliance on 'discursive deracialisation' provides the mechanism for the framing of legislation which is not expressly racist in intent, that is, according to its formulators. Certainly, the support generated for Britain's immigration laws since 1962, which we'll discuss in Chapter 2, owes much to the careful and deliberate avoidance of reference to the overtly racist conceptions of citizenship which the legislation both sought and ultimately sanctioned.

Avoiding explicit racial references also authenticates a scenario in which culturalist explanations of the way things are assume pre-eminent status. In the field of education, for instance, 'culture' has become the fulcrum on which policy and debates about the education of ethnic minority children and their white classmates balance. Not only in Britain but in other western democratic societies such as Canada, the United States, Australia and New Zealand, multiculturalism remains a key concept in contemporary educational discourse. In Australia, for instance, Brian Bullivant, whose other work we look at in Chapter 6, has embedded his most recent research into the differential academic performance of pupils from 'Asian', non-English speaking background (NESB) and Anglo-Australians in a culturalist framework. He asserts that the 'ethnic-success-ethic' of the 'Asian' and NESB pupils must be contrasted with the 'shirk-work-ethic' of Anglo-Australian cultures in order to account for the relatively more successful performance of 'Asians' and NESB pupils in school (1987). Similarly, in the UK, culture is conceived as a robust variable in analyses of the performance in public examinations of white indigenous pupils and those of South Asian and Afro-Caribbean origin. Here, culture is seen as both the cause of and the solution to the apparent tendency for pupils of Afro-Caribbean origin to leave school with relatively fewer or less prestigious qualifications. Thus in its forlorn attempt to explain 'the reasons for the very different school performances of Asian and West Indians', Lord Swann and his colleagues on the committee of enquiry into the education of children from ethnic minority groups looked to their 'respective cultures'. The result: 'Asians', we're informed, 'are given to "keeping their heads down" and adopting a "low profile"', thereby making it easier to succeed in a hostile environment. West Indians, by contrast, are given to "protest" and "a high profile" with the reverse effect' (DES, 1985, p. 86). Now, putting to one side our objections to what one of us has argued before is a cultural-deficit interpretation of differences in school performance, let's look at where this analysis led the Swann committee (Troyna, 1988). Having nailed its colours firmly to the mast of a pathological model in which the victims are blamed for their failure, the Committee then set sail in search of an organizing principle for schools which when implemented might, amongst other things, attenuate differences in academic performance. And where does it drop anchor? Why, in the sea of cultural pluralism. *Education for All* was both the title and rallying call of the Swann committee's report. It recommended that all cultures — even those whose members are losing out — should be acknowledged and reflected in the way schools are organised and in what they teach. The illogical relationship between diagnosis and prescription is plain to see. Diagnosis: Afro-Caribbean culture contributes largely to educational failure. Prescription: include all cultures in the curriculum and organisation of schools.

Swann's report did not attract an uncritical response. For some, its analytical prowess left a lot to be desired, it was peppered with logical inconsistencies and, most significantly, it failed to engage directly and forcibly with racism as it impacts routinely on the educational landscape. As Bob Carter and Jenny Williams have pointed out, racism is incidental rather than central to the Swann committee's analysis and where it does feature it is construed primarily as 'individual prejudice, based on negative cultural stereotypes' (1987, p. 172). Later we will examine the significant differences between racism as an individual property and something which is more pervasive. Of course, this interpretation of racism as an individual property has led a number of writers to hitch their wagons to a teaching approach in which information about other cultures is expected to dislodge children's unfavourable and stereotypical views of other cultures and countries (e.g., Lynch, 1987). But the 'wishful thinking' of this proposition has been exposed by a number of critics. Research suggests that increasing knowledge of other groups either directly through enhanced physical contact, such as twinning, say, all-white and ethnically-mixed schools, or vicariously, through teaching about minority ethnic and cultural lifestyles might have the effect of *enhancing* children's identification with their own group and underlining their negative view of others. 'When individuals interact with persons from other cultures, the differences that separate the participants tend to become salient', writes Stephen Bochner. 'We immediatly place such people into the category "they", distinguishing "them" from "us" ' (1982, p. 10). Multiculturalism may thrive in the UK but racism is far from dead.

Other reactions to the Swann report tended to see its championing of a cultural pluralist ideology as subversive; a potential threat to the sanctity and well-being of 'our' culture and 'our' nation. In his valedictory speech as Secretary of State for Education, Sir Keith Joseph insisted that whilst he did not endorse a virulent brand of assimilationism in which 'our education system should in effect take no account of ethnic mix' he was equally anxious that the Swann report should not be the harbinger of a period in which schools are turned 'upside down to accommodate ethnic variety' or encouraged 'to jettison those many features and practices which reflect what is best in our society and its institutions' (1986). For Joseph, then: 'Community by community we have much more in common than dividing us . . . A British school for British citizens is surely right to transmit to all its pupils a sense of shared national values and traditions'.

It is precisely what constitutes these 'shared national values and traditions' which have been contested with such vigour since the publication of our original

CULTURAL DEFICIT
Often, when victims of racism and various other forms of oppression continue to suffer across space and time, explanations are sought in their culture. In other words, they are not blamed as individuals, but neither is the society in which they live. It is the culture to which they belong that is seen as somehow flawed and inferior. So, according to this interpretation, their culture is identified as the main contributory factor to the oppression because of its (alleged) deficiency.

text. Government rhetoric continues to assure that its obligations in a multicultural society will be met. However, the commitment seems perfunctory. For instance, the Education Reform Act (ERA) 1988 and the changes to the curriculum, organization and entire system it brought crystallized the Tory government's view of what values and traditions should be inculcated in pupils. With total disregard for the fact that by the year 2000 12 percent of the school population will be of ethnic minority origin, the ERA reflects a specious conception of British culture as monolithic and undifferentiated. Consequently, we find the ERA insisting that the daily act of collective worship in schools must 'be wholly or mainly of a broadly Christian character' unless special dispensation is granted. Further, any new syllabus in RE 'must reflect the fact that the religious traditions in the country are in the main Christian . . . '. Hardly compatible with Kenneth Baker's view that the ERA and proposed National Curriculum will be 'very helpful in holding together a multi-racial and multi-cultural society' (*The Guardian*, 17 August 1988). Indeed, the so-called 'entitlement curriculum' seems to be suffused with a brutal assertion of an Anglocentric ideology. The direction of history teaching, for example, seems to be heading away from the 'warts and all' approach favoured in an increasing number of schools in the 1980s. In the National Curriculum, we're likely to see a syllabus predicated on a concern to eulogise British 'achievements'. 'I'm not ashamed of our history', Kenneth Baker told colleagues at the 1988 Conservative party conference, 'it has given many great things to the world. That's been our civilising mission' (quoted in Troyna and Carrington, 1990). This view is, of course, supportive of those sentiments expressed by Mrs Thatcher in the early 1980s to which we referred earlier. In the chapters that follow we'll be scrutinising closely this New Right, monocultural interpretation of British history. Suffice it to say here that it encapsulated what Baker, and his successor as Secretary of State for Education, John McGregor, envisaged as the defining characteristics of history teaching within the National Curriculum. And what of the English syllabus? In setting up the working party to report on a suitable English syllabus, the Secretary of State informed its chairperson, Brian Cox, that: 'The Working Group's recommendations on learning about language and its use should draw upon the English literary heritage . . . ' (quoted in Troyna and Carrington, 1990).

All in all, the trajectory of educational policy in general and the ERA and National Curriculum in particular bear testimony to the restrictive and racist conception of 'British schools for British citizens' which prevails in the late 1980s. If there was 'a liberal moment' in educational policy and discourse when antiracist education secured some purchase on the way Local Education Authorities (LEAs), their schools and individual teachers conceived of their role in a multicultural society, then it has passed. The ERA and the systemic changes it has mobilised has restricted the 'space' where challenges to Thatcherite conceptions of 'British schools for British citizens' might be most effective: the level of the local state. Proposals for open enrolment, for example, whereby parents are given greater 'freedom' to choose which schools their children attend is likely to increase 'white flight' and create segregrated schools; a scenario which, on the face of it, is at variance with the commitment to a multicultural society. Despite this, Baroness Hooper, the government's spokesperson in the House of Lords, was adamant that parental choice would remain sacrosanct in the operation of this clause: 'Segregation is no part of this Bill. We underline the fact that in giving parents choice, we do not wish to circumscribe that choice in any way' (*Times Educational Supplement*, 13 May 1988). As a number of commentators have noted, this abdication of responsibility for the consequences of this clause is likely to lead to the recurrence of events witnessed in Dewsbury, Yorkshire in 1987 when a group of white parents refused to send their children to a school where Asian pupils predominated. Within a year the courts gave them the legal right to send their children to 'white' schools. One implication of this is a reversal to the type of busing witnessed in the UK during the 1960s (see Chapter 6).

One way of making sense of educational policy imperatives in the late 1980s and the early 1990s is to recognize that they are imbued with a fundamentalist conviction which demands, when necessary, the cultural resocialization of 'aberrant' (i.e., ethnic minority) pupils. Above all else, then, the education system is being geared up to treat these pupils as 'trainee whites', to use John Eggleston's phrase (quoted in Alibhai, 1988). Like their parents they are accorded only conditional citizenship. The ideology which underpins this policy approach rose to the surface in early 1989 in response to fundamentalist Muslims' objections to *The Satanic Verses*. Alongside increasing calls amongst this same group for separate schools, their vociferous demands evoked a hostile (and illuminating) response: simply put, 'only if' conceptions of citizenship greeted their demands. 'Only if' for example, the group showed a sound business sense, an assiduous commitment to industry, a devotion to family life and an avoidance of the kind of conflict in which Afro-Caribbean youth have been embroiled. South Asians have demonstrated all of these and have received bouquets for their efforts. But these bouquets turned to brickbats when fundamentalist Muslims, previously regarded as a chameleon presence in Britain, openly campaigned for their cause. The Rushdie affair showed this community in a new light: ablaze with anger and, in some cases, prepared to kill after a violation of the received wisdom of the Koran by an author and his publishers who were seen to have contrived mortally to insult all Islam — in fundamentalist eyes, at least. Thoughts that British-born, young Muslims had left their parents' ethnic identity behind were made to look forlorn as fundamentalist Muslim youths raged, prompting the kind of police attention more usually reserved for their Afro-Caribbean peers.

The ethnic renewal, of which these incidents are part, has been accompanied by a distinct tightening of social control. After the Brixton disturbance of 1981 and its contagion (covered in Chapter 7) the police force was prompted to rethink its approach to maintaining public order. A year before, in the wake of the Bristol uprising, the then British Home Secretary, William Whitelaw, had expressly rejected the idea of paramilitary riot squads. But, after Brixton, the Royal Hong Kong Police (RHKP) Force was called in to advise on how most effectively to deal with riots (the RHKP had experience in quelling major disorders in the 1960s). The result was what Gerry Northam describes as a 'paramilitary drift' (1988): the British force, drawing on the colonial experience for its examples, began to gear up for future disturbances. Riot training became mandatory and anti-riot equipment became standard. This included CS gas, plastic batons and short shields.

The 'unveiling' of the paramilitary force came at Orgreave in South Yorkshire in May 1984 when about 1,800 pickets confronted 1,500 riot-trained police officers wielding state-of-the-art equipment. Sixty four people were injured and 84 arrested in the single bloodiest episode of the 1984/5 miners' strike. Little over a year later, the riot gear came out once more after outbreaks of violence in London, Birmingham and other major British cities. CS gas was deployed (but not used) for the first time in mainland Britain. One of the centres of conflict witnessed two more 'firsts', as Northam notes: 'Broadwater Farm Estate marked the first riot in post-war Britain where the police themselves were under fire from at least one shotgun in the surrounding tower blocks. It also saw the injuring of 200 police officers and twenty civilians, and the killing of a community policeman' (1988, p. 7). Many commentators, before and after 1985, have talked of the police's siege mentality, but, after Broadwater Farm, they began to accumulate evidence. For instance, Roger Graef quotes a London Home Beat Officer: 'There's a very, very hostile relationship between me and the black activists in the community. There is virtually no relationship other than open hostility. They despise the uniform I wear with a pathological hatred, and I have little or no contact with them' (1989, p. 102–3). This has been reflected at policy levels, a zeal for 'overpolicing' becoming evident in situations such as Wolverhampton's Heath Town area in May 1989 when 120 officers in riot gear raided a pub and arrested twenty people, twelve for drug offences. Support was called for after barricades were set, bringing the total police involved to 250. All that was recovered was a small amount of the cocaine derivative 'crack' with a street value of about £500. Over the next month, police used anti-riot gear and techniques or massed troops operations on two independent occasions, once to curb a Muslim demonstration in London and once to dispel groups congregated at Dewsbury, Yorkshire. None of the episodes would warrant being called a riot and perhaps not even a serious breach of the peace. Yet they each occasioned the use of riot control tactics by hundreds of officers.

Police efforts have not been directed only at ethnic minorities, though it seems fair to suggest that Afro-Caribbean youth has been used as a virtual metaphor for the urban disorders and street violence that have allegedly threatened law and order. Yet police efforts have proceeded along another plane also. As well as 'arming for the armegeddon' (as a US reporter once put it), police have redoubled their efforts in the sphere of community relations. Following Scarman's report and the Police and Criminal Evidence Act, 1984, they have established statutory community liaison committees. They have tried to tackle the problem of racialist attacks by setting up 'helplines', monitoring response times in some areas and publishing 'Best practice guidelines for recording and monitoring racial incidents'. Many forces have mounted recruitment campaigns aimed specifically at ethnic minorities. Some would see them as appeasements, calming the anger at the paramilitary approach. If they are, they may still not work: in the UK, as in the USA, there has, over the past decade, been a hardening of feeling against the police by some groups, especially young blacks who have borne the brunt of some very special police attention in the 1980s, as a whole sheaf of evidence shows (for instance, Gilroy, 1987b; Gordon, 1985; Solomos, 1988). In the 1990s, more and more black youth may see police statements of intent undermined by paramilitary actions and find some relevance in the messages of bands like Public Enemy who call police the problem and urge their followers to 'Fight the power'.

Mutant racism

In spite of the tumult and trauma caused by these events, none of them explicitly invoked the 'race issue'. Nowhere do we find racism as an acknowledged reason for a controversy, at least not in the more conventional understanding of racism

— which is the definition we adopted in the original edition of this book (see Chapter 2). A protean concept at the best of times, racism has virtually challenged analysts to redefine it in the light of changing events, or leave it behind in the mists of history. A fairly orthodox rendering of racism would be: a set of ideas or beliefs assembled into theories, arguments or ideologies that purport to explain differences in the world's human population by reference to biological characteristics which fall naturally into discrete categories, or 'races'. The main premise on which the theories or arguments stand is that there is a fundamental inequality between various roles and, from this, derive all manner of propositions. Revisions of this have relaxed the biological aspect so as to allow the inclusion of functional equivalents. These may have no biological connotation but their effect is much the same. Identifying a particular group by its possession of distinct cultural characteristics may not seem pejorative at first glance. But, when these characteristics are used as the basis for exclusion or for unequal treatment of some kind, then a value is placed on them. One type of culture may be devalued: not just different, but inferior. Non-biological ideas can work very effectively to legitimate unequal treatment, as we have seen. In some instances, we might even say that notions like nation and culture are symbolic of race. This makes them just as damaging — or useful (depending on one's interests and political perspectives).

This tendency to class beliefs that have no explicit reference to race as racism has led to what Miles has called a 'conceptual inflation' (1989, ch.2). He writes of racism: 'A number of writers . . . have inflated its [racism's] meaning to include ideas and arguments which would not be included by those who initially formulated and used it'. Other writers have inflated the analytical meaning of the concept so as to refer largely to individual and institutionalised practices which have as their outcome the determination and/or reproduction of "black" disadvantage, regardless of the intention and legitimating ideology (p. 66). The first meaning is clear enough; the second means that some bottom-liners are not interested in intentions, only in consequences. An organization might have what it consideres to be a perfect equal opportunities policy. But, if ethnic minorities don't get recruited and promoted in the numbers one might expect, then the end result means racism is at work. This equates roughly to what is often described as *institutional racism*, which works to protect the advantages of white groups, often unwittingly. 'A bridging concept, linking and blurring the distinction between the material and the ideological', is how Williams, in her critical evaluation, describes institutional racism (1985, p. 335).

There are seveal consequences of this inflation, one of which is that it was able to capture many diverse forms of inequality, or more accurately, arguments that justify inequality. Simply excluding reference to race or 'natural inferiority' isn't enough to escape the disapproval racism carries with it. The kinds of events we covered in the last section may not have held an explicit racial component, but, by inference, they were about racism in the sense that they involved exclusion and a nationalist or cultural elitism.

Miles' term invites the metaphor of a balloon: inflate it to a degree and it assumes a shape and gravity sufficient for it to float satisfactorily; try to blow in too much air than its mass can accommodate and the whole thing will burst. The same with racism: enlargement works if accompanied by analytical precision and accurate indicators of how to recognize racism. But beyond a certain point, it loses all utility and becomes a mere slogan. To scream 'racism!' at every instance of injustice or inequity involving ethnic minorities may reap practical rewards in the short-term. It may also take away the concept's incisiveness and luminosity over a longer period.

For example, the Centre for Contemporary Cultural Studies (CCCS) reminds us that racism must be regarded as a moving concept, neither hunters nor prey standing still. CCCS write of pluralities of 'ideological configurations', meaning that there may be different patterns of thought, each of which is affected by the specific social contexts in which they emerge, contexts which themselves are shaped by 'endogenous forces', (influences that originate outside the society in question). CCCS writer Paul Gilroy has extended this by offering the idea of a 'reciprocal determination' between 'race and class, neither being a fixed category of people, but each having potential as organizing agents in conflict situations' (1987a). Gilroy sees them as fluid, changeable, but always related. Unlike earlier Marxist formulations which reduced racism to an aspect of class antagonism, this argument approaches racism and class conflict as relatively autonomous features of society, each with a high degree of elasticity. Racism isn't just a reflection of society: it can act back on that society and introduce changes. Given the changeable nature of racism in this view, we might more properly talk in terms of racisms.

The value of this approach would be enhanced had the CCCS authors tried to nail down at least some lowest common denominators of racism rather than assume we all know intuitively what is and isn't to qualify. We can accept the important observation that the phenomenon, or phenomena, is or are ever-changing and so resist(s) formal definition. We can also accept CCCS mentor Stuart Hall's recommendation to investigate not racism *per se*, but the ways in which racist ideologies have been 'constructed and made operative under different historical conditions' (1980, p. 341). But we crave clearer guidelines on how to recognize racisms in all their forms. CCCS point us in a new direction but without a compass.

Barker's lodestone leads us to the conclusion that racism refers to all arguments and theories based on the assumption that groups are biological, when they are, in fact, social. This means that a racist theory may refer to

COLONIAL MENTALITY

A mode of thinking that has its sources in the racist philosophies of the eighteenth and nineteenth centuries. These purported to explain — and justify — the white Europeans' demonstrable superiority over groups falling under their domination, many of which were of unfamiliar backgrounds, with unusual beliefs and, crucially, of different colours. The central principle of the mental outlook is that whites are, in some sense (or many senses) naturally suited to dominate; it follows that any attempt to challenge that dominance should be rebuffed. Although its origins are in colonialism, this style of thought has a very modern, pervasive presence and manifests itself in many spheres (such as work, where white-dominated trade unions have resisted the blacks' attempts to gain parity and equality in some respects). The colonial mentality that whites are superior impels whites to try to maintain their historical edge with whatever means possible.

groups being different because of biological reasons, but not necessarily superior or inferior. This is an inclusive conception and covers so many possibilities that it is virtually unusable. The concept is inflated so much that white women might well fit in: they are different biologically to men, but they are also members of gender, which has been built out of social artifacts, not genetic ones. It would also be possible in theory to find two groups which co-exist peacefully, but believe each other to be biologically quite different. No conflict here; but racism aplenty. In his effort to embrace what he sees as the newer forms of racism, Barker loses sharpness of definition.

Does our treatment in this book allow us to escape the same criticism? We do, after all, set our limits widely and the key to our approach is the fact that race is arbitrary. It's a convenient label applied to some groups to legitimate, justify or explain treating them unequally. And, while it refers, often explicitly, to biological differences, our interpretation of race is as something quite independent of physical phenomena. Race exists in the mind of the believer only. There is a biological element present, but it resides in the seemingly universal propensity of *Homo sapiens* to congregate into portions which may be selected on assumed physical similarities or cultural affinities. Humans possess a striking faculty for defining not only their confederates, but also those who clearly don't belong. Physical characteristics are reliable indicators of 'them' as they are of 'us'. This is a worldwide, historical pattern: it seems to recognise no boundaries nor time limits. Human beings simply have this proclivity for dividing up the world in this way.

It takes a racist form when quite specific criteria are selected. Those criteria are physical and observable in nature and work as signs of a person's race. Hair texture and skin colour have been serviceable in the past. Possessors of such features are considered as parts of races that are not just different, but permanently different. The permanence is thought to be fixed by biology. Conventionally, racism attempts to justify or explain inequality: why 'they' are inferior to 'us'. But, following those who stress racism as a moving concept, we need to modify this, asking whether people necessarily see those they deem other races as inferior. If people lift up their heads and look around, they find that 'they' are patently not inferior. Even those with colonial mentalities who comfort themselves with thoughts of the past glories of the empire can't deny the evidence of their senses. Some of 'them' are business-owners, professionals and politicians. These are not inferior beings, but they're discomfiting nevertheless.

The startling thing about 'them' is that they're wilful, remote and living according to their impenetrable wisdom in some cases. They're on the move, either snatching '*our*' housing, taking '*our*' jobs or sucking up to the powers-that-be. They might even *be* part of the powers-that-be and aren't going to be dislodged. This is the image of ethnic minorities as races, but not inferior ones; threatening, self-serving, possibly intimidating and maybe even malicious, but clearly not inferior.

Racism nowadays, whether it operates at personal, institutional or political levels, makes no necessary assumption of inferiority. This seems to be the major change in racist thinking over the past decade and applies *mutatis mutandis* to the USA and parts of continental Europe as well as the UK. Groups that were once held at arm's length because of their supposed inabilities and inherent limitations have stripped such suppositions of any empirical support. They have done so by simply proving themselves beyond dispute as capable of performing tasks at all levels as well as their white counterparts. Whether in industry, the professions, business or any other sphere where race has been used as a basis for separate and unequal treatment, groups that have felt the brunt of racism have demonstrated their adequacy. How, then, can racism persist when the alleged inequality that functioned as its pivot has been removed?

In 1948, Robert Merton wrote an article, 'The self-fulfilling prophecy', in which he showed that: 'ethnic out-groups are damned if they do embrace the values of white Protestant society and damned if they don't'. The second part is plain: arrangements are made in such a way as to prohibit, say, blacks from scaling the walls of discrimination and exhibiting the values and virtues of white society and they're disparaged and condemned for their failure. But, according to Merton: 'The systematic condemnation of the out-grouper continues largely *irrespective of what he does*'.

This occurs through a process of 'moral alchemy' in which virtues are changed to vices. For example, in whites' cognizance, young Paul Jones who works into the night is industrious, resolute, perseverant and eager to realize his capacities to the full. But if Paul Patel does the same, it bears witness to Indians' sweatshop mentality, their ruthless undercutting of British standards and their unfair competitive practices. If young Jones is thrifty, shrewd and intelligent, why is young Patel sharp, cunning and too clever by half? Simply because the right activity by the wrong people becomes a thing of contempt, not honour.

There is nothing contrived or disingenuous in this: the reasoning has its rationale, its own logic. Whites have been — to use an unfashionable, but accurate word — indoctrinated with an appreciation of the 'proper order' of things. It is an order in which, historically, white groups have held positions of authority and dominance. Even working class whites situated at the bottom of the social scale have been imbued with the idea that they are part of a population that is, almost as if by divine right, suited to rule. This helps smooth out the inconsistency in seeing others as, in most important respects, equal, yet begrudging them legitimate right to assume positions of high rank in society. This is an example of racism, but the concept of 'race' is only *implied* by the suggestion of natural order. 'Name-calling is avoided by the modern racists', who nevertheless 'express strong opposition to moves to advance the position of blacks', write Michael Billig and his research associates. 'This opposition is typically justified in terms of traditional values, and, in particular, in terms of equality and fairness' (1988, p. 106). There's no paradox in condemning Asians and Afro-Caribbeans when they do *and* when they don't demonstrate the right virtues, while insisting that race doesn't enter into it. Nor is there a paradox in actually encouraging equal opportunities and accepting a group's achievements as a warrant of its essential equality with one's own group while still believing in the rightness of their being assigned an inferior status in society. In both cases, the special importance attached to ethnic minorities can be seen as eminently reasonable; all part of *The Logic of Racism*, as the title of one of our books expresses it (1987). We wrote earlier of a transmutation of racism and this is an instance: reshaping virtuous accomplishments that demonstrate equality into vices befitting only groups lower down the scale.

Assimilation fits into the picture because it *hasn't* happened. Since the war, there has been, as we have seen, a constantly renewed ethnic diversity. This has accentuated the absurdity of labelling ethnic outgroups inferior: it's not just the ones who have dropped their culture and forgotten their ancestry who have managed to avoid the underclass department. There have been few attempts to minimize the manifest differences which remind whites that old myths about their intellectual superiority are redundant. Events over the past decade show that ethnicity has not just burned quietly, but has been ablaze. Assimilation

UNDERCLASS
**Rather a vague concept used in many different ways, but defined by
Douglas Glasgow in his book *The Black Underclass* as 'a permanently
trapped population of poor persons, unused and unwanted.' Poverty is the
key criterion: blacks, as a group especially affected by poverty, comprise
an increasingly bigger portion of the underclass.**

would disguise the anomalies in white racists' thought by removing from their
vision the reminders. Presumably, this is roughly the reason behind attempts to
encourage it: minimising manifest differences would salve racists' discomfort;
discomfort, that is, with the sight of more and more ethnic minorities
destroying age-old beliefs and arguments about white superiority.

Here then is a conception of racism not as the beliefs, arguments or theories
themselves, nor as a property of those who believe in them, nor even as a broader
category of thought to which people can appeal. Racism is a relationship
between 'insiders' and 'outsiders' that is given potency by ill-defined but
efficient beliefs that have been passed down through the generations, though
with many tortuous changes. The historical experience of outsiders who have
been identified by their alleged race leads us to conclude that Britain remains
unremittingly exclusive. It excludes those who fail, for whatever reason, to 'fit
in', to assimilate. And even, if they do, there are no guarantees. The British even
today are always looking backwards to confirm that they are still best. Events
such as those covered in the last section do no damage at all to this process.

If, as we argue, racism is best seen as a quality of relationship, rather than a
category of beliefs, then we should recognize that it is possible to conceive of a
'reverse' or black racism. Blacks' relationship with whites has been structured by
history and filtered through the experience of modern times. And, as whites
have drawn reference points from lost empires, blacks have maps of their own
history. The perspectives, of course, contrast. Actual beliefs, arguments or
theories are used as resources, supplying supports or defences for particular types
of relationship. Though, as we've seen, they are more than mere ingenious
expedients in changing times: beliefs about natural orders cling like barnacles to
the sunken hulk of empire.

Black equivalents are drawn from a different experience, but the contents of
some beliefs and their practical implications suggest direct comparisons. 'There is
no doubt, for example, that many of the statements made by the American
"black" Muslim leader, Louis Farrakhan, warrant description as racism',
observes Miles (1989, p. 6). While he doesn't spell out his point, Miles
presumably refers to the acerbic anti-semitism that pours from Farrakhan and his
followers in the Nation of Islam movement. This proved something of an

embarrassment to Democratic presidential nominee, Jesse Jackson, when he made a public reference to New York as 'kike city'. Previous Nation of Islam leaders, such as Malcolm X and Elijah Muhammad, had also attracted accusations of racism in the 1960s and 1970s. But Farrakhan and his acolytes, in the late 1980s, added new dimensions with the idea of wealthy Jews encouraging the flow of narcotics, particularly the cocaine derivative 'crack' into black ghettos to induce dependence and enforce control over blacks. The theory had a disarming symmetry with the purported Zionist world domination conspiracy of the *Protocols* which has inspired white racist organizations for generations (see Chapter 8). In one notable interview in 1989, an aide to Eugene Sawyer, then Mayor of Chicago, was quoted as saying that Jewish doctors had infected blacks with the HIV virus, thus precipitating the spread of Aids in US ghettos (reported in *Sunday Times*, 18 June 1989). You might call this historical revisionism; you might call it paranoia. The conspiracy theory has gained currency only among some portions of the American black population. But, it's current enough to prompt questions about whether it really is a form of racism. In a sense, it's a negation of whites' racism: accepting the basic categories imposed by whites to justify their domination, then denying the validity of the meanings attached to those categories, according to whites' doctrines. Accepted is: the fact that blacks constitute a distinct race. Rejected is: that the race is inferior and degenerate. Viewed in terms of content, this mirrors ideas and ideologies of white racism. Some interpretations closely resemble white supremacist visions, especially in regard to Jews, who are depicted as spiders at the centre of a vast web they have surreptitiously spun about the world.

If it were a straight question of beliefs, then there would be little argument about the existence of black racism. But, content is only one component of the relationship. Black populations have been affected by the accumulated experience of forcible migration and enduring oppression. The material element of blacks' relationship with whites has affected both parties' mentalities, outlooks and approaches to each other. One big difference is that white racism, as we will see in chapters to come, is a direct legacy of imperialism, whereas the black version is a reaction to the experience of racism. We believe that this qualitative difference is disguised by the term 'black racism' which implies too simple a comparison with its white counterpart. Blacks' reaction to white racism may take many forms: accepting racial categories and articulating them in a way that mimics white racists is but one of them. We don't believe analytical purposes are served by calling this black racism. The term misguidedly suggests that modern racism can be studied without careful consideration of the vastly different historical experiences of groups involved.

By implication, we have to resist describing the kind of conflict witnessed in recent years on both sides of the Atlantic and featuring only ethnic minorities as *racialist*. Later in the book, we use 'racialist' synonomously with 'racial discrimination' to mean actions, or practices, that are motivated by racism. Afro-Caribbeans clashing with Asians in Birmingham, England, or black Americans locked in combat with Cubans in Florida, USA, may resemble other forms of violence associated with racism. But, in these conflicts, a resentment or rivalry is recognizable. Rivalry in the inner city isn't novel. So how do we explain this?

Historically, we all tend to assess our material circumstances and progress against tangible points of reference. We find such reference points in our immediate environment as well as in society-at-large. Class, gender, age and ethnicity are obvious indicators. Living in the constricting environs of the inner city encourages comparisons: ethnic minorities might easily evaluate their own progress with that of other ethnic minorities, some of whom may be regarded in racial terms. These may or may not be outpacing them in material terms. Asian or Cuban businesses may be small beer objectively speaking, but signs over shop fronts reading 'Dhorajia' or 'Diaz' can give different impressions to recipients of income support or welfare benefits. They can stir exactly the kind of enmity that flares into *inter-ethnic conflict* (a term that carries no presumption of a natural hierarchy). Such conflict is parodied, with only minor exaggeration, in Spike Lee's film *Do the Right Thing* (1989), in which an angry exchange between blacks and Italians on a scorching summer's day in Brooklyn's Bedford-Stuyvesant district spirals into a calamitous scene involving Puerto Ricans, Asians and every other ethnic minority in the polyglot area. This shows the USA not as a melting pot, but as a witch's cauldron that spits, sizzles then boils over when left outside in a heatwave. The eeriest aspect of the plot is its plausibility. No single person shoulders responsibility: a tense, but seemingly trivial, dispute rumbles towards a climactic conflict almost independently of the personnel involved. With final quotations from Martin Luther King condemning violence and Malcolm X approving violence as 'intelligence', Lee leaves us with more questions than we started. We intend to pay our readers the same compliment. Our method is to ask questions at the beginning of each chapter, then offer possible ways of approaching them, without suggesting there are pat answers.

But what is race? It strikes us as one of the great diabolic probelms of our time — and as with most problems, there are creators and victims. In the next chapter we show how the problem was created in history and how, even centuries ago, it was closely related to issues of power and class. Briefly stated, race was originally a unit of classification, a principle for understanding the characteristics by which segments of the world's population were divided. With the expansion of European colonialism, the white-skinned adventurers came across darker-skinned peoples who were less advanced technologically and who subscribed to different religious beliefs. The Europeans judged them on these, reasoning that they were, in many senses, inferior to their 'enlightened' white counterparts.

The subsequent domination or enslavement of these peoples to further the interests of those prospering from colonialism and the growth of the empire reinforced the feeling that the world was composed of different types of groups and that some groups were superior to others. The theories abounding in the eighteenth century gave added force to the view that fundamental inequalities between races of people existed. Further, in an era when the church taught a philosophy based on the fixed, unchangeable order of things, it was believed that the inferior dark-skinned races could simply not be educated sufficiently to become the equal of whites. Thus, no opportunities for improvement were offered them and the original evaluations were seen to be validated as the gaps between white and dark-skinned peoples widened. The theories of racial inequality appeared to be accurate and the reality of race was not in doubt.

The original creators of these equalities are long gone, yet their legacy remains. The exact nature of race has been the subject of many a controversy at both the scientific and the street level. But people still rightly or wrongly believe in it; and so they act on it; and this, according to the argument we develop in chapter 2, makes it real. No matter how offensive we find race and how unimpressed we are by the scientific research on it, it remains a great motivating force behind peoples' thought and behaviour. It cannot be wished away.

Race is as real as people want it to be and we do not wish to deny its reality. However, we are not interested in its biological basis. This is not denying that humans do possess genotypes, that is the genetic set of instructions for physical and intellectual development; a person may be born genotypically big and strong. But environmental conditions like poor nutrition might make it impossible for that person to develop in this way and, instead, may facilitate their development as small and weak; this eventually would be the person's phenotype. Much of the biological research into race has been directed towards locating and establishing the nature of genotypes, though, of course, the absence of controlled breeding and regulated environments has complicated matters.

Somewhere, somehow, it may be technically possible to determine the exact genotypical nature of different races. But this in no way negates the arguments we propose throughout this book, because we are interested not in the genetic aspects of race, but in the social reality of race. In other words, the reasons why people believe in the existence of race and the ways in which their behaviour is affected by their beliefs. This, in essence, is the starting point of the study of race relations — as against the study of race in itself. People fashion their relations with others on the basis of what they believe about others; if they believe those others belong to a group which is genetically and permanently different and possibly inferior in some respect, then we have a situation of race relations.

Robert Miles has strongly criticized the concepts of race and race relations and all those who use them as 'analytical categories'. He acknowledges that race and race relations exist 'in the sense that human agents believe them to exist, but uncritically to reproduce and accord analytical status to those beliefs is nevertheless to legitimate that process by giving it 'scientific' status (1982, p. 33). In other words, Miles wants to investigate what he calls 'the social construction of race': how and for what reasons race is generated and reproduced? In this sense, his task is broadly in alignment with our own, though we are much less inclined to make hard and fast distinctions between what Miles calls 'commonsense categories' (like race) and 'structural realities' (such as class and relations of production) (see Miles, 1982).

In contrast, Michael Banton has defended the use of the race relations term: 'Just as there is a folk concept of race, so there is a folk concept of race relations, but that need not prevent the latter expression being used as a name for a field of study' (1979, p. 137). Miles reckons Banton contradicts himself by making the parallel between social scientists and doctors of medicine and stating that medicine would not proceed if doctors accepted their patients' conceptions of their complaints. Maybe not, but the doctor is invariably dependent on the patient's experiences for a full understanding of the problem; and, in any case, we do not share Miles's view that social science bears direct comparison with medical science. We are not setting ourselves up as surgeons, scalpels at the ready, poised to dissect our patients and rid them of their maladies. Social scientific work is of a quite different nature and, as we hope to show, requires accepting a great many viewpoints including those of such people as the recipients of racial attacks as well as the instigators of them. The racist has a conception of social reality and one which we, as social scientists, cannot afford to ignore or dismiss.

This then is the focus of our book and in the chapters that follow we will explore the different dimensions of race relations, mainly in the UK and USA, but with references to elsewhere. We highlight the key issue of social inequality, in chapter 4, showing how it has reared itself in the workplace and, in chapter 5, as it operates in the sphere of housing. Education is seen by many as the instrument for the removal of inequalities but by others as the perpetuator of them; we give air to the arguments in chapter 6. In all these chapters, we close with an assessment of the ways in which this inequality can be either minimized or squashed.

There has been a trend over recent years to change the whole field of study to ethnic relations. Given our theoretical position on race, we see no reason to follow this trend and, in any case, we work with a very specific definition of ethnicity as elaborated in chapter 7. Without preempting our argument, let's say that an ethnic group is a collection of people who feel themselves to be distinct in some way and united in some common cause, usually because of their distinctness. Ethnicity, then, is a subjective feeling of sharing and, possibly, being oppressed. A racial group, by contrast, is a label stuck on a collection of people by others, like white Europeans, who feel themselves to be different, maybe superior, to those people. Historically, the main and most effective labellers have been white and those to whom the labels have stuck most fast black or brown.

Chapter 8 is a more detailed examination of the white groups who have been most resolute in their labelling and have taken it to extremes by mounting campaigns aimed at either the expulsion or elimination of so-called inferior races. This type of white reaction to blacks has a long history, but took on greater virulence more or less immediately after the end of slavery and continues to the present day. We trace its development.

The media bear important influences on how we think and, therefore, how we act and in chapter 9 we assess their role in depicting race and related issues with a view to appraising the extent to which television, newspapers, books, etc. have affected race relations.

This then is the plan for the book and it is directed towards our concluding chapter in which we make a clinical assessment of and prognosis for race relations. Each of the chapters follows a logical sequence and builds into a general argument which is that race relations today cannot be understood without one eye on history and that this history is one steeped in the traditions of conquest, colonialism and empire. We argue that the whole structure of colonialism may be disintegrating, but the remnants of it remain in people's thinking. This is what we term the colonial mentality and its sense is expressed perfectly by a Punjabi interviewed in the BBC-2 series, *The Promised Land*: '200 years of seeing someone as a coolie does not end in thirty-five years' (12 August 1982).

The whole book is organized inside this framework, but the individual chapters are also self-contained in the sense that they isolate particular, relevant areas of race relations and make specific points, arguments and conclusions about each. As this book is intended as much for beginners as the advance students of race relations, we have included in the text more detailed definitions of some of the 'trade terms' and ended each chapter with a number of suggestions for further reading.

Further Reading

'Culture, nation and "race" in the British and French New Right' is Gill Seidel's contribution to **The Ideology of the New Right** edited by Ruth Levitas (1986). Alongside David Edgar's chapter, 'The Free or the Good' in the same volume, it provides a clear insight into the New Right's anti-egalitarian ideology and the cultural basis of its racist convictions. Seidel's chapter in particular engages critically with some of the seminal articles of the New Right in the UK written by 'luminaries' such as Roger Scruton, Raymond Honeyford and Anthony Flew.

'Race' in Britain: Continuity and Change, 2nd edition, edited by Charles Husband (1987) examines the concept of race in contemporary British society and culture through the writings of a number of scholars. The chapters by Husband on the construction of racial ideologies, by Miles on racism and nationalism in Britain and one of us (BT) on how the media promote limited conceptions of British citizenship are especially pertinent to the themes argued in this chapter.

Black Youth, Racism and the State by John Solomos (1988) examines some of the key issues in British race relations in the 1980s, black youth–police relations being the fulcrum of the argument. It is also valuable in highlighting the ways in which ethnic minorities are actually 'made' into social problems.

Ideological Dilemmas: A social psychology of everyday thinking by Michael Billig and his research group from Loughborough University (1988) deals with a variety of issues, including 'prejudice and tolerance' where the discussion centres on the distinction between the 'modern racist' and the 'redneck racist'. The former avoids expressing crude racist views and phrases his or her 'negative opinions' of ethnic minorities in 'reasonable' and 'respectable' terms. 'The modern racist' according to the authors, 'believes that black people are "getting more than they deserve" and are receiving unfairly generous, and thereby unequal, privileges and "they", despite the good qualities of some of "them", are held to be different from "us" '.

Communicating Racism by Teun A. van Dijk (1989) investigates how racism is communicated in everyday language. This microlevel analysis is based on extensive research interviews and embedded in a multidisciplinary framework. His focus is 'the reproduction of racism . . . through a detailed analysis of communicative interactions'. Communicating 'prejudice' (his term) is seen to be functional, for instance in 'signalling group membership, the display of social competence, the sharing of socially relevant experiences and cognitions, or the illustration and prescription of effective social action against minorities.' His analysis of 'Racial discourse' complements the insights provided by Billig and his colleagues.

Minorities and Outsiders is the second of three volumes on *Patriotism: The Making and Unmaking of British National Identity*, edited for Routledge by Raphael Samuel (1989). Alongside its companion volumes it explores changing notions of patriotism in British life. In this collection Samuel argues in his introductory chapter that: 'Minorities have not normally had an easy time of it in Britain' and the case studies which follow exemplify the point vividly. What's more, they demonstrate the truth of Samuel's claim that, whilst tolerance 'enjoys an honoured place in the pantheon of national virtues', it is a feature of British life that hardly survives historical scrutiny. More realistic is the view that 'Britishness' is formed mainly through processes of exclusion and 'in relations of opposition to enemies both without and within'.

2
Race — power — prejudice

- What is race? Something natural?
- Are race and inequality inseparable?
- Is race connected with power and domination?
- What are the causes of racial prejudice?
- How is race related to ideology?

That remarkable urge

A distinctive feature of human beings, as compared to animals, is the ability to act purposefully and intentionally. We behave not instinctively or as if subjected to governing forces, but with a consciousness of what we are doing. We are, for the most part, rational, often calculating and frequently goal-directed and we guide the way we act towards specific objectives. To have such objectives we need knowledge about them and how they might be achieved; we can then act on the basis of such knowledge.

A strange way to begin to study of race relations? Not really, for it is the human capacity to draw on knowledge and act out intended courses of behaviour which makes such things as race relations possible. People relate to each other in terms of the knowledge they have of each other. They are not drawn together or thrust apart by innate drives or external powers — though, in some situations, it might appear to be the case. People organize their social arrangements in terms of what they think, so there is always a very close connection between what goes on inside their heads and what they actually do in their everyday lives. The connection is an ill-defined one, but ideas and actions are inseparable.

Of course, the ideas which comprise the stock of knowledge available to us are not uninfluenced by the societies in which we live. As we will argue, no knowledge is ever neutral: it is always, in some way, affected by the social contexts. What we think has to be seen as relative to our environment. It is for this reason that race relations has to be seen not simply as the way in which people act towards each other. This is merely one dimension of study and, important as it is, it tells us little of the complusions behind the actions. Race

ENVIRONMENT
Very basically, this refers to everything external to the individual: a social environment may be composed of other people; a physical environment of actual material products. In both instances, the individual is susceptible to outside influences. The importance of the idea of environment is in the observation that 'no man is an island': she or he always responds to and is shaped by the influences of other people and things. So, she or he may be influenced by prejudiced friends and become prejudiced in her or his own ideas. In chapter 5, we show how the physical environment of the city can have effects on relationships.

relations also involves how people think about each other, the ideas they hold about one another. It's for this reason that we accept Banton's view that to understand the nature of race relations we 'should approach it from the standpoint of the growth of knowledge' (1977, p. 5).

As our knowledge of others develops, we become aware of possibilities for action. Maybe that action is to restrict contacts, maybe it is to intensify them. There is, of course, an endless array of possibilities, and race relations study is about analysing them. But it must also find out what it is in peoples' heads that makes them organize social relationships in certain patterns.

There is nothing natural or inevitable about blacks in the UK and USA of the 1980s living in tight constellations in the inner cities — places commonly called ghettos. Nor is there anything natural about the high number of South Asians in manual work. For that matter, we can look at any conceivable aspect of race relations, historical or modern, whether it's slavery, rioting or underachieving at school, and argue that each deserves investigation as patterns of action — and, therefore, the results of ideas. A sociobiologist might say something like racial hostility or prejudice is 'bound to happen...human nature' (see, for example, Tiger, 1969; Wilson, 1975). But we feel that this fogs the issue. Dismissing social events as natural outcomes is ultimately obscuring and only inhibits understanding of the frequently complex processes underlying race relations.

Yet, it cannot be denied that resorting to vague theories of human nature or innate propensities to action is a beautifully convenient and, under some circumstances, plausible way of explaining what might otherwise be mysterious events. Take, the concept of race itself: it seems to contain some element of a biological reality quite separate from social relations. To talk in terms of a race implies that the world's human population is divisible into discrete portions distinguished by biological properties. We still hear, for instance, about having our race's 'blood in our veins'. Qualities like skin pigmentation are commonly thought to reflect inner characteristics. In this way, skin colour divides humanity: people fight, abuse or just despise each other simply because of skin colour. But, while the belief in the reality of race can be seen as responsible for prompting the antagonisms, it can slso be invoked as an explanation of them: 'It's only natural.'

Yet, on closer examination, we can see there is far from universal agreement on exactly what race means. The concept is notoriously fragile when subjected to biological analysis, but is incredibly powerful as a force in history. Or rather, the belief in race has been — and still is — a powerful force. What we will argue is that race is real and it is part of our stock of knowledge. Our justification for this derives from Peter Berger and Thomas Luckmann who argue: 'It will be enough, for our purposes, to define 'reality' as a quality appertaining to phenomena that we recognize has having a being independent of our own volition (we cannot ''wish them away''), and to define ''knowledge'' as the certainty that phenomena are real and that they possess specific characteristics' (1972, p. 13).

For our purposes too, this seems to suit, for, if people recognize that race exists, undesirable as it may be, it cannot be 'wished away', it is real. The consequences it will have in their behaviour towards others will serve to reinforce its reality. If teachers believe that black students are ill-equipped intellectually compared to whites, then they will tend to have depressed expectations of their school performances and so treat them differently to whites.

Race, then, is real and, as we will see, it is real in its consequences. But it has a multifaceted reality and part of its attraction — if we can call it that — is due to its unfathomable ambiguity. Its roots are in what Jacques Barzun has called: 'That remarkable urge to lump together the attributes of large masses' (1937, p. 18). It has been defined in a bewildering variety of ways and has given rise to an equally bewildering variety of actions. In some cases, as we will document, the definition followed the action and, was invariably, manipulated to suit the action or even provide a rationalization for it.

It's possible, however, to trace a unity, for underlying all the conceptions of race there is the simple conviction that human beings are separable into types that are permanent and enduring; that there are a limited number of types and these are races fixed by biological characteristics. In itself this conviction is fairly innocuous; it constitutes an attempt to classify human populations in terms of immanent physical features.

We can imagine the classification along a horizontal parameter and think it interesting, if without immediate relevance save for aiding our comprehension of how physiological and, perhaps, psychological differences between individuals and groups occur. It is when the classification turns on its axis that its overtones become more sinister. No longer is it a simple ordering of groups on the basis of racial characteristics: now it takes on a moral complexion with some groups, or races, appearing higher than others in a ranked hierarchy. The vertical dimension introduces pernicious typologies. Races are better or worse, superior or inferior and these flow easily into ideas about dominant and dominated races. A dominating group can easily justify its position along the lines of: 'Well, we're the superior race, so we deserve to be in our dominating position. After all, it's only natural!'

In history, we find this kind of reasoning in the heart and blood of all theories about race. The concept was given life and maintained its being by this specious logic. Its vitality and power derives from inequalities and is a source of inequalities. Race and inequality are, as we shall see, intimately connected — perfect partners. The scientific bases on which the ideas of race rest may be disinterested and detached from the issues of inequality, but there again, race is not simply the preserve of academics. It is when it is in the hands, or, more accurately, heads of 'men-in-the-street' that it takes on its more powerful form. Our first approach to understanding this power, then, has to be historical. We will take Banton's advice and look at race as a growth of knowledge, a knowledge which has early origins.

Sources: from the Bible to Darwin

The protean concept of race has as many uses as it has definitions. Barzun notes a very early interest in physical appearances of various groups taken by the ancient Greeks, including Aristotle and Hippocrates, though: 'In recent times, the first systematic division of mankind into races is that by Bernier in 1684' (1937, p. 51).

Medieval thinkers, following Aristotle's example, tried to sort out things into their essential generic properties, when stripped of their superficial features. Herbalists classified plants and herbs, mainly for medicinal purposes and one notable botanist, Linnaeus, in 1735, published a system of classifying all living phenomena. As an item of classification, the concept of race was already available; it was regarded at the time as a sort of lowest common denominator of biological forms.

The sources of the concept? Well, it's extraordinarily difficult to locate the origins of what was even then an obscure concept. The idea of separating out men on a biological basis is found in the Bible, particularly in Genesis X where the three sons of Noah are said to form three distinct lines of descent. Significantly, they all had a common ancestor in Noah, a point picked up by St Paul in Acts, xvii: 24–6: 'God . . . hath made of one blood all nations of men.' The New English Bible translation of this passage reads: 'He created every race of men of one stock.' The theme would seem to be that there exist several

---

MONOGENESIS
The view that all humans are descended from one essential source; it derives from the Bible but was given credibility by Linnaeus who advocated 'The great chain of being' concept, meaning that all creation is arranged in strict hierarchical sequence with creatures distinguished from each other in a series of linked gradations. This contrasts with **POLYGENESIS**, the thesis that argues that the differences existing between living creatures was due to their being separately created, i.e. from distinct, unrelated sources; thus there is separate development.

---

separable types of human beings, though they are ultimately unified at source through their sharing of a single ancestor. This is called monogenesis.

Whatever its origins, race was available and in use as a scientific concept by the eighteenth century when it became the basis of identifying the common descent of sets of people. Obvious physical differences were taken for granted and race was thought to account for how they came to appear so markedly different.

Up to Linnaeus, biblical stories of the earth's history were largely accepted, but the discovery of fossil remains of creatures raised severe doubts about the accuracy of Genesis and the Adam and Eve scenario. There were various attempts to reconcile the new findings with the Old Testament, most revolving around the problem of human divisions. Prior to 1800, the concept of race itself was generally taken to refer to the way physical differences between human groups were the results of the circumstances of their history. So, as the Bible alluded to it, race was more to do with lineage. But then, as Banton points out: 'In the nineteenth century race comes to signify an inherent physical quality. Other peoples are seen as biologically different. Though the definition remained uncertain, people began to assume that mankind was divided into races' (1977, p. 18). And it's in this sense of the word that race came to take on the significance it has in the modern world.

What followed the changed conception of race as a physical, fixed category is what Banton calls the 'racializing' process, whereby people began to organize their perception of each other in terms of permanent physical differences. It was a very short step from theorizing about the differentness of peoples to theorizing about inequalities between them: if people were of different races, those races may not all be of equal standing; some might be superior to others. Exemplifying this principle is the work of Joseph Arthur, Comte de Gobineau (1816–82), whose historical interest lay in the question of why once-great societies seemed destined to decay.

The answer, Gobineau thought, might be the fundamental inequality of races. Gobineau floated the idea of a threefold division of humans into white, yellow and black races, each of which possessed specific characteristics, such as whites with leadership, and blacks with sensuality. 'Civilizations,' replete with government and art, result from the mixing of races, but this inevitably led to the dilution of the 'Great Race' and the decadence, or *dégénération*, this brought. Gobineau accepted the prevalent monogenist view that all human descended from a single pair of ancestors but did not take this to imply that all were equal. On the contrary, some races occupied higher intellectual positions than others.

Gobineau's theories were most influential in the middle 1800s, particularly in Europe where there was widespread debate over the race issue. The counter to Gobineau's view came with Georges Pouchet who stressed the physical and mental diversities of races which he felt all had separate origins — the polygenist viewpoint. The monogenist school maintained that humans had a single origin, but since races were manifestly different, there must have been evolutionary changes. Pouchet and his school believed in prehuman ancestry giving rise independently to several species of man which were more closely related to their ancestors than to each other. In this perspective, races were fundamentally different, unrelated and irredeemably divided even at source.

The publication of Pouchet's theory in 1858 preceded by one year the release of Charles Darwin's *Origin of the Species*, and of course this work was to transform our knowledge of human evolution (though Darwin was rather guarded in his speculations in the first edition). Darwin precipitated the development of new perspectives on race as John R. Baker notes: 'If man had originated not by special creation but by evolution, it was perhaps natural to suppose that the human races might represent stages in this process, or the branches of an evolutionary tree' (1974, p. 39).

This meant a complete re-thinking of the concept of the finite number of permanent types, all of distinct origins (interbreeding would have no lasting impact as hybrid stocks were eventually sterile). Variations of human forms were seen as only superficial. In contrast to this and the degeneration that it implied through people like Gobineau, Darwin and his followers forwarded a process of natural selection in which the existing diversity of human forms would be reduced to a smaller number of races best suited to the prevailing environment — the survival of the fittest races. Hence, they were confident of a human progress towards an ever-improving series of races.

The principle of evolution offered an open challenge to orthodox Christianity in seeming to offer an explanation of the origins of humans in scientific terms. Adam and Eve stories were relegated to the realms of fairly tales as Darwin proposed a model of the human being as the extension of animal ancestors. In the Darwinian perspective, people were animals, albeit special ones, with a history stretching back to the Cambrian period when fossils were first preserved in rocks. All living creatures belonged to species, or distinguishable generic groups, but, crucially, they were subject to mutations; they were in a constant process of change.

Not surprisingly, after Darwin, the study of man commanded the attentions of many zoologists; humans were animals, so they were fair game for study. The German, Karl Vogt, for example, postulated a process of convergent change: he believed that, if the various races could be traced back to their origins, no single human type could be found. But, over the centuries, humans came to resemble each other in several important respects. Human races were essentially different but converging towards similarity.

Vogt's work was seen as radical in the mid-1800s and his polygenetic conclusions were tantamount to heresy. So were the theories of another German zoologist, Ernst Haeckel who, with Vogt, considered that prevailing human races were unequal in many respects. In particular, Haeckel identified the 'Indogermanic' race as intellectually superior. Small wonder than that his famous work, *The Riddle of the Universe* (1899), became a best-seller as the Nazis grew to prominence. According to Haeckel there was a scale of development with 'woolly haired Negroes' being much closer to their animal origins than the more mentally developed race.

Though it is unclear as to whether Darwin himself would have agreed with Haeckel, we can be sure that his impact in Europe was enormous, perhaps because, as Daniel Gasman argues, the Germans saw Darwin through the distorted lenses of Haeckel (1971). Nevertheless, repercussions of Darwinism were felt in the nineteenth and twentieth centuries principally in two social phenomena: imperialist slavery and Nazism. In these two, we begin to see the practical significance of the race concept. It was not only an idle idea of philosophers or speculators on the nature of humanity that helped us understand convergences and cleavages of groups. Ideas are not spontaneous; they have authors, people who try to sell their theories. And sellers need buyers who can see the practical utility and seek to use the theories as ways of augmenting actions. We do not have to question the motives of the original conceivers to recognize the significance of theories of race. Their rise to power through their adoption by others, however, often smacks less of the imperative to further understanding than the impulse to rule. As Barzun writes: 'The irony of race-theories is that they arise invariably from a desire to mould other's action rather than to explain facts' (1937, p. 284).

There is a popular though indefensible misconception that ideas about race grew out of the series of contacts betwee European explorers and the peoples whom they encountered on their voyages to the Americas, Africa and parts of Asia. We've already noted that the concept itself has much older origins than the contact period of the fifteenth and sixteenth centuries. Certainly, its meaning changed and interest in race grew rapidly after this time, but its presence lurked even before.

It is, of course, no coincidence that the growth in currency of race occurred at roughly the same time as Europeans were widening their colonial nets and enslaving vast proportions of populations. Improvements in transport and communications meant more and more contacts with unfamiliar peoples with different physical appearances, different languages and different cultures. This inspired many to try to make sense of this new-found diversity in human beings. Race was an obvious tool of analysis; but it had other purposes.

Supposing we accept the basic principle of human inequality implicit in Darwinism. We are a country of conquerors; our conquests prove fruitful if we make full use of the materials available in the new lands. We must exploit the natural materials and make full use of the human resources. It makes sense to use our obvious military power to compel the natural populations to obey our commands. They're not compliant so we introduce a strategy: we make them our property and demand total obedience. So much so, in fact, that we lock them in irons, take them wherever we see fit, force them to do any task we desire and punish them severely if they disobey. *Ergo* slavery.

Now this poses a serious dilemma if we accept the fundamental unity and equality of all people, for it seems blatantly wrong for one group to dominate absolutely another and enforce its domination with the utmost cruelty. But a view of the world in which populations divide up naturally into distinct and unequal races is much more accommodating. The argument for slavery can be advanced much more confidently because there is nothing wrong in reducing other races to the status of chattel as long as they're seen as inferior. After all, it was obvious that the conquerors of natives must be, by the mere fact of victory, superior and therefore the better-equipped to survive.

This reasoning lay at the base of a branch of Darwinism that applied itself to whole societies and this was an enormous convenience for slavers, as Barzun argues: 'It was good Social Darwinism for the white man to call the amoeba, the ape, and the Tasmanian his brother; it was equally good Practical Darwinism to show that the extinction of the Tasmanian by the white colonists of Australia was simply a part of the struggle for life leading to the survival of the favoured races by natural selection' (1937, p. 69).

The Darwinian sword could cut both ways. It could maintain that all forms of animate life were related so 'all men were brothers.' But it could also be used to support the view that races, having been established by what Darwin vaguely called 'variation', were struggling for survival and some, the superior ones, were coping better than, and at the cost of, others.

It's easy to understand why many see the concept of racial inequality as little more than a rationalization, a means of intellectually justifying the

SOCIAL DARWINISM
An approach to the study of society. It emerged in the late nineteenth and early twentieth century and gained impetus with the acceptance of Darwin's doctrines of evolution. Basically, the idea was to transfer Darwin's principles on natural selection to the social world. Societies were said to evolve in patterns whereby some institutions and 'races' of people survived because they were better suited to the environment. Thus there was a gradual evolution towards perfectability.

EXPLOITATION
The act of bringing people into service and using their labour to gain profits or advantages.

wholesale exploitation of human beings. It was quite possible and common to entertain a Christian view, yet continue to be a slaver. Darwinism added substance to the view that blacks were not as adequately endowed as whites in the struggle for survival and would probably die out eventually. Slavery assisted a natural process.

Race had great utility in this role and served its masters well in maintaining a semblance of morality in their gross endeavours. But it is certainly not just a rationalization: although it facilitated slavery and even encouraged it in some respects, it did predate it, even if it took on very different meanings in the context of slavery and encouraged pronouncements such as the Lord Chief Justice Mansfield's when summing up the case of the slave ship *Zong* from which slaves were ejected into the sea. Mansfield informed the jury that the drowning of slaves 'was the same as if horses had been thrown overboard'.

Slave-owners, armed with a theory of inequality and the practical experience of plantations to back it up, could quite credibly argue against those who wanted to abolish slavery that slaves were ignorant and illiterate. They were; but because of the denial of any educational facilities. Slavers ignored this and contended they were so because they belonged to an inferior race and were therefore incapable of learning. Their conduct and apparent lack of awareness was not seen as the result of the horrendous conditions they had to exist under nor the animalistic treatment they were subjected to. Race was much simpler: they had inherent natural differences and no amount of education could remove them. Phillip V. Tobias sums up the slave-owner's approach: 'It is easy to deny a subservient people the benefits of civilization and then to describe them as uncivilized' (1972, p. 27).

Race as a concept and the inequality that it entailed was given a massive boost by slavery, which was thought to prove the existence of natural inequality. In effect, it was itself supported by the belief and, once in motion, gained impetus from the debates about the subject. The concept of race both fed a theoretical justification for slavery and was fed nourishment by the results of slavery. The ideas and the actions had a symbiotic relationship: they supported each other. But it was not only in slavery that race had application.

All great civilizations...

Darwinism percolated across Europe, seeping through the theoretical filters of people like Haeckel and, more importantly, Houston Stewart Chamberlain, son of a British naval admiral who studied zoology under Vogt in Geneva. He later moved to Dresden where he developed a historical perspective that was to influence world history.

Published in 1899, Chamberlain's work was a gigantic exploration of what he called 'the foundations of the nineteenth century'. He traced them back to the time of the ancient Israelites, locating the critical year as 1200, the beginning of the 'middle ages' when the race of *Germanen* would emerge 'as the founders of an entirely new civilization and an entirely new culture (quoted in Baker, 1974, p. 49).

A large part of this work, which was to take on a prophetic status, was to play down the parts played by Jews, Romans and Greeks in the development of European culture. In fact, Baker notes of Chamberlain: 'He deplored the increasing influence of Jews in the government, law, science, commerce, literature, and art of Europe' (1974, p. 49).

On the unwanted effects of indiscriminate hybridization or mixing of races, he was in broad agreement with Gobineau, but without the *Leitmotiv* of gloom; Chamberlain was convinced that the strongest, best-equipped and, therefore, fittest race would be able to assume at any moment its dominance and impose itself, thus curbing the tendency to degeneration. That race was derived from the peoples of Germany who constituted a unique race. Chamberlain defined the race as created 'physiologically by characteristic mixture of blood, followed by inbreeding; psychically by the influence that long-continued historical-geographical circumstances produce on that particular, specific, physiological disposition' (quoted in Baker, 1974, pp. 49–50). The influence of Darwin in this context is very apparent.

Of course it would be misleading to cite Chamberlain as the central theoretician in what was later to become Nazism. There is a very clear complementarity between Chamberlain's version of history and National Socialist philosophy. Interestingly, however, he was rather imprecise on the exact meaning of race. The name *Germanen* refers to a mixture of northern and western European populations which are said to form a 'family', the 'essence' of which is the *Germane*. It seems that his general thrust about the inherent superiority of one group over all the rest was more important than the accuracy of his concepts in elevating him to the role of a Nazi prophet. (He died in 1927, before the Nazis came to power.)

Of course, social movements such as Nazism pay scant respect to the intricacies of theories or the complexities of concepts, when they are on a rising curve. The appeal of the movement was based on a crude and selective utilization of theoretical themes by a receptive population and a successful manipulation of them by a coherent, focused organization — the party. Chamberlain's work was selectively used, as was Gustaf Kossina's.

The idea of *Volk* came from Kossina and was meant to emphasize the essential unity of the German character with its self-assurance, reserves of strength, willingness to be led, and intractible urge towards freedom. Such attributes were thought to have enabled Germanic people to overrun large parts of Europe as Roman power declined and to establish themselves as a ruling elite.

Volk was also invoked by Otto Spengler, though with him it was less a biological or anthropological concept and more a cultural one, 'a society of men that feels itself to be a unit.' He made it clear that *Volk* was not to be equated with race in any physical sense, though he stressed the cultural superiority of the Germans and for this reason his work was enthusiastically siezed upon by Nazis.

There are other less influential writers, but uniting them all is a sense of basic inequality: the race set apart and variously defined as *Germanen* or, to use the more obscure Indo-European term, Aryan, was thought to be superior and therefore destined to dominate.

Hitler's *Mein Kampf*, published in two volumes in 1925 and 1927, is a much less violent appraisal of the theories than his actions might suggest. It was a biology of animals and of human beings, noting particularly the tendency of both to draw mates from amongst their own taxa or type. On to this is built a theory of natural progress, an innate impulse to the self-improvement of species under natural conditions.

This was the theoretical foundation for a political philosophy that posited the presence of two main races, Aryans and Jews. The latter was depicted in terms of their astuteness, cunning and wile and their rise to power was seen as self-motivated and in total disregard of other groups. This power, Hitler contended, must be terminated and the purity of the Aryan, or Germanic, race be restored. 'All great civilizations of the past,' he wrote 'only perished because the original creative race died out from blood-poisoning.' His attempts to regain the racial purity of the Aryans barely need going over, though there is little indication of his future intentions in *Mein Kampf*.

In both the examples of slavery and Nazism, incomplete theories of the

ARYANS
Originally, the Aryans were thought to be wandering tribes from Northern India. But the infamy of the concept of the Aryan grew with Hitler's Nazism, which was based on the myth of a supreme race called the Aryan. Influenced by Nietzsche's predictions on the future race of supermen, Hitler experimented with eugenics to further his aim of creating what he thought would be a pure, unpolluted race of people which would lead all others.

origins of humanity and the natural inequalities of people were used in fragmented ways. Doctrines of the racial inferiority of blacks reached their full pitch in the late eighteenth century; the Nazi ideology proliferated prior to World War II. In neither case were there attempts to fuse elements of existing theories into logically coherent complexes. And this tells us something very important about the relationship between ideas, knowledge and action.

Ideas do not have to be clear nor knowledge sound to commission action. The action, however misguided, can then serve in such a way as to enrich the original ideas. The issue of race in the slavery case was invoked to settle moral dilemmas posed by groups of people who were in the business of making capital out of exploitation. In Nazism, it was selected to support the drastic actions of a movement trying to salvage the remnants of a society in steep economic decline. Race was an expedient in both circumstances; it stood as a call to action and, as Manning Nash put it, it 'persistently crops up wherever the political and social circumstances make it functionally pertinent' (1972, p. 113).

So, we see its pertinence in the UK of today: with unemployment affecting about one in seven people, particularly the young, and prices rising at unprecedented rates, race has surfaced as a most urgent call to action. The growth of such neo-Nazi movements as the National Front and the British Movement plus the incorporation of race into mainstream political debate attests to the persistence of the concept even thirty years after UNESCO had denied its validity as a scientific concept and government bodies decried its use as a political expedient. The point is that race means different things to different people and it's very hard to be even a little more precise than that, if only because even the biological, genetic evidence we have available today is perplexing and contradictory (see Banton, 1979). About this, we aren't concerned; we will not complicate our argument by entering into debates about the actual biological bases of race. As social scientists, this matters less to us than the way in which everyday people think about race. We're interested in the social reality of race rather than the search for the essential nature of the phenomenon.

Race is not a problem: it's something that people create as a problem.

Questions about just how fundamental are the differences between human beings are not in themselves causes for outrage, nor for abuses, less still for rioting. Yet, wherever it becomes possible to conceive and delineate those differences in terms of natural properties, there arise certain groups who seem only too eager to justify privilege or even persecution because of those properties. That's when the race question takes on social dimensions. The ideas provided by Gobineau, Darwin, Chamberlain and the others were, in themselves, harmless. But they provided, however inadvertently, criteria for exploitation, murder and genocide.

The theorists themselves were about as much to blame for these as Einstein was for the wipe-out of Hiroshima. Not a perfect parallel admittedly but one meant to convey the importance of how knowledge is used in practical circumstances. This is what we need to examine in very close detail. Some would argue that there is no complete, exhaustive set of conditions we can specify to explain and predict when and how race emerges as an instrument — something to be socially used either to instigate or justify inequalities. The range of historical circumstances in which the concept has been given purchase is very wide indeed. There are others who have tried to develop theories purporting to explain the existence of the race issue without resort to actual theories about race itself. In this type of perspective, race is seen as a distortion of reality, a way of protecting the interests of groups which hold power and intend to hang on to it with whatever means they have available.

Race and capitalism

Oliver Cromwell Cox was interested in race relations, which he defined as 'that behaviour which develops among peoples who are aware of each others' actual or imputed physical differences' (1948). He was not particularly interested in race itself: his focus was on contacts between groups who are conscious of each other having physical, racial differences. So, if a man looks white in the USA, but he is called black everywhere, then he is a black American; but if a man of identical physical appearance is recognized everywhere in Cuba as a white man, then he is a white Cuban — for Cox's purposes. Conversely, if two people or groups of what Cox calls 'different racial strains' come into contact with but are not conscious of each other's differences, there does not exist a situation of race relations. This may sound rather obvious to social scientists in the 1980s, but, in the 1940s, when Cox is writing, it was an important reorientation in thinking. The sociologists, Robert Park and Ernest Burgess, had, between 1930 and 1940, pushed study in a social direction, detailing the ecological influences on relationships between various groups (we consider their work and influence in chapter 5). But Park and Burgess tended to study segments of social life in isolation, looking at the ways in which race becomes an issue by examining the interactions of people living in the cities.

For Cox, this approach lacked a critical component: power. Race manifests as an issue and prompts conflict between different groups because it is a convenient device for power-holders who need any weapon they can get to prise open gaps between the working classes and thus keep them fragmented.

Cox's argument, simply stated, was that people are encouraged to think in terms of race and, therefore, inherent inequality because it benefits capitalism. This system is based on a basic split over the ownership of the means of production: the owners, capitalists, continually need to exploit the nonowners, or workers, on whom they depend for labour. Their remaining in power as owners is contingent on their ability to maintain their grip over the workers and this is best done if those workers don't perceive their common exploitation, unite and present opposition. So, it becomes necessary to keep them divided into fractions, if possible by introducing and perpetuating antagonisms between them.

The race issue performs the function perfectly: it encourages the workers to regard each other as inherently different and unequal. They arrange their relationships with each other so as to align themselves with members of their own race whom they perceive as allies. The capitalists' heaviest weapon is open racial conflict when groups organize their allegiances along perceived racial lines and clash with those of other races (see chapter 4). But at a covert level, a simmering or latent conflict is also useful in preventing the workers from perceiving their real allegiances — with each other — and their real opposition — the capitalist class. Racial antagonism was, according to Cox, a 'fundamental trait' of capitalism. Race as a socially defined category is a product purely of the development of capitalism and Cox points to the end of the fifteenth century as the crucial date when the system began to introduce the concept as a method of dividing workers. At this stage, the Europeans were extending their links in colonizing the world and needed the racial facility to justify and promote the exploitation.

Interestingly, Cox noted that the white workers in the early stages of capitalism were as savagely exploited as blacks and capitalists invoked the race issue to justify their unequal treatement of them too, claiming that social class characteristics are transmitted through heredity. Race was an additional weapon in their arsenal.

So, the concept of race facilitated the exploitation of blacks in particular and the working class in general. It provided a justification for consigning workers to degrading employment and treatment by stating that they were innately degenerate and naturally suited to such conditions, and served the purpose of

---

RACIALISM
The action of discriminating against particular others by using the belief that they are racially different, and usually inferior. It is the practical element of the race concept.

---

fragmenting the working class and inhibiting a united challenge against the system of domination.

In Cox's view, all the phenomena of race relations had to be seen as part of the economic system of exploitation. Race as a functional concept had clear utilities, but so had racial prejudice — the hostile or negative attitudes towards groups seen to be a different race. There is obviously no natural reason why some groups should feel antagonistic towards another: in fact Cox reasoned that, without capitalism, the world might never have experienced racialism. Everything to do with race and race relations was, for Cox, epiphenomenal: a mere symptom of the underlying reality of capitalism, a spin-off rather than a cause of antagonism. This is, of course, in sharp contrast to the early views that race was a natural cause of antagonisms between unequal groups. In this way, Cox prompted a completely new approach: race had to be seen as a by-product, albeit a most important and functional one, of the economic system.

Cox specified 'situations of race relations' in which there was, to a greater or lesser extent, an awareness on the behalf of one or more of the groups of the different racial type of the other or others. Perceptions are organized so as to demarcate lines of alignment and cleavage and these are drawn on the basis of race. Here we return to our original theme: for all the race relations situations as depicted by Cox stress the close link between ideas about race and the social actions implied by them.

The sources of the race ideas are, from Cox's marxian vantage point, the product of material relations, meaning that the holders of power (or of material resources) also have the power to influence the thoughts of the rest of society through ideology. Karl Marx's dictum that 'The ideas of the ruling class are in every epoch the ruling ideas' is the basis for this observation. Cox's argument here was, in a sense, a reaction to an earlier work by Gunnar Myrdal, *An American Dilemma*, published in 1944, in which it was suggested that the 'American creed' lay behind the racial conflict in the USA. Myrdal identified the problem as a 'white problem' because the system of values accepted by whites emphasized nationalism and Christianity yet encouraged self-interests which were incompatible. Crudely put, Myrdal saw the conflicts causing race problems as arising from what whites think. Cox objected to this as superficial: for Cox, what goes on inside peoples' heads is a reflection of their material circumstances.

IDEOLOGY
In one sense, this describes a general apprehension of the world, a way of
interpreting and explaining things that go on about us. But a marxian view
would be that ideology is a false way of interpreting the world — a way
that is disseminated by the ruling classes and accepted by those who are
ruled. In this way, domination is facilitated by the ruled group's lack of
questioning. In both senses, an ideology is a picture of the world, an
attempt at comprehending its complexities and an effort to situate oneself
in the world.

Beliefs are not primary causes of action, but are part of the ruling ideas of that epoch and are, therefore, instrumental in perpetuating class inequalities and the domination of the working class.

Now, this is a critical feature of race relations studies. We will argue that it must be, for our contention is that all situations in which race is a relevant factor involve a consciousness of race; and that consciousness must be an element of study. Being conscious of race is always a condition of race relations situations. Where there is no active consciousness of race, there is no issue. Race does not become important until people start thinking about it as such.

About this point, there would be no disagreement: race is in the consciousness. There is, however, little unity in theories about its source. Cox would argue that it derives from unequal power relationships and the ensuing ability of dominating groups to impose their conceptions on the rest of society. Others would find this insufficiently detailed at the psychological level, finding the Cox line rather too broad, if not too crude.

That people do think in terms of race and arrange their perceptions of each other so as to accommodate the concept is beyond doubt. This is the everyday form of racism; on a national level, it can express itself in full-blown doctrines such as that of South Africa where apartheid makes sure the idea of racial inequality pervades the whole of society. Actions based on such ideas, we call racialism. Racism is a kind of theoretical basis of or justification for racialist behaviour.

But, some would argue, racism and racialism are expressions not so much of the forces of capitalism, but manifestations of more fundamental human prejudices, reducible to what psychologists call inter-group tensions. In contrast to Cox's approach, theorists of this persuasion try to examine race at the level of the individual or group personality. Let's see what light these throw on our subject area.

APARTHEID
The political system which strictly enforces total separation of groups designated as different races. Different races have different legal and moral rights and are prevented from mixing with each other. In South Africa, for example, whites are given privileges in all areas of society. Nonwhites are given separate facilities and barred from using the same living areas, recreational areas, etc. In effect, it constitutes a rigid political caste system with whites enjoying innumerable advantages.

RACISM
The doctrine that the world's population is divisible into categories based on physical differences which can be transmitted genetically. Invariably, this leads to the conception that the categories are ordered hierarchically so that some elements of the world's population are superior to others.

Prejudice

'Do all whites suffer from unpleasant body odour?' A ridiculous question, maybe, but in it are hidden the elements of racial prejudice. Let's look at it more closely: the two give-away words are 'all' and 'whites', the former generalizes, the latter specifies. Implicit in the question is the assumption that a segment of society can be distinguished by an observable characteristic — skin colour, in this case, white — and that we can impute properties to all those sharing that characteristic. As soon as we do this, we establish a basis for prejudice.

Prejudices are usually based on faulty or incomplete information. For instance, if a person is prejudiced against blacks, we mean that they are oriented towards behaving with hostility to blacks: they think that, with the odd exception, all blacks are very much the same. But, the characteristics they assign to blacks are probably inaccurate or, at best, based on a grain of information that the person can apply to blacks as a whole. This generalization is called stereotyping and it involves attributing identical properties to any person in a group regardless of the actual variation among members of the group. Like all blacks are gifted in sport, but are limited intellectually; this is based on the evidence that some black sportsmen are very competent and some black schoolchildren do not achieve good examination results. But not all. The stereotyping is a way of simplifying our view of the world. Yet it can get insidious.

Examination results might make it easy to think of blacks as stupid and this can lead to a justification for depriving them of an education (in the same way as the early race theoriest used incomplete biological knowledge to construct a

PREJUDICE
An inflexible mental attitude towards specific groups of others based on unreliable, possibly distorted, stereotyped images of them.

STEREOTYPE
A mental image held about particular groups of people constructed on the basis of simplified, distorted or incomplete knowledge of them. An example would be a stereotype of Jews: all of them are mean. This isn't accurate, but is a widely held stereotypical image of them.

stereotype that justified slavery). In a similar way, feminists argue that the stereotype of women as biologically equipped only for domestic or menial jobs has been serviceable for justifying sexual inequality in employment. We don't necessarily have to be aware of working with stereotypes; often we are brought up to accept them and cannot entertain alternative images. But, crucially, the stereotype images function in such a way as to prejudice us against another group.

In all race relations situations, there are prejudices based on stereotypes. Historically, the more politically and economically powerful groups cultivate the images and act towards disadvantaged groups using them as gauges for their behaviour. As we have seen, race and the stereotype of distinct racial groups served their masters adequately and so were useful for justifying action. They helped to keep the slavers from feeling immoral and un-Christian.

This makes prejudice seem merely an afterthought, whereas there may be many other factors lying behind it. Competition over scarce resources is an obvious one. as we will see, prejudice against blacks and South Asians in the UK seemed to rise in proportion to fluctuating demands of the labour market in the 1950s; as the number of jobs being sought after diminished, West Indians and Asians became more threatening competitors in the job market and hostility against them increased. This type of situation is almost exactly parallelled in John Dollard's study of a small American industrial town in which there was initially no apparent prejudice against local Germans. The jobs got scarcer and 'scornful and derogatory opinions were expressed about these Germans' and these tended to give the whites some self-satisfaction (1938). This goes to show that prejudice is by no means limited to visibly different groups.

Related to this is the scapegoat production: deteriorating prospects on the job front might lead to worsening material conditions, like deteriorating standards of living, poor housing, limited diets and so on; so people look for possible causes. Of course, the deep-rooted social and economic causes of the

---

SCAPEGOAT
Term taken from the ancient Hebrews who used to transfer symbolically their sinful deeds to a goat which they let loose in the wilderness; the scapegoat is an object or group of people which others blame for their problems, when in fact those problems are caused by other factors.

---

decay are usually complex and obscure, so something more comprehensible is looked for. A quite logical move is to turn attentions to visible and powerless groups, like immigrants. People transfer the causes of their own problems to what they deem racial groups.

A famous American study by Carl Hovland and Robert Sears related precisely the number of lynchings of blacks between 1882 and 1930 with the changing price of cotton (1940). Similarly, the rising importance of racist movements like the National Front and the British Movement in the UK of the 1970s and early 1980s was largely a response to unemployment figures exceeding three million (see chapter 8). The activities of these organizations prompt comparisons with Hitler's scapegoating of Jews in Nazi Germany.

In fact, it was mounting anti-Semitism which gave rise to one of the most famous studies into prejudice conducted by Theodor Adorno and his associates. Unlike the two previous explanations of prejudice as grounded in social processes, the study identified what was called *The Authoritarian Personality* (1950). People possessing this showed certain tendencies such as being anti-Semitic, anti-black, intolerant to weakness, rigid in beliefs and extremely suspicious of minority groups. The values and attitudes associated with these people were thought to stem from childhood experiences rather than social circumstances. People learn prejudices and develop them in later life.

Thomas Pettigrew used the Adorno study's scale for measuring prejudice for a separate research project that came to the conclusion that prejudice is very simply a matter of conforming to norms (1958, 1959). In other words, if everybody you associate with resents Asians, then you tend to as well. Prejudice is not seen as an inbuilt component of the personality, but as a fluid processual thing, coming and going, depending on where a person lives and whom she or he uses as reference groups. It is a socially transmitted phenomenon.

Racial prejudice, then, can be viewed as a result of self-justification, competition, personality or conformity; we can approach it as a social phenomenon or an individual one. What is certain is that prejudice against racial groups is a factor in all situations of race relations. Being conscious of other groups as sharing properties that are undesirable is a necessary condition. And this observation reinforces our statement that race relations studies must take account of what goes on inside people's heads as much as how people actually behave towards each other.

These studies of racial prejudice seem to be light years away from the early investigations of people like Linnaeus and Gobineau, yet they are linked, however tenuously, by the concern with race. No matter how much we object to its presence or how vile we find its intrusion into our lives, it is there and it has consequences. We accept that race was in use scientifically and that its history predates colonialism, yet we also believe that no satisfactory account of race relations in contemporary society can proceed without reference to colonialism and the 'racializing' process accompanying it. As we pointed out, the concept of race prior to the nineteenth century was markedly different to the one that both facilitated and justified the colonial exploitation of peoples of a different colour. Race was anchored to a basic premise of human inequality and it has remained in that sea-bed ever since. Where people have perceived others as racial groups, they usually grade them higher or, importantly, lower on some scale of status or prestige. It is as well to remind ourselves at this stage that being conscious of race, though it may work as a tool of ruling groups, can also pervade the consciousness of ruled groups, the exploited.

This we take to be of the utmost significance, for an argument in this book is that it is through the transference of ideas on race that the inequalities are perpetuated. But, whereas such ideas are explained by some as the result of ideological domination, 'the ideas of the ruling class' theme, we prefer to see ideas also as flowing from the underclass groups themselves. Groups designated racially inferior contribute to the maintenance of inequalities by believing in them or even not rejecting them. So racial inequalities are often generated and confirmed within groups as well as imposed from the outside.

None of this is meant to indicate that we intend to ignore the vital parts played by state agencies and institutions in creating and maintaining ideas about fundamental divisions and stratifications. These do arise historically from material dominance and exploitation. By including the ways in which the ideas are embodied in the culture of disadvantaged groups, we do not intend to reverse the flow of ideology. In fact, in the next chapter, we will examine the influential role played by central government in the disseminating of ideas pertaining to race.

Further reading

Theories of Race and Ethnic Relations edited by John Rex and David Mason (1986) is a collection of conference papers which attempts to cover the full panoply of theories of race and ethnic relations: marxian; sociobiology; pluralism; Weberian and others.

The volume reveals two main features: 1. there is a perplexing diversity of theoretical positions which prohibits the establishment of common ground; 2. even in a volume as large as this many contemporary interpretations have been omitted. This work is intended for the advanced reader.

Racial Consciousness by Michael Banton (1988) is a short book on 'racial classification' systems. In contrast to our perspective, the author advances a liberal argument, which includes a rejection of the term 'black' as a generic concept to capture groups experiencing racist oppression. For Banton, black is 'inaccurate, emotionally-loaded and implies an over-simple division of the population'. This type of approach is at variance with the anti-racist imperatives of the present volume.

The Ideology of Racism by Samuel K. Yeboah (1988). The author's own words describe the tone of this largely historical work: 'Until one understands *why* white people racially discriminate against black people, one cannot understand the nature of obstacles in the way of equal opportunities and racial equality, and, hence, one cannot prescribe effective solutions to the problem'. Yeboah's task is a grand one and his effort interesting if not entirely successful.

'Marxism and racism', 'pluralism', 'race', 'race relations' and 'sociobiology' are entries in **Dictionary of Race and Ethnic Relations**, 2nd edition (1988). These important theories of racism are crisply summarized by leading international scholars.

Racism by Robert Miles (1989) is a difficult, challenging, but rewarding book which examines the many-sided concept of racism and suggests ways in which it might best be understood. The author argues against what he calls the 'conceptual inflation' of racism and for an understanding of racism as a 'specific form of ideology'. But, 'ideologies are never only received but are also constructed and reconstructed by people responding to their material and cultural circumstances in order to comprehend, represent and act in relation to those circumstances'.

3
Laws — labour — migration

- How did the 'blacks/Asians = problem' equation emerge?
- Why is the fact of empire so important?
- Why did blacks and Asians come to live in Britain?
- What is the numbers game?
- How have governments tried to combat racialism?

The empire

Readers of *The Magnet* and *Schoolboy's Own Library* in the 1930s would have been acquainted with Hurree Jamset Ram Singh, probably the first Indian to be encountered by generations of British schoolboys. To his creator Frank Richards, he was the 'dusky nabob of Bhanipur'; to his Greyfriars schoolmates, of whom Billy Bunter was the most celebrated, he was 'Inky'. In the comics, he was depicted as bright and studious — a 'top-hole' Englishman who always played with a straight bat. All in all, then, a far cry from the popular image of Indian residents in Britain today.

We use this example to show that, contrary to popular opinion, the Asians' presence in Britain is by no means new. In fact, there was a period long before the onset of mass immigration from South Asia (that is, India, Pakistan and what is now Bangladesh) when they played a prominent and distinguished part in British public life and moved smoothly in the upper echelons of society. The same holds true for blacks whose presence in Britain can be traced back even further to the mid-sixteenth century when they were brought over to serve as valets and manservants to the planter aristocracy. Indeed, despite efforts by the privy council in 1596 to curb their import, their numbers increased, mainly as a by-product of colonial expansion. By the end of the eighteenth century then, they constituted a sizeable minority of between 14–15,000, most of whom lived in London. Douglas Lorimer tells us that the vast majority of them received some education and a few also gained 'extensive training in the arts of gracious living' (1978, p. 206). Such an existence was obtained, for the most part, at the expense of their individual liberty. But, like the Indians, blacks were in frequent contact with the aristocracy — often filling strikingly different roles from those which the majority of them fill in the UK today.

Slavery, as we've seen, was not then in top gear though the race issue was still of some importance; only intermittently did it emerge as a matter for political and public concern, however. For instance, in the late sixteenth century — just after Linnaeus's writing — when the country was afflicted by hunger and poverty, the privy council issued an edict banning the future entry of black slaves. It was anticipated that this would lead to more domestic positions becoming available to the white population which, in turn, would alleviate their economic problems. The results were disappointing, however, and, in 1601, Queen Elizabeth I, 'tendering the good and welfare of her own natural subjects', issued a Royal Proclamation ordering the expulsion of all 'Negroes and blackamoors' from her kingdom (quoted in Walvin, 1971, p. 64).

These brief historical snapshots provide an interesting backcloth to this and subsequent chapters where we move from our general discussion of race and associated concepts (such as racism and prejudice) to a more focused analysis of the significance of these ideas in the contemporary UK. We've already seen in this chapter how those who held power in Britain at the turn of the sixteenth century saw the restriction and subsequent expulsion of the black population as the appropriate cure for the country's ills. By beginning our analysis with an appraisal of the policy response of successive governments to mass immigration into Britain after 1945 we can demonstrate the remarkable resilience of this blacks = problem equation in the social consciousness.

The equation is a powerful one and one clearly having tremendous impact psychologically; as we saw in the section on prejudice, this type of explanation of perceived social problems is an enormous boon for those wishing to locate simple causes for often complex social and economic phenomena. But there's no necessary, logical reason why blacks and other nonwhite immigrants should be identified as the scapegoats any more than people with big families (because they occupy more space and put pressure on housing) or people over 200lbs (because they have big appetites and tax food supplies). There are reasons and these are deeply rooted in history.

The race issue, as we've seen, flourished in the period of slavery; and slavery itself was part of a system of often raw exploitation of human labour and natural resources called colonialism. The total structure was the British empire. This system of supreme and extensive political dominion in which the British sovereign exerted total control over vast and wide portions of the globe was secured and justified by the belief in racial inferiority and inequality.

EMPIRE
A large commercial network encompassing many territories controlled by an extensively powerful source known as the metropolitan centre with the outlying regions of the network being the peripheries.

The empire has been in a process of dissolution since the late eighteenth century. But, once set in the consciousness, beliefs are often more difficult to remove than the structures of which they were originally part. What we're suggesting is that, while the empire itself might have dissolved, the consciousness associated with that empire has been transmitted through generations and remains largely intact. The idea that being white denotes superiority is not some natural fact, but a remnant of the colonial mentality. The enormous flux of immigrants which the UK received after World War II was possible precisely because of the old system of empire: the territories from which the migrants came were parts of the old regime and the new arrivals in the post-war years were, in a real sense, reminders of the empire. The reactions they eilicited from both politicians and people in the street can be seen as a legacy of the colonial era which maintained the white man's innate superiority over both black and brown men.

Before we move on to a discussion of the introduction and development of laws that served to bolster (if not extend) this mentality, we need to recognize that every facet of modern race relations has to be seen as derived from the imperial expansion of the seventeenth century: the settlement of the West Indies and the expansion of the trade in slaves, gold and sugar between Africa, the Americas and Britain. The system of slavery that glued the empire together meant that whites maintained their domination over blacks and other populations and so kept a rigidly structured inequality that was believed, conveniently enough, to rest on racial grounds. Such an inequality has been modified and refined in the decades since emancipation, but whites have never quite removed the notion of social superiority from their collective consciousness and this fact is reflected in the ways the UK implemented laws in relation to immigration control.

A reserve army

The enormous movement of blacks from the Caribbean and Asians from India (including Pakistan until 1947) was precipitated by economic and demographic phenomena. These can be specified in terms of 'push' and 'pull' factors. The former refers to the predisposing factors within the sending societies of the Caribbean and South Asia, the latter to the unique attractions of the receiving society, Britain. 'Pull' factors are especially important in influencing why migrants choose to head for one country in preference to others. 'Whether they go at all,' writes Sheila Allen, 'and how many leave, in the case of migrants who are moving mainly for economic reasons, seems to depend less on the conditions at home than on the migrants' assessment of the demand for labour in the country to which they are going' (1971, pp. 37–8).

Migration from the Caribbean islands, particularly Jamaica and Barbados, and from India has been a long-established routine, and the 'push' factors which operated after 1945 were basically no different from those which had prompted previous waves of emigration. Quite simply, emigration was seen as one of the main ways of escaping from the twin problems of overpopulation and under/unemployment, both of which have been enduring, characteristic features of these societies. The main difference from earlier waves lay in the destination of the migrants. Those from the Caribbean, for example, had traditionally headed for the USA, partly because its proximity made it an inexpensive journey, partly also because of the wide range of job opportunities to be found there. In 1952, however, the USA government passed the McCarran-Walter Act which limited the number of immigrants from this source to 100 per year; in effect, the USA had closed its doors on the Caribbean migrants.

Such Draconian immigration measures had not been introduced in Britain — at least, not yet. And, as E. J. B. Rose and his colleagues have pointed out, the only restrictions on entry into the UK from these countries in the immediate post-war period were 'the ability to pay the fare and the prospect of finding employment' (1969, p. 43). The attraction, or 'pull' of Britain for the migrants lay precisely in the fact that the 'prospect of finding employment' was extremely good. The late 1940s and early 1950s saw the UK embark on a process of extremely rapid economic growth; although, along with other Western European countries which were also experiencing this 'boom', Britain faced a chronic shortage of labour. Its first attempts to alleviate this problem saw the introduction of the Polish Resettlement Programme which led to over 16,000 Poles coming into the UK, according to Jerzy Zubrzycki (1956). This programme was subsequently augmented by the European Volunteer Workers Scheme (EVW) which allowed displaced persons or prisoners of war to volunteer for jobs covered by twelve-month work permits. Although the EVW attracted another 100,000 workers to the country this was still not enough and it was at this juncture that the UK, almost in desperation, turned to its colonies and ex-colonies in Africa, India and the Caribbean. Here lay a vast reservoir of cheap and alternative labour which could be attracted into the country. The migrants collectively came to be known as a reserve army of labour to the British economy.

The period between 1948–57 was an interesting one in the development of race relations in Britain: it was the only time after the war when blacks and Asians were not obviously labelled as some sort of social problem. Yet after 1957, as we will argue, barely a year went by when the migrants or their children (or both) were not identified as contributory figures in important social problems. Before 1957, however, political and social considerations about black and, later, Asian settlement in the UK were subordinated to the country's economic priorities and the migrants filled the gaps in the job market perfectly. As one works superintendent told the researcher, Peter Wright, it was a time when 'you couldn't get an armless, legless man, never mind an able-bodied one' (1968, p. 42). The immigrants, initially from the Commonwealth territories of the Caribbean and later, from South Asia, readily accepted the jobs which the white workers steered clear of doing, as Ken Pryce has called it, the 'shit work' (1979).

As we mentioned before, the UK at that time did not have any relevant legislation which could impede in-migration from these areas. Nor did it want any. The introduction of the Nationality Act in 1948 merely facilitated access to the army of labour, allowing citizens of the British Commonwealth to enter Britain freely: 'to find work, to settle and to bring their families' as Tom Rees has put it (1982, p. 83). These years were characterized by the British government's *laissez-faire* approach to immigration; that is, it didn't interfere with the flow of in-migration from the Commonwealth. But perhaps this non-interventionist posture was carried too far. After all, there was no centrally directed attempt to coordinate the inflow of migrants from the Caribbean or South Asia. The steps taken by public and private organizations such as the National Health Service, London Transport Executive and, from 1956, the British Hotels and Restaurants Association to set up recruitment posts in Barbados and to match entrants to existing vacancies, were the exception rather than the rule. The immigrants were allowed to enter the country willy nilly and, once in the UK, were left to their own devices. This was in sharp contrast to the Polish Resettlement Programme which included a coordinated effort to facilitate settlement in the UK by the provision of educational, housing and welfare advice and facilities. There was, in other words, a steadfast refusal by the government to recognize anything other than the economic dimension of Commonwealth settlement. To put it bluntly, these migrants were seen and treated simply as factory fodder.

It wasn't until the British economy began to take a turn for the worse in the mid-1950s and the shortage of labour in Britain's major industries began to recede, that the social consequences of this mass, unregulated arrival from the Caribbean and, increasingly after 1956, India and Pakistan, began to make a significant impact on British politicians. In this familiar scenario of imminent social and economic stress, race, as it had done in similar conditions in the sixteenth and the early twentieth centuries, emerged as an issue for political and public debate. As the conditions continued to deteriorate, demands for a response from central government increased, culminating, as we shall see, in the creation and implementation of legislation by Westminster. This legislation was propelled by racist assumptions and was based on logically inconsistent premises. The belated development of immigration policy in the 1960s and 1970s, and the direction it assumed bears out the argument of John Rex and Sally Tomlinson: 'Notions which would have been dismissed by nearly all parties in the early 1950s became the unspoken ground assumptions of the most respectable politicians and leader writers by the end of the 1960s' (1979, p. 37).

Those 'ground assumptions' were that black and brown Commonwealth citizens spelled trouble and measures had to be introduced to curtail any further entry.

Policy of surrender

By the time the British economy had entered a recession in the mid-to-late 1950s, the number of people from the Caribbean and South Asia in the UK was estimated to be somewhere in the region of 200,000; this is, 0.5 per cent of the total population of England and Wales. They were not evenly distributed throughout the country, however. Instead, the early migrants, quite logically, had tended to gravitate towards areas where labour, and especially unskilled labour, was reputed to be in greatest demand. This is why minority groups tend to be found in cities such as London, Birmingham, Manchester and Leeds. Those who followed the early migrants tended to reproduce this settlement pattern and to head, understandably, to those districts within these areas where friends and relatives from 'back home' had already established themselves. (We shall be returning to this theme in chapter 5.)

Although the rationale for this pattern of settlement was, as we've explained, quite obvious, the concentration of migrants in particular parts of the cities clearly strained the limited resources of those local authorities affected. But still central government did nothing to help. Because of this, Commonwealth immigration simply 'sneaked up on the local councils without warning,' as Paul Foot remarks; nor, as he continues, was there any 'guidance from Health or Education Ministries on the possibilities of different health and sanitation standards or on the difficulties of teaching children who could not speak English' (1965, p. 162). In this situation, the imperative for central government seemed clear: provisions along the lines of those prepared for the Polish settlers in the late 1940s should have been made available to the relevant local authorities. Yet two sets of things were happening, one inside Westminster, the other outside it,

NEW COMMONWEALTH
Contrasted with the Old Commonwealth, which refers principally to the white dominions of Canada, Australia and New Zealand, the New Commonwealth embraces Caribbean, Asian and African colonies and ex-colonies of the UK.

and the confluence of these two tides served to deflect government attention away from this course of action for the settlers.

Calls for the control of immigration from what has now come to be called the New Commonwealth had been voiced almost from the day in June 1948 when the SS *Empire Windrush* arrived in Britain carrying the first intending immigrants from Jamaica. These cries had been taken up with fervour by some right-wing Conservative MPs, such as Cyril Osborne and Norman Pannell in the early 1950s, but, as the problem of solving the labour shortage in certain sectors of the economy overruled all other considerations at that time, these demands remained confined to the 'lunatic fringes' of the House. However, throughout the 1950s, Conservative party leaders found themselves under increasing pressure both from this small but vociferous group of MPs and from some sections of Whitehall, to introduce controls. So, in 1955, the Central Council of the Conservative party passed a resolution in favour of this proposal. But it was still not a priority of the party. What changed the situation was the outbreak of violent disturbances apparently about racial issues in 1958, first in Nottingham in August and then, a month later, in the Notting Hill district of London. Whether these disturbances had been generated more by racialism than by youthful hooliganism was, in many senses, irrelevant. (We return to these disturbances in chapter 8.)

'The immediate effects of the disturbances,' wrote Rose and his colleagues, 'was to blow away the complacency in which the subject was still clothed and leave the Government's lack of policy indecently exposed' (1969, p. 213). This we accept. But the long-term effects of the disturbances were even more profound as they helped to shape the direction of future government policy.

If we accept for the moment that the violence had more to do with racialism than hooliganism, then the government had at least two ways to respond in policy terms. On the one hand, it could have begun to frame policies designed to ameliorate the social problems which existed in these and other decaying inner city areas where the migrants had settled. This might have had the effect of reducing the tension between black and white residents in those areas. The alternative was to restrict the number of New Commonwealth migrants entering Britain. Certainly we've already seen that there was growing support in Westminster for this second course of action. Yet, as Ceri Peach's analysis demonstrates, selective controls were unnecessary (1968). Peach shows that as the British economy entered a downward phase and the number of job vacancies gradually diminished, the number of in-migrants from the Caribbean had fallen accordingly. In other words, this migration was self-regulating, it 'rose and fell to the demand for labour from year to year', according to Peach (1968, p. 93). Similarly, Vaughan Robinson has shown an association between Indian and Pakistani migration to, and unemployment within, the UK (1980). Nor was there much prospect of long-term unemployment in Britain at that time, so it was unlikely that recent immigrants would spend months drawing social security benefits. Even so, the government did little to assuage these and other anxieties which had led to the disturbances in Nottingham and Notting Hill.

In the event, the Conservative government of the day eschewed the more constructive and, as we've emphasized, more logical step of attacking social problems through policies to improve the lot of inner city residents. Instead, it accepted the racist definition of the situation, namely, that the unrestricted entry of blacks and Asians had caused these problems and the solution therefore lay in curtailing the numbers allowed into the UK. The subsequent Commonwealth Immigrants Act of 1962 thus marked the end of Britain's *laissez-faire* posture on immigration by qualifying the right of free entry into the country for New Commonwealth migrants. In contrast, there was no attempt to impose contols over the entry of migrants from the Republic of Ireland, even though the Republic was not a member of the Commonwealth. The aim and implications of this legislation were clear and in this context we can see why Ann and Michael Dummett refer to it as a 'policy of surrender' to racist agitation (1969).

The 1962 Act marked the start of 'the numbers game' in Britain and, since then, the overriding concern of politicians, the media and the general public has been with the numbers of New Commonwealth migrants entering, or having potential to enter the UK. Since 1962, then, efforts to minimize the number coming in have completely overshadowed all other aspects of race relations policy. The act established a precedent from which a series of progressively restrictive and, *de facto*, racially discriminatory immigration measures ensued in 1965, 1968, 1971 and 1981. These measures have successively and systematically emasculated the legal rights of blacks and Asians to enter the UK. By the time the 1971 Commenwealth Immigration Act came into force (in January 1973), workers from New Commonwealth countries found that they had less rights than workers coming from the Irish Republic or EEC countries. In other words, they held the legal status of aliens and were compelled to apply for short-term work contracts. They were allowed into this country as migrants not settlers and their rights were roughly equivalent to those of the guest workers,

---

GASTARBEITER
German for guest worker; in recent times this has become synonymous
with the Turkish migrants who travelled to West Germany in the hope of
finding employment; they were given temporary permits which enable the
government to expel them or return them in accordance with the demands
of the labour market. Interestingly, in the early 1980s, when West
Germany experienced high unemployment, working-class hostilities
towards Turks mounted quite seriously.

---

or *Gastarbeiter*, in West Germany and other Western European countries whose
experiences are so vividly described by John Berger and Jean Mohr (1975): their
continued presence has become dependent upon continued demand for their
labour.

And it didn't stop there. Recently, as these external immigration controls
have become more restrictive, so the government's reliance on internal controls,
such as passport checking and police surveillance of 'suspected' illegal
immigrants has become correspondingly greater. The 1981 Nationality Act,
which made a significant change in the UK's citizenship laws, has already led to
further increases in the enforcement of these internal controls.

All in all, we can now see how much influence this move towards a
selective immigration policy has in defining and confining the race relations
debate. Although the immigration laws may officially be part of external policy,
'they express,' as Ann Dummett reminds us, 'by means of their definition of
wanted and unwanted newcomers, what kind of society' the government is
aiming for (1978, p. 14).

We've made it clear in this section that, while the onset of an economic
recession in the 1950s focused many people's minds on the number of New
Commonwealth migrants entering Britain, it was racist and not economic
considerations that persuaded the Conservative government to rescind the
principle of free entry in 1962. By 1965, the Labour party, recently elected to
power, had also submitted to the numbers game. 'Without integration,
limitation is inexcusable; without limitation, integration is impossible' declared
Labour MP, Roy Hattersley, in favour of his party's 1965 White Paper which
amongst other things, extended the controls on entry from the New
Commonwealth. This syllogism has come to typify the two-party, or bi-
partisan, policy on immigration and race relations ever since. In effect, it has
provided explicit legitimacy to the racist argument that it is the actual presence
of blacks and Asians which constitutes the problem and the elimination of
virtually all future inflows from the New Commonwealth that provides the
solution. It's in this context that legislation designed to ensure that blacks and

---

THE NUMBERS GAME
Refers to the belief that the starting point for the debate about race relations is the absolute numbers of immigrants entering and settling in the host countries, their fertility rate, number of relations, etc. It avoids paying attention to the actual quality of relationships between different groups by concentrating only on numerical features of their presence.

Asians in Britain are not worse off than their white counterparts in their access to jobs and houses seems at best, half-hearted, and at worst, merely an empty gesture. The former Labour Minister of State for Race Relations and Immigration, Alex Lyon, put it well when he said in 1976:

> One cannot say to a man who is black: 'We shall treat you as an equal member of the society; as a full citizen of this community; and say to him at the same time, we shall keep your wife and children waiting seven years before they can come and live with you'.

From the massive to the substantial

'If you want a nigger neighbour, vote Labour' read one of the slogans supporting the Conservative party candidate, Peter Griffiths, during his campaign for the Smethwick constituency in the 1964 General Election. His shock success at the expense of Patrick Gordon-Walker, on such an obviously racist platform, demonstrated the growing importance of race as a political issue and precipitated the start of the bi-partisan agreement on race and immigration policy in the UK. It was an agreement defined, as we've already indicated, by a concern over numbers and was directed by the guiding principle: 'Keeping numbers down is good for race relations.' In other words, as long as there was strict control over the numbers of blacks and Asians allowed in the UK, the problems thought to derive from their presence would be minimized. Put differently, it was alleged that if they weren't here there wouldn't be any problems. This rather short-sighted principle was the one on which the outgoing Conservative government organized its policies in relation to nonwhite migrant groups, neglecting the fact that they *were* in the UK and *were* experiencing problems. The Conservative policies had been about immigration control and not race relations, because the government had equated the one with the other. The newly elected Labour government, on the other hand, distinguished between the two rather more. Its introduction of more restrictive controls of entry, again largely on the basis of skin colour, was accompanied by

---

INTEGRATION
In race relations, this is one of the ideals governing many policies aimed at producing a situation in which groups of different cultural backgrounds and different beliefs can participate in society on an equal footing without losing their essential distinctness as individuals. People retain their cultural identity but are accepted as equal if total integration is attained. This ideal replaced the more outmoded ASSIMILATION.

---

legislation designed to combat what was becoming an increasingly apparent issue — racial discrimination. This was also the start of policies aimed at alleviating the privations of inner city residents.

The attempt to unify these concerns into one formal policy strategy was not without its difficulties, however. Indeed, we would argue strongly that the Labour party's avowed aim to create a society in which 'every citizen shares an equal right to the same freedoms, the same responsibilities, the same opportunities, the same benefits' is no nearer its realization in the 1980s than it was when it was first declared in 1968 by the then Home Secretary, James Callaghan.

The Labour government's first steps along this tricky road of trying to integrate these policies into one formal document was in 1965. The result? The White Paper, *Immigration from the Commonwealth* (Cmnd 2739), which the Dummetts have referred to as 'possibily the most logically incoherent government paper ever produced' (1969, p. 39). We can see why: on the one hand, it repudiated many of the accusations commonly directed at the black and Asian immigrants in the UK, namely, that the vast majority of them scrounged off the welfare state, that they were depriving white people of jobs, that they had lower health and sanitation standards than whites, and so on. At the same time, however, the document endorsed the need for futher immigration controls, and declared that the government was to limit further New Commonwealth immigration to Britain. So, while attempting in the first part of the document to dissociate itself from any form of racialism, the Labour government, through its proposals for immigration controls, was helping both to orchestrate and support racist views. In effect, then, its policies were self-contradictory: how can you denounce racialism, then implement policies which deliberately exclude groups of certain colours?

But the White Paper also marked the first official recognition of the need for protective laws to combat racial discrimination. The reduction of racial discrimination, argued the Labour party, would help the integration of blacks and Asians into British society. Although it was an important start, the 1965 Race Relations Bill was very limited in scope, particularly in comparison to similar initiatives in Canada and the USA. It outlawed racial discrimination in 'places of public resort' such as restaurants, hotels, places of entertainment and on public transport. The government set up the Race Relations Board which was charged with the responsibility to deal with complaints of discrimination and resolve them through conciliation. Even before the bill reached the statute books, however, critics were pointing to significant gaps in its provisions, most notably in the areas of employment and housing where racialism was said to be rife.

The veracity of these criticisms was underlined in 1967 when the findings of the PEP survey into racial discrimination in England were published. 'In employment, housing and the provision of services,' wrote William Daniel in his summary of the report findings, 'there is racial discrimination varying in extent from the massive to the substantial.' Nor did he leave any doubt that the dominant expression of racial discrimination in England was along colour lines. The experiences of 'black or brown immigrants, such as West Indians or Asians' were, according to Daniel, demonstrably worse than those of 'white immigrants, such as Hungarians or Cypriots' (1968, p. 209).

The PEP provided the first systematic evidence of the extent to which white people received preference over blacks and Asians in areas not covered by the existing anti-discrimination legislation. But this posed enormous political problems for the Labour government. On the one hand, it recognized that the level of racialism amongst the white electorate would render any extension of anti-discrimination laws very unpopular; the party would stand to lose considerable electoral support. On the other hand, if it failed to respond positively to the PEP findings and did not extend these laws to the spheres of employment and housing, it would undermine its avowed commitment to assist integration. The concept of integration had been defined by Roy Jenkins, then Home Secretary, in 1966, as 'equal opportunity, accompanied by cultural diversity, in at atmosphere of mutual tolerance' (quoted in C. Jones 1977, p. 148). Reference to the notion of 'equal oppotunity' is important here because, although Jenkin's definition was vague and lacked any specific policy directives, it was clear that he was receptive to the 1967 PEP's find that the black and brown communities in Britain were being continually and systematically denied equal opportunities in the allocation of jobs and housing.

It was also around this time that events in the United States were to send tremors throughout the western world. The open racial discrimination of the 1930s and 1940s with 'whites only' and 'for coloured' signs had gone, but blacks were persistently disadvantaged relative to American whites and were, as Douglas Glasgow puts it, 'locked permanently into the underclass' (1980, p. 7). Riots in the Watts district of Los Angeles in 1965 signalled a volatile reaction of blacks to a shared situation in which, according to Glasgow:

ASSIMILATION
The process of incorporating a freshly arriving group with a distinct culture into the host society in such a way as to make the incoming group conform to established cultural patterns and, eventually, disappear as an identifiable group of people.

They were jobless and lacked saleable skills and the opportunities to get them; they had been rejected and labelled as social problems by the police, the schools, the employment and welfare agencies; they were victims of the new camouflaged racism (1980, p. 1).

It doesn't take much imagination to realize that British politicians were very much aware of the civil disturbances in the USA and were mindful of the developing situation in this country. Although the migrant groups in the UK were nowhere near as proportionately significant as blacks in the USA, they were fast growing and were, according to research such as the PEP's, having to put up with similar conditions. It was with one eye on Los Angeles that politicians moved to new legislation in the UK.

The 1968 Race Relations Act replaced the 1965 Bill and was based more on the American model which had as an organic part of its anti-discrimination laws a partially independent statutory enforcement agency. The British equivalent was the Race Relations Board, empowered to investigate complaints brought to it by members of the public, although without the power to prosecute. In the terms of the 1965 Bill: 'A person discriminates against another if on the grounds of colour, race or ethnic or national origins he treats that other . . . less favourably than he treats or would treat other persons' (1965, s. 1(i)). The 1968 Act enlarged the scope of the law to the important spheres of employment and housing and gave the Race Relations Board the power to instigate court proceedings. But crucially, the definition of discrimination was not expanded and this made the board a reactive body: it was designed to respond to complaints rather than initiate investigations into racialist practices.

The new act was intended to take heed of the lessons of the USA, though at this stage it was apparent to Americans, if not to the British, that a law that required proof of deliberate acts of discrimination by and against individuals would have only limited effect on the more widespread patterns of inequality between blacks and whites (see Pollack, 1974). Although it was designed to reduce racialism and so avoid similar occurrences to Watts, the 1968 Act failed to tackle what Glasgow has identified as one of the central causes of the American riots — 'camouflaged racism'. In other words, the act was a tool designed to combat only the open and visible expression of racial discimination and could do nothing to cope with the more subtle forms.

The potentially disastrous effects which these anti-discrimination initiatives might have had on electoral support for the Labour party were largely mitigated by the re-emergence of the numbers game in 1968 and the party's legislative response to the impending inflow of increasing numbers of Asians holding UK citizenship into Britain from Kenya. Spurred on by parliamentary and press campaigns for further restrictions, James Callaghan, then Home Secretary, passed a new Commonwealth Immigrants Act to prevent the in-migration of Kenyan Asians. Referred to in the *New Statesman* as 'the first incontestably racialist law to be placed on the statute book', the 1968 Act ensured that only those British passport holders with 'substantial connections' with the UK had an automatic right of entry. 'Substantial connections' was defined in the Act as having at least a grandfather born in Britain, a condition which facilitated the entry of many white British passport holders living in Australia, New Zealand, Canada and Rhodesia (now Zimbabwe), but which effectively blocked the entry of Asians in Kenya holding equivalent passport credentials.

Harold Wilson's claim that 'the criteria for exemption' from this latest wave of immigration controls 'were geographical not racial' was seen through by critics of bi-partisan policies on immigration and race relations, as well as by the black and Asian communities.

The recession of the 1960s, though relatively mild compared to present day standards, had once again provided the scene for the re-emergence of race as a salient issue in political and public debate. The issue was given further dimensions through the widely reported speeches of Enoch Powell, who started his 'immigrant-as-threat' campaign in 1968 (we discuss his impact in chapter 9).

It was against this background of increasingly widespread resentment and animosity towards the black and brown populations that these groups were, for the second time in three years, implored to accept a message from the Labour party's legislation, the gist of which was: our anti-discrimination laws should assure you that we're doing all we can to ensure your right to exist as equal citizens in the UK, but our immigration laws make it clear — we don't want any more of your kind here! And as we've already suggested, this message has continued to go out to the groups throughout the 1970s and 1980s. The 1971 Commonwealth Immigration Act, which effectively ended all primary immigration from the New Commonwealth (that is, the admission of heads of households rather than dependents), and the 1981 Nationality Act, along with various internal immigration controls have been seen as complementary, indeed essential to the ultimate success of legislation aimed at eliminating racial discrimination and relieving the disadvantages related to life in the inner cities.

It was not unitl the mid-1970s that the anti-racialist laws were further

INSTITUTIONAL RACISM
The policies of institutions that work to perpetuate racial inequality
without acknowledging that fact. Douglas Glasgow refers to this as
camouflaged racism, meaning that it is not open and visible but is
concealed in the routine practices and procedures of organizations such as
industries, political parties and schools.

amended and extended, however. The main stimulus for the new legislation, the 1976 Race Relations Act, was provided once again by the series of surveys carried out by the PEP between 1973–4. Broadly, the surveys were designed to answer the following questions: how effective had the 1968 Race Relations Act been in reducing racialist practices in the allocation of employment and housing and what was the relative impact of racialism, generally, on the material living standards of the minority communities? Briefly, the researchers found that 'there has been a sharp decrease in the extent of discrimination in the field of housing since 1967' (Smith, 1977, p. 311). The PEP findings also suggested a similar decrease in discrimination in the sphere of employment, although different research techniques in 1967 and 1973–4 meant that direct comparison was not possible. Did this mean that the 1968 legislation had been an unqualified success? No, because as David Smith, the senior researcher on the surveys, pointed out, there was still 'substantial and widespread discrimination' (1977, p. 312).

Generally, the PEP results had shown that the liberal pretensions of the 1960s were no longer tenable, if they ever were. The unique disadvantages experienced by blacks and Asians in their search for jobs and housing did not derive from their newness in the UK. By the time of this latest PEP investigation, it was clearly no longer appropriate or legitimate to characterize blacks in Britain as 'dark strangers' as Sheila Patterson had in 1963. The PEP report made it clear that, despite its proscription by law, racialism was still extensive in the UK and that those of Caribbean origin were exceptionally affected by such practices. Indeed, it is plausible to argue that one of the major consequences of the 1968 legislation had been not to reduce the incidence of racialism but to replace its more visible expressions with less detectable practices and procedures. 'Camouflaged racism', to use Glasgow's term again, remained undisturbed.

The PEP surveys had shown a further inadequacy of the existing machinery to combat racialism, namely, the complaints-based system. Two PEP researchers, Neil McIntosh and David Smith, demonstrated this point vividly when discussing the operation of racialism at job-recruitment level: 'Asians and West Indians applying for unskilled jobs faced discimination in 46% of cases. This finding implies that there are tens of thousands of acts of discrimination of this kind in a year. By contrast, the Race Relations Board dealt with only 150 complaints of discrimination relating to recruitment in 1973' (1974, p. 35).

Through the 1976 Act, parliament resorted to civil law to regulate behaviour not reckoned serious enought to merit control by criminal law. Discrimination was declared unlawful (as opposed to illegal) and victims were provided with redress by way of compensation. But it was not a crime to practise discrimination. The Race Relations Board, and the Community Relations Commission (which had been set up under the 1968 Act to promote 'harmonious community relations') were both abolished and their respective functions integrated into a new body, the Commission for Racial Equality (CRE) whose functions were specified in Section 43 of the 1976 Act as:

(1) To work towards the elimination of racial discrimination.
(2) To promote equality of opportunity.
(3) To keep the workings of the Act under review.

The CRE was given power to issue notices requiring unlawful practices to cease; if they continued, then injunctions could be taken out from civil courts; persistent offenders could then be imprisoned for contempt of court. Significantly, the discriminatory behaviour was not deemed bad enought to be made criminal.

Since its inception, the CRE has been assailed on all sides, one of the most extreme criticisms coming from Remi Kapo, who reckons: 'The Commission for Racial Equality is the off-shoot of a permanent tranquillizer mentality, a pre-dated programmed relief, erected in order to satisfy the programmed paranoias of the whites in their immemorial one-sided arguments' (1981, p. 123). (See also the report of Home Affairs Sub-committee on Race Relations and Immigration, 1981.) Malcolm Cross emphasizes that the CRE 'has too much to do' because it operates not only in the continuing absence of a centrally coordinated policy on race relations, but also in a political climate which is wholly antagonistic to such a policy (1982a). After all, we have already shown in this chapter that central government tends to specify and prioritize race only in terms of immigration control. Both parties have been habitually fearful of stirring up a 'white backlash' in their preparation of other race-related policies. That is to say, even if both parties were in favour of extensive anti-racialism laws — and the Conservative party is not — progress on this front would be inhibited by their belief that the white population would be antagonistic to such policies. Whether or not this assumption is valid is difficult to gauge, but it is clear that the work of the CRE is severely constrained by this assumption. And, as Smith has remarked: 'a policy to combat racial discrimination — however determined and well organized — will not be enought to ensure equality between racial groups' in Britain (1977, p. 320).

The reluctance of governments to specify race in policies outside the realm of immigration control is illustrated clearly in efforts aimed at alleviating the impact of urban deprivation. Survey after survey has shown that while blacks and Asians in the inner cities experience many disadvantages also shared by their white neighbours, they tend to have them in much larger measures; they also have extra problems. As we said before, the argument that this is due to their newness and unfamiliarity with the society can no longer be upheld legitimately. It is due, to a greater or lesser degree, to racialism. Despite this, successive governments, while tentatively recognizing that black and Asian residents have special needs over and above those of their white neighbours, steadfastly refuse to formulate policies which address such needs explicitly and directly. Perhaps the conspicious exception to this was the Labour government's Ethnic Needs Bill which reached its second reading in the Commons before the 1979 General Election but which was then discarded by the Conservative government. On the whole, however, these policies have been based on the assumption that the specific and additional disadvantages of blacks and Asians were being addressed by anti-discimination legislation and that any residual disadvantages would be caught by wider packages aimed at the inner area in general. Certainly, this was the ground assumption of the Urban Programme which was launched by Harold Wilson in May 1968, in the wake of Powell's infamous speech. Both Wilson and his Home Secretary made it clear from the outset that finance under this programme would be channelled to those 'urban areas of general need' and that the presence of a sizeable immigrant population in a particular area constituted only one of the criteria used in assessing 'need' (Edwards and Batley, 1978, p. 41).

It would appear that this original formulation is being adhered to as the Urban Programme is being phased out in favour of proposals outlined in the Labour party's 1977 White Paper, *Policy for the Inner Cities* (Home Office, Cmnd 6845). While, once again, recognizing that 'race problems are by no means coterminous with inner area problems' and that the government 'intended to ensure that [ethnic minority] needs are taken into account' the thrust of the initiative remained the same: 'Where members of the ethnic minorities in inner areas suffer the kinds of disadvantage experienced by all those who live there, they should benefit directly through measures taken to improve conditions, for example, in housing, education and jobs' (1977, p. 4, para 19).

The principle of non-discrimination which is embodied in the 1976 Race Relations Act effectively ensures that this diffusion of resources and finance throughout the inner cities is to continue in preference to more specific policies on the needs of blacks and Asians in those areas. The following three chapters on employment, housing and education will show, however, just how necessary such policies are.

Swamped?

Unlike some countries, the UK has never operated racialist immigration control. Not openly, anyway, though we have seen how many of its policies have worked effectively to exclude nonwhites from entry. Race has often appeared as an issue in a disguised form. The appointment of Margaret Thatcher as prime minister in May 1979, has, according to Martin Barker, enhanced this trend and heralded the onslaught of what he calls *The New Racism* (1981).

Barker's view is that the political rhetoric and action of the Tory government are geared to the notion of a 'way of life' that is threatened by outsiders. Constantly alluded to in the 1970s and early 1980s was the core of the new racism: 'Human nature is such that it is natural to form a bonded community, a nation, aware of its differences from other nations . . . feelings of antagonism will be aroused if outsiders are admitted' (1981, p. 21). Barker contends that the new racism has its roots in Powell's ideas but have flourished with Thatcher who, in 1978, asserted that, 'the British character has done so much for democracy, for law and order and so much throughout the world that, if there was any fear that it might be swamped, people are going to react and be hostile to those coming in' (*Daily Mail*, 31 January 1978).

This pre-General Election declaration of intent for future policies was to be a central statement for later Thatcherism replete with the idea of homogeneous culture being 'swamped'. Although there was no obvious reference to race, prejudice, inequality or even xenophobia — that is, a dislike of foreigners — there was a sense in which the fear of being saturated with others of different beliefs, customs and languages, registered very similar thoughts in public consciousness.

The British Nationality Act, 1981, which was introduced by the Conservative government illustrates the point perfectly. Ostensibly, the bill was designed to clarify the concept of British citizenship thereby tidying up administrative confusions. There are now three classes of British citizenship and one of the important consequences of this is that UK citizenship is not automatically gained by birth and residence in Britain. In other words, if neither parent was born in the UK or was not lawfully settled there, then the child would not be able to obtain citizenship, until he or she can prove that they have not been absent from the country for more than ninety days in any one of the first ten years of their life. Despite this, it's clear that the principle of cultural separateness across generations has now been recognized and enshrined in law. It's a principle which is informed by a biological deterministic view of culture and which adheres closely to Powell's assertion in 1968 that: 'The West Indian or Asian does not, by being born in England, become an Englishman. In law he becomes

IMMIGRATION ACTS OF THE UK

1962 Commonwealth Immigrants Act introduced a system of employment vouchers for New Commonwealth immigrants. Three grades of vouchers were related to different job opportunities.

1965 Immigration White Paper limited the number of New Commonwealth migrants allowed into the UK to 8,500; of these 1,000 were reserved for migrants from Malta. The bill also abolished the lowest and most flexible grade of employment voucher.

1968 The Commonwealth Immigrants Act was rushed through parliament by the Labour government in response to the expected arrival from Kenya of Asians holding UK citizenship.

1971 The Commonwealth Immigration Act introduced the concept of 'patriality' which effectively changed the status of New Commonwealth citizens to aliens by insisting that only those with British passports born in the UK or whose parents were born there had the 'right of abode'. It put New Commonwealth citizens on the same footing as workers from other overseas countries.

1981 The British Nationality Act established three classes of British citizenship; under the new act UK citizenship is no longer automatically gained by birth and residence in the UK.

a UK citizen by birth; in fact he is a West Indian or an Asian still' (quoted in Smithies and Fiddick, 1969, p. 77).

The 1981 British Nationality Act was a most logical development of the legal traditions started in 1962: the imperative was to control and preserve. By curbing the numbers coming in, it was thought that the alleged 'way of life' could be retained; though, interestingly, in-migration from Australia and Europe has generally been greater than that from the New Commonwealth. The majority of migrants to the UK aren't black or brown, but white.

This is where we see surfacing again the colonial mentality: the idea that the UK was a metropolitan cultural preserve. The migrants came from the West Indies and South Asia because British post-imperial policy was to use those places as recruiting areas for workers; yet they were repelled when the demand for labour diminished.

As we've seen then, there is a very obvious relationship between demands for labour in the metropolitan centre and immigration policy: before 1962 when demand was high, there was no control over the inflow of labour. As the economic recession began to bite, however, and demand for workers receded accordingly, controls tightened. At the same time there were, at political levels, pronouncements on the fears and anxieties of the general population and parallel attempts to retain the allegedly unique 'British way of life'. To understand the development of the UK's immigration laws therefore there must be a consideration of both internal economic factors, deriving initially from the system of empire, and more recently, from the changing demands of the home labour market, and of the persistent and resilient belief in the blacks/Asians = problem equation — itself a legacy of the empire. On both counts, we are forced to consider the critical role of empire in history and in modern times as both an organizing principle behind government policy and a theme in the consciousness of the British population. No area illustrates this more clearly than work. This will be the focus of our next chapter.

Further reading

Staying Power (1984) and its companion volume, **Black People in the British Empire** (1988), both by Peter Fryer, are historical accounts of the experience of ethnic minorities in Britain and its colonies. Both are detailed and illuminating.

Here for Good: Western Europe's new ethnic minorities by Stephen Castles and Tina Wallace (1984) is a comparative analysis of migration patterns from former colonies to European nations and the experience of migrant workers in, for example, West Germany, France and Holland.

Black and White in Britain is the third set of results produced by the PSI (1984). Written by Colin Brown, it demonstrates an enduring pattern of ethnic inequality in which a racially demarcated labour force is complemented by racial segregation in the housing market. Furthermore, it indicates that the mechanisms of racial inequality in the UK have become progressively more entrenched and self-sustaining.

European Immigration Policy: A comparative study is edited by Tomas Hammar (1985) and explores the official policy responses of six European countries to the migration and settlement of foreign workers and their families, especially in the years 1945–74. The authors distinguish between *immigration* policies, which control the ebb and flow of migration and the *immigrant* (i.e., domestic) policies which they engender. Case studies of each country are followed by a detailed, comparative analysis by the editor in which he locates individual policies in a broader and common economic and political context. Whilst underplaying the significance of internal immigration controls and over-emphasizing the governments's commitment to multiculturalism as a policy imperative, Layton-Henry's chapter on the UK provides some useful insights.

Citizenship for Some? by Paul Gordon, of The Runnymede Trust (1989), looks at the effect of ten years of Conservative party rule on race relations in the UK. Gordon carefully scrutinises policies on immigration and various aspects of social policy before concluding that, under Thatcherism, the 'otherness' of black people in Britain has been emphasized and rigidified.

'The return of "sus"' by Jolyon Jenkins (**New Statesman and Society**, 4 August

1989) is a short but interesting account of how immigration law has been used as 'an all-purpose police tool for harassing black people'. It details how blacks are picked up on the streets for alleged immigration offences, which, in some cases, leads to their deportation. In police parlance, this operation is termed 'Big Silver Bird'.

4
Work — class — inequality

- Why is work so central to our lives?
- Do colonial migrants always stay in low level jobs?
- Are trade unions racist organizations?
- Are Asians successful businessmen?
- What is positive discrimination?

Centre and periphery

Tommy and Phil were both 18. They'd been out of work since they left school. They hadn't got a qualification between them. Neither had much idea about what to do for a job. Every day, they'd get up at about 11.00, except on dole days, when they had to sign on at 9.30. Then they'd drift into town, play pool or space invaders (if they could afford it) and meet friends. If the weather was okay, they might play soccer in the park; if not they'd go back to Phil's place and play records. It is two years since Phil left school and his mother is sick of telling him how he should get a job. One night, she comes home from work expecting to find her son and Tommy dossing in the front room with the music blaring away. 'Philip! Where are you?' she shouts. No reply. She puts on the kettle for a cup of tea. 'Philip!' Nothing. Strange: it's raining, so they won't be playing soccer. She looks upstairs. They're not in the bedrooms. They can't be far away. The kettle starts whistling, so she heads back downstairs. At the foot of the stairs, there's a window through which you can see the back garden. Phil's mother glances through it. She tries to scream, but can't. The horror mutes her. Tommy and Phil are hanging by their necks from an oak tree. They have left a note on the record player. It says: 'We can't carry on like this all the time. We can't get a job and everything has lost its point . . . ' There's more, but the first sentences are all the press need and the following morning's headlines read: 'Dole queue suicides' and 'Out-of-work youngsters in suicide pact'.

This story may sound even more exaggerated than the headlines, but it's not; it's based on actual events. The precise reasons behind the deaths were never accurately determined, but the note strongly suggested that the youths experienced a kind of work deprivation in which they lost morale and direction, found life meaningless and hollow and experienced their own attempts to change the situation as futile. So they killed themselves. Obviously, the story is extreme, but it points up in a most dramatic way the power of work in structuring people's lives: take it away and the structure collapses and people are left disorganized and without purpose.

We live in an age in which the work ethic prevails: people believe that we are how we work. 'What are you?' 'I'm a postman . . . , a lecturer . . . , a rep.' Work determines who and what we are. Its importance to people's lives is not peripheral, but central. So when we lack it, we're stripped of a vital element. So, the way we work affects our whole lives. It may seem an obvious point, but it's one that simply can't be overlooked in the context of race relations. Work has central significance to all humans: the manner in which we labour to produce has a critical influence on all other aspects of our life.

There are other key areas, of course, and in the chapters immediately after this we will be looking at two of the most important ones, examining how the places where people live and the manner in which they are educated have important consequences on their total existence. Yet, despite the significance of housing and education, there is a sense in which employment is the decisive factor in life, if only because, as Sheila Allen points out, 'the relationship between occupation and income level is sufficiently close to make employment patterns crucial in the setting of life style, including, for instance, access to certain education opportunities and residential areas' (1971, p. 103).

Peter Braham and his colleagues make a similar acknowledgment: 'Access to the educational system and to leisure facilities, patterns of housing and health, and many other areas of social concern are all likely to be related to employment location in one way or another' (1980, p. 11). This makes work the single most important feature of our lives — whether we like it or not.

The total work experience has constituent parts, all of which play important roles in the workers' lives: the kinds of jobs done, the ownership of the materials and tools involved, the rewards derived from doing the work, the degree of involvement in it, the hours taken to perform it, the physical conditions in which it's done and the amount of supervision over it. These factors affect everybody, regardless of their background or colour — or any other feature for that matter.

But work has a special significance when it comes to race relations because these situations invariably implicate one or more of the groups involved undergoing unusual, if not unique, employment experiences. Many would argue that all situations of race relations actually arise out of one group's determination to keep control of the production process and, in order to do this, maintain power over workers — a point made forcefully by Cox.

Members of groups designated racially inferior are rarely provided with job opportunities equal to those thought to be their superiors. Crudely stated, discrimination and disadvantage usually ensure that the work experience of the powerless groups are less enriching than those of the powerful; the jobs themselves are generally less crucial to the total production complex and the possibilities for advancement they offer more limited.

The reasons for this are rooted, as are most other phenomena of race relations, in the historical experience of empire. This system of domination ensured an easy regulated flow of labour to the system's centre of gravity, the metropolis, from the outlying regions that were brought under its control, the periphery. In the first phases of conquest, the transference of peoples to where their labour was required was made possible by simple force, slavery being the obvious example. But, in more recent times, migrants have moved voluntarily within the system, though, as we've seen, the options available to those who eventually move are often more apparent than real.

Frequently, the dire lack of work opportunites combined with the possibility if not probability of better job prospects in the new environment fuse to motivate the migration. On and for some time after arrival, the migrants tend to be disadvantaged relative to the metropolitan population and are compelled to accept only the undesirable jobs. Thus, migrants are almost always disproportionately represented in the lower grade employments, or what Glasgow calls 'cellar jobs'. This has the double effect of making promotion or any kind of advancement rather harder than for native workers and of reinforcing native workers' images of migrants as fit only for menial tasks. The latter effect leads to the sort of stereotyping perfectly suited to the colonial mentality and migrants soon become stigmatized as low ranking workers naturally suited for the cellar jobs. In this sense, the colonial worker remains, as John Tierney puts it, 'caught in the most vicious of vicious circles' (1982, p. 8).

In the USA, the situation regarding black workers is slightly different and has to be traced back to the migration from Africa forced by slavery. The Emancipation didn't completely destroy the system and remnants endured in the southern states where blacks supplied cheap, unskilled agricultural labour. A system of peonage was developed in which the ex-slaves were held in servitude and the white stayed in domination. The early twentieth-century expansion of industry opened up new gaps in the labour force which the incoming European immigrants could not adequately fill. So, a new source of labour was found: blacks. In the north particularly, they came to be a sort of subgroup, for, as

James Geschwender points out: 'Blacks were shunted to the harder, least desirable, more dangerous and more poorly paid jobs' (1977, p. 4).

As well as providing the American equivalent of the reserve army, the blacks in industry tended to inhibit white militancy; according to Geschwender: 'Whites could always use the threat of replacing white strikers with black workers' (1977, p. 4).

After World War II, the civil rights movement stimulated considerable improvements in the general and working conditions of blacks but did little to change the basic picture of a stuctured inequality and left blacks excluded from prestigious, rewarding, decision-making positions.

The processes in the UK were not dissimilar, though, of course, there was no massive internal migration comparable with the American shift northwards. Labour migration was nothing novel as British employers had, for years, used labour from Southern Ireland, Europe and isolated parts of the New Commonwealth, though matters after 1945 necessitated new measures in recruitment. The gaps in the labour market prised open by the post-war expansion were filled with the appreciable help, first, of Caribbeans, then, of South Asians. Together, these formed a subgroup tending to occupy positions not wanted — or, indeed, needed — by native workers, who were prospering from the market's widening choices. They stepped up from the cellar, leaving the new arrivals to occupy the left-over positions.

In profile, blacks and Asians formed a fraction of the working class: they occupied similar positions in relation to the means of production; they supplied labour not capital and worked for others rather than having others work for them. In this sense, the interests of the migrants were basically those of the broad working class. But common interests are not always visible and the hostility of the white workers to what were then 'dark strangers' indicates the extent to which they regarded them as unwelcome threats to their improved positions in the rejuvenated labour market.

So, the introduction of a new source in the labour supply to industry served to divide working-class loyalties and set people with similar interests against each other and, perhaps, deter whites from being over-militant, the underlying idea being that owners of the means of production could say: 'If you don't like your job, there's always a coon ready to take your place!'

This kind of principle led to New Commonwealth workers being not only disadvantaged and discriminated against, but actually dislocated or separated from the total system of production; collectively they were outside the main occupational sphere and used as what were in effect ancillary workers. Their roles were to augment the labour force but, at the same time, they effectively introduced divisions within in.

One result of this was the enormous maldistribution of immigrant labour.

KONJUNKTURPUFFER
The political strategy of admitting migrant workers to a country for the purpose of working for a set period of time, but not allowing them to settle permanently.

Obviously, the migrants headed for the areas most fertile in job opportunities — London, the Midlands and, later, the Bradford-Leeds area — and took up the types of jobs available in those areas: many became engaged in the heavy manufacturing and textile industries (Runnymede Trust, 1980, pp. 55–72).

Since the 1950s, there have been many modifications in the employment of migrants and their offspring, yet the fact remains that they are still concentrated in the least desired, nonskilled, manual positions. But, while this pattern of disadvantage persists, black and Asian workers were — at least until 1973 — something of an elite when cast alongside other migrant working groups, particularly in Northern Europe. Like other major European societies, the UK was committed to large economic growth policies and full employment and so sought expedient measures to remedy labour shortages. All the expanding European countries, expecially West Germany, solved this problem by recruiting foreign labour, thus giving their home workers the chance to leave less wanted jobs and improve standards of living. Migrants from less developed places like Turkey filled the gaps such as in agriculture in Germany and mining in Belgium. They were cheap, available and ready to travel. The strategy of bringing in pliant outside labour was a common one amongst industrial capitalist societies.

Most European states in the post-war phase adopted what's called the *Konjunkturpuffer* approach, making the political decision to admit migrants for the specific purpose of working for set periods of time, but not allowing them to settle. In this way, temporary shortages on the labour front could be alleviated without taxing the economy in times of unemployment; the workers were sent packing when their work ran out. It's easy to see how immigration control, when augmented, as it usually is, to employment demands, is a most convenient instrument with which industry can regulate its supply of labour.

A study of Canadian immigration control since 1867 illustrated the very close links between government policy and manpower requirements, giving rise to the idea that Canadian immigration laws were legislative innovations which acted as responses to the necessity of providing a mobile, docile and inexpensive work force for a variety of powerful groups (and of course to make a substantial contribution to the demand for manufactured items, food and land) (Cashmore, 1978, p. 428).

One of the rawest examples of the exploitation of immigrant labour was

---

UNDERDEVELOPMENT
Refers to the inferior conditions which certain countries and societies experience relative to the advanced capitalist nations of Western Europe and the USA. It frequently originated from the emasculation of those countries and societies which took place through imperialist and colonial conquest. The process entails, in early phases, exploiting the labour, stripping of the natural resources, and the use of the underdeveloped country as an ancillary market for goods manufactured in the metropolitan centres.

---

the recruitment of Chinese workers to help build the Canadian Pacific Railway; conditions were so treacherous that local whites refused to work under them. In 1885, the railway was completed and it seems more than just a coincidence that this year also saw the passing of legal measures to restrict non-European immigrants' entry by imposing what was then a heavy 50 dollars entry tax that few Chinese could meet.

There are too many parallels with the UK developments to conclude anything other than that immigrant labour has been used, often wantonly, to serve capitalist interests. The host country's ability to operate the *Konjunkturpuffer* rests on the willingness of migrant groups to travel and work; research tells us that they were, if only because of the 'myth of return' — the preservation of the idea that, at some stage, they could return to their original lands enriched with the spoils of a lucrative spell in the metropolis. Such an idea is best nourished under conditions of hardship and deprivation, such as in the peripheral colonies that were supported in the early phases of empire building, stripped of their natural resources in later stages and left to deteriorate in modern times. The seventeenth and eighteenth centuries saw Britain and other Western European powers occupy vast portions of Africa, Asia and the West Indies. Colonialism laid an economic basis for the development of western capitalism; the colonies provided cheap labour, raw materials and, in some cases, markets. In the process, however, there was a 'perversion', as A. Sivanandan puts it: 'colonialism perverts the economy of the colonies to its own ends, drains their wealth into the coffers of the metropolitan country and leaves them at independence with a large labour force and no capital with which to make that labour productive' (1982, p. 102).

The colonies and ex-colonies habitually experienced extreme poverty and offered, at best, seasonal or contract employment, or at worst, no work at all to the vast majority of their populations. One of the major consequences of colonialism is that it creates a labour force ready and willing to travel thousands of miles on the promise of employment and the possibility of profound improvements in living conditions.

DUAL LABOUR MARKET
The concept of the dual labour market suggests a basic division between employers operating in two distinct spheres: 1) the primary market, providing high wages, internal structures with career opportunities, non-arbitrary management and secure employment; and 2) the secondary market providing low wages, no career opportunities, arbitrary management and insecure employment. More recent developments of this theory have suggested a more highly differentiated situation in which visible signs, like skin colour, have become important criteria. These signs may be a legacy of the colonial past, but they have relevance to contemporary social conditions.

Stephen Castles and Godula Kosack call the labour migration 'a form of development aid given by poor countries to rich countries' (1973, p. 8). Inhabitants of these poor countries, having lived through depressions, endured multiple deprivations and adapted to poverty, glimpsed the prospect of employment at the metropolitan centre, uprooted themselves and set forth with the optimism of a latter-day Dick Whittington; like he, they were to find no streets paved with gold.

What they did find we will examine next, but let's remind ourselves of two things: (1) That the present situation of black and South Asian groups has to be seen in the historical perspective of migrant labour's response to developments of imperialist capitalism, particularly the post-war reconstruction of Europe; (2) That work is the most central feature of life and has ramifications in all spheres of activity. Having been pulled or pushed from the peripheral homeland to the more promising centre, the immigrants confronted only a limited range of job opportunities and so settled for low-level jobs that yielded less money than positions occupied by native workers; let's look at this situation in more detail.

No way out and up

The distorted profile of employment patterns in the contemporary UK hasn't arisen accidentally: the low level of migrant workers was almost pre-determined, and the types of work available to them was severely affected by the decaying empire. As Rex points out, in metropolitan societies such as the UK, 'there develops a set of unwanted economic and social positions which can most readily be staffed by colonial or immigrant workers' (1973, p. 202).

The skewed distribution of migrant workers in the UK was demonstrated in a number of surveys throughout the 1960s (see Daniel, 1968; Davison, 1962;

Patterson, 1968; Peach, 1968; Wright, 1968). One of the most exhaustive of these early analyses was carried out by Rose *et al.* using evidence from the 1966 10 per cent sample census (1969). They considered, amongst other things, the occupational distribution of what they called 'coloured immigrants' in the two main areas of settlement in the UK, London and the West Midlands. Rose *et al.* pointed out that 'coloured immigrants' did not constitute an homogeneous group and that there were wide occupational variations between and within the immigrant communities. Nevertheless, the general conclusion was that the immigrants were 'less well-represented than the total population in those occupations usually considered most desirable, and over-represented in those considered most undesirable' (1969, p. 165). They were undesirable not only because of the wage level, which in some cases, say, shift work, may have been relatively good, but also because of the conditions and hours of employment, or their exceptional vulnerability to economic fluctuations. Such jobs are said to be located in the secondary labour market. The vast majority of the immigrant workers found themselves in the low status, largely unskilled positions in the textile and clothing industries, engineering and foundry works, hotels, hospital and transport services.

It might be said, of course, that as migration from the New Commonwealth had been stimulated largely by the desire to find better employment, then almost any job in the UK, regardless of wage level or conditions of service, was likely to have brought a distinct improvement in the migrants' job statuses and, therefore, life styles. At the same time, it could be contended that the sorts of jobs they obtained were commensurate with the levels of skills they brought with them.

It's certainly possible that this was the case for migrants from India and Pakistan. Coming mainly from rural areas, their skills, inevitably, were of limited use in a modern technological society such as the UK's. In the case of the migrants from the Caribbean, however, the picture is not so clear because of the problems involved in trying to establish with any precision their occupational background and level of skill prior to migration. Whether or not they experienced an elevation in job status in the transition to the UK remains a matter for conjecture. Some, like Ruth Glass, would say that they actually had to take a drop in job status (1960, p. 29). Others, like Nancy Foner, say there was little difference (1979, p. 86). Whatever the case, it's clear that their work background or qualifications from their societies of origin made little difference; they were constrained, as David Pearson reminds us, irrespective of their background, 'to enter occupations which (were) labelled suitable for them in Britain' (1981, p. 52). Even those who did go through some occupational upward mobility and managed to secure material and status improvement would have had their satisfaction tempered by a reception suffused with racism.

SOCIAL MOBILITY
The process by which individuals or groups move upwards in terms of job status and income relative to their parents. As most occupations require qualifications for entry, education is seen as one starting point for social mobility. In race relations, the popular view is that the sons and daughters of immigrants should, because of the advantage of their education, experience some upward social mobility and advance beyond their parents' positions. In fact, events do not quite bear this out.

In the sphere of employment racialism affected not only migrants' chances of getting a job but also their opportunities for promotion. As Dennis Brooks found in his study of London Transport, the idea of a black worker in a higher occupational position than a white colleague was wholly at odds with stereotyped images of black people as subordinate; so, the appointment of a black bus inspector, according to one busman interviewed by Brooks, would 'cause resentment. Some would say "I'm not taking orders from a black b..." ' (1975, p. 105).

Quite clearly, the persistence of racialism reinforced the subordinate position of migrant workers in the labour market while their role in the reserve army of labour made them especially vulnerable to unemployment when the economic situation deteriorated (Field *et al.*, 1981, pp. 21–2).

All migrant communities were, to a greater or lesser extent, disillusioned with life in the UK, so much so that some writers, like Rex, have found it surprising that there wasn't an emergence of 'a politically militant movement of coloured people fighting for their rights' (1973, p. 109). Of course, the various communities were not totally unmoved by their experiences in Britain and in the late 1950s and throughout the 1960s a number of minority organizations were formed (Sivanandan, 1981, pp. 117–18). But, on the whole, these initiatives were fragmentary and, unlike the experience in the USA, did not cohere into a unified civil rights movement — a development outlined by Harvard Sitkoff (1981). Instead, the response of the migrants to the daily iniquities of British racialism was generally muted and there was an acceptance of subordination. How do we explain this? Well, we believe that it is explicable in terms of the colonial mentality theme. Blacks, in particular, were nurtured in colonial ideology and accepted it, were prepared to accept cellar jobs and maybe even internalize negative self-images during their settlement in Britain. Other commentators, however, like Stuart Philpott, have suggested that there was a general adherence to the 'migrant ideology' (1973). That is to say, a large proportion of the migrants saw themselves as transient workers and were prepared to tolerate what Foner called the 'pain of being black in Britain' until they had accrued

SELF-IMAGE
The conception persons have of themselves; their sense of identity. In race relations, the negative self-image of migrants (and their children) is often invoked to explain the lack of militancy or challenge to subordination. Briefly, this means that the migrant accepts what seems to be a prevalent definition of him or her self; if the rest of society believes all blacks to be inferior and suited for degrading work, it may well be that the immigrant comes to accept this negative image and settles quite happily for degrading work.

sufficient money to return home (1979, p. 123). Whatever the likelihood of this happening, it's clear that it had some effect on the migrants' behaviour in Britain. Another explanation is that the migrants expected that their children, born and brought up in the UK, and therefore not encumbered with an immigrant culture, would not have to confront the racialism they had faced.

In view of our argument about how the colonial legacy has helped to shape race relations in modern Britain, it should come as no surprise to learn that the migrants' aspirations and expectations have remained unfulfilled. The disadvantages of the colonial worker in the metropolitan society are only tenuously associated with newness and are therefore unlikely to diminish substantially with the passage of time. It's precisely because of the colonial system that these disadvantages are unique to the worker from the New Commonwealth; according to Rex, for example, they can be distinguished from the experiences of other immigrant workers in at least two ways:

First he is more severely confined to the position of replacement worker and resident, and second and most important, he cannot expect with confidence that his children or grandchildren will have been accepted into the stratification system of the host society . . . . In the second generation his children find that there is no way out and up for them (1970, p. 109).

There are now a number of studies which support Rex's contention through a careful documentation of how far migrant workers and their British-born children continue to occupy inferior positions in the labour market. Not only do they tend to have poorer jobs and to earn less than whites, but also tend to face a much higher risk of unemployment (Field *et al.*, 1981; D. Smith, 1977, 1981). For school-leavers, of course, the chances of finding a job, irrespective of background, are uniformly bleak. But for young people of Caribbean and South Asian origin these chances are even more remote. In the Brixton area of South London, for example, the number of registered unemployed young blacks between 19–24 rose by 71 per cent between April 1981–April 1982 (*Sunday Times*, 4 April 1982). Malcolm Cross and his colleagues report a similar trend in Birmingham between 1980–1; then, registered unemployment amongst black youths rose at twice the rate of young people as a whole in the city (Cross *et al.*, 1982, p. 3). School-leavers of South Asian origin confront similar problems according to research carried out in Bradford by Mike Campbell and Doug Jones. They report that: 'a staggering 72%' of South Asian youngsters in the city were without real jobs 12 months after leaving school, when the 1981 school leavers were also entering the job market; this compared with 31 per cent of school-leavers as a whole in Bradford (1982, p. 51). When these local patterns are translated into national trends the disproportionate effect of youth unemployment on minority youngsters is starkly revealed: 'The overall change among the unemployed aged under 18 in Britain for the 12 months to January 1980 was a *reduction* of 2.4%; the *increase* among ethnic minorities was 7.3%' (CRE, 1980, p. 14).

It could be argued that the higher rates of minority youth unemployment reflect their lower educational qualifications rather than their skin colour. Without doubt, there is as relationship between educational achievement and the chances of finding a job, but this relationship is not as clear-cut as is often assumed and there is substantial evidence to show that colour has an independent and powerful impact on the chances of success in the search for a job (see Troyna and Smith, 1983). Studies carried out by the CRE in the Lewisham district of South London, and in Nottingham, indicate that direct discrimination against young Caribbean and South Asian job-seekers persists (CRE, 1978; Hubbuck and Carter, 1980), while camouflaged racism through the operation of particular recruitment strategies also serves, in effect, systematically to disadvantage black and South Asian applicants (Carby and Thakur, 1977; Jenkins, 1982). A study by Gloria Lee and John Wrench has also shown that it's more difficult for black and South Asian school-leavers to secure apprenticeships, relative to whites (1981). The evidence, then, is clear: disadvantage in trying to get work is being reproduced among generations born and educated in Britain, and that with the economic recession, conditions for migrants and their children have actually deteriorated over the last twenty years. Employment has been one of the main issues confronting migrants not only in the UK but elsewhere in Europe since the war. Indeed, we've argued that, because its impact on all other areas of life is so massive, it's the single most important issue. However, if the indications of the early 1980s are anything to go by, it may not be work that is the chief issue in the lives of the migrants' children, but rather the chronic lack of it.

Unemployment, of course, is something which trade unions can do little about, yet their function is to defend and further the interests of the working class of which migrants and their offspring are a part. Yet unions have not been spectacularly successful in their task, as we will now see.

Unions

'A remarkable state of affairs' is how Peter Ratcliffe describes the situation regarding blacks and Asians and trade union membership (1981, p. 268). His study of Handsworth in Birmingham reinforced the earlier PEP (1977) conclusion that 'trade union membership is, if anything, higher among the minority groups than among the white population.'

On the face of it, there are forces that would seem to militate against this high TU membership. Unions have a rather poor record of defending black or Asian members in conflicts where race has appeared to have been a factor and have, on occasion, been guilty of overtly discriminatory practices. Also, when specific groups have organized themselves into movements based on background or colour rather than class position, they have been appreciably more effective in furthering their members' interests than conventional unions. Added to this is, as we noted earlier, the fact that groups of Caribbean or South Asian origins or descent tend to be structurally dislocated from the main occupational sphere.

Then why do so many join unions? Ratcliffe's answer can be summarized like this: (1) They don't want to remain outside formal union movements and so appear to reject 'the integrationist perspective'; (2) The power of minority unions, in particular the Indian Workers' Association (IWA), in relation to the established unions has seemed deficient on some occasions; (3) The lack of a show of solidarity on the shop floor might simply reinforce their sub-working class status — and, by implication, further dislocate them.

So, the reasons for joining unions are more defensive than provoked by the positive desire to improve conditions through union activity and the 'marked indifference' to union issues Ratcliffe found seems to bear out the idea that, although membership is high, commitment is low. This is not to suggest that immigrant workers have been — or, indeed, will be — entirely apathetic: periodically, they've been mobilized impressively to defend their interests — interests, significantly, that they've seen to be based on colour or background rather than the relationship to means of production, class.

Industrial conflicts in modern capitalist society tend to have a common origin in the relationship to the means of production: between owners, who live off profit, and those who work for them, who live off wages. As we've seen, the majority of migrants belong to the latter group; but, also they undergo quite specific experiences that mark them off from the rest of the working class and influence the manner in which they react to disputes arising in the workplace.

In May 1972, an Asian employee of the Midlands firm of Mansfield Hosiery Mills Ltd complained to the Race Relations Board of racial discrimination in promotion procedures. His complaint was referred to the East Midlands Conciliation Committee. An investigation revealed that the firm had unlawfully discriminated against Asian workers. While deliberations were taking place, a wage claim by other Asian workers erupted into a strike which was eventually recognized as official by the National Union of Hosiery and Knitwear Workers (NUHKW), though white workers were not required to withdraw their labour too, 'presumably because it (the union) was well aware of their hostility to the advancements of the Asian workers,' according to Robert Miles and Annie Phizacklea (1981, p. 254).

A government committee of inquiry was set up to try to settle the dispute and two of its conclusions were that, (1) the NUHKW had not adequately helped its Asian members and, (2) those members might well break away in future and form their own organization should the union fail to represent their interests.

Shortly after the Mansfield affair came a rather more important conflict at another Midlands town, Leicester, where Imperial Typewriters Ltd was the subject of considerable dispute between Asian workers on the one hand and management and trade unions on the other. This three-cornered business escalated with both management and union accused of racial discrimination. In both incidents at Mansfield and Leicester, allegations of racism by trade unions were rife and the TUC as good as acknowledged this at its 1974 Congress when a representative recognized that, while union officials never sanctioned such actions, rank and file members might well refuse to work with blacks or Asians (Select Committee, 1975, p. 459).

The contradiction surfaced again in 1980 when Birmingham-born George Jones was refused a fitter's job at British Leyland despite having the requisite qualifications and experience. 'The reason for not appointing him was not because he was black but because others would not work with him because he was black,' a BL spokesman explained to the *Birmingham Post* (6 November 1980). The plant superintendent was told by shop stewards of the Amalgamated Union of Engineering Workers 'that some fitters were prepared to pack in their jobs if a black fitter was employed.'

Officially, the trade union movement condemns racialism and encourages the membership of groups of all backgrounds: it has insisted on an equal opportunities clause in collective agreements with employers, has released several publications about race relations and has held public demonstrations with the theme 'united against racialism' (Trade Union Congress, 1981). At the same time, the movement expressly refuses to single out specific groups of members, predicating its policy on the principle: workers are workers irrespective of colour and background. Yet there are occasional episodes like at BL which seem to reveal that, below the surface, many rank and file union members are prejudiced and do racially discriminate. And clearly this is an influence in discouraging union commitment from Caribbean and Asian workers.

We've noticed that, in the thirty years after the war, New Commonwealth workers tended to be concentrated in the least desirable and unrewarding jobs. Race was an important factor in this and unions were singularly unsuccessful in removing it. Small wonder that there was at least some dissatisfaction with the rate and scope of progress; and it was precisely this dissatisfaction which fuelled such movements as the Indian Workers' Association (IWA) formed in the late 1950s.

The IWA was the UK's nearest equivalent to the Detroit-based League of Revolutionary Black Workers which was active in the period 1968–73 and organized black auto workers, held wildcat strikes, conducted demonstrations, participated in union electoral politics and, generally, fought for black workers. The reasons underlying the formation of the league, which was geared to black interests rather than class interests, are pertinent to the UK experience. Geschwender points to one important reason:

> Black workers confront racism much more directly than they confront class exploitation. That is, they may suffer more from class than racial exploitation but class exploitation is more difficult to observe and identify and its recognition requires more political sophistication (1977, p. 183).

His argument is that black workers see that white workers in the main have better jobs and more income and so perceive that they are exploited not as members of the working class but as black people. 'It may be difficult for many black workers to accept the suggested relationship between capitalism and racism as anything other than a diversionary ploy designed to retain white skin privilege by undermining the fight against racism,' argues Geschwender (1977, p. 183). Conversely, white workers feel that they are better off than blacks and want to maintain their edge, so have a 'vested interest in racism and the status quo' (1977, p. 218). The whole thing gets into a situation in which, as Geschwender describes the Detroit scene: 'Black workers generally viewed labour unions as organizations of white men concerned with white men's problems' (1977, p. 26).

So, accepting Geschwender's argument, we can say that blacks see unions as not only unhelpful, but as inimical to their particular interests as blacks (rather than as members of the working class). This goes a long way to helping us understand why official union commitment is low whereas commitment to splinter movements is on the increase. Objectively, many would argue that movements structured along such lines are 'an exacerbated postponement' of the eventual class confrontation, as Cox would put it (1976, p. 190). But, given that racialism is practised (if not preached) by trade unions and that people respond to problems they perceive as immediate and apprehensible, then we can surmise a sprouting of black and Asian alternative unions in the 1980s, a possibility that was clearly on the mind of Ken Gill, the chairman of the TUC's equal rights and race relations committee, when he said that black workers 'might press to form their own trade unions' if they weren't allowed to express themselves in the mainstream unions (*Guardian*, 10 September 1982).

Such movements we anticipate will be inspired by an awareness of belonging to a distinct underprivileged, disclocated group and are expressed in a 'ghetto consciousness' rather than a class consciousness, though Phizacklea and Miles instance the convergence in their study of West Indian workers in North West London: 'It is therefore possible for black migrant labour to develop both a class and a racial consciousness' (1980, p. 39). Geschwender's study illustrates how a black revolutionary movement cultivated a complementary consciousness of belonging to a group of black people and to a working class which shared a common enemy and so organized along black lines to confront it.

Parallel developments in the UK are possible, though improbable in view of the circumstances of widespread working class and, in particular, trade union racialism. Blacks and Asians have little faith in the efficacy of unions and none in the integrity of them.

Not that a sizeable portion of migrants seem to need unions to push their interests for them: a great deal seem to advance quite smoothly outside the main industrial spheres and detach themselves from their assigned class location in the UK; though, as we'll see in the next section, they are not always as sizeable or successful as they seem.

Asian prosperity: a hollow façade

We've depicted colonial migrants as conscripted into a labour force, where they are virtually compelled, due to a variety of circumstances (both current and historical), to stay rooted at the bottom of the occupational ladder. Involvement in the trade unions has yielded little improvement in their overall position and it is a position rendered fragile by fluctuations in the economy. In all, the rates and standards of occupational progress have been minimal, as Smith reports: 'All the minority groups have penetrated comparatively little into non-manual jobs, particularly the better ones classified as "professional" or "management" positions' (1977, p. 73). Yet a walk through the Manningham district of

---

ENTREPRENEUR
One who attempts, through enterprise, calculated risk and initiative, to make profit by dealing or other commercial activities; in doing so, he escapes the situation of being dependent on wages paid by an employer for his existence.

Bradford, or along the Melton Road in Leicester, or through the main streets in Southall, West London, provides a contrasting profile of colonial workers.

In these areas, there is a profusion of small businesses owned and staffed by Asian migrants. The emergence of these businesses has made a significant impact on the townscape of areas such as Belgrave in Leicester, as Amit Roy discovered:

> Belgrave and Melton Roads, once apparently a dilapidated and decaying part of town, has developed into a large Asian shopping centre. The rows of sari shops, curry restaurants, groceries, jewellers and travel agents and cinemas might look foreign, but they also exude an air of confidence, prosperity and even excitement (1978, p. 2).

This trend towards self-employment amongst the Asian communities in Britain is not an unusual phenomenon, however. Stephen Aris, amongst others, had discussed a similar pattern amongst the Jewish population in the UK during the nineteenth and twentieth centuries (1970). Similarly, in the United States, the Chinese, Japanese and Jewish communities have shown a predilection towards opening their own shops and firms. Ownership of a business enhances the sense of independence and self-esteem and so has been an obvious goal for minority groups.

On the face of it, the apparent scale and success of Asian-owned businesses in the UK would seem slightly to undermine, some might say invalidate, our argument about the lower status and structural dislocation of at least this group of colonial migrant workers. 'Out of nothing they seem to be able to create enormous wealth' is how one 'expert' on this area characterized Asian entrepreneurs (quoted in Forester, 1978, p. 422). And Tom Forester, apparently, found nothing to contradict this view in his study of Asians in business. Amongst those he interviewed was Mohinder Singh Chera who had arrived virtually penniless from Gulunda in 1958 and then became founder and sole owner of Bradford Grinders (UK) Ltd, a firm which employed twenty-three mostly skilled workers. Kewal Singh Bhullar's experiences were fairly similar to Mohinder's, according to Forester. Twelve years after he had arrived with no money from the Punjab he bought a business comprising one room and a few decrepit sewing machines for £150. By the time Forester met him, 'thousands of anoraks and nylon housecoats' later, the situation had changed dramatically. His son Ajmair drives a £16,000 Mercedes, lives in a big house and insures his wife's jewellery for £10,000. Dad is virtually retired, they have built a new house for themselves in India and the firm employs a total of 150 people in Leeds. They are suppliers of lined nylon anaroks or 'poor man's sheepskins' to Woolworths, Hepworths, Burtons and other well-known chainstores (1978, p. 422).

Rags-to-riches stories such as these have become elements of popular folklore: Forester's description of most Asians that they 'have turned to self-employment and entrepreneurial experimentation' is now a common stereotype (1978, p. 422). If, indeed, this is an accurate characterization, then the Asians seem to be well on the way to achieving parity with whites. But are these impressionistic accounts supported by statistical as well as visible evidence?

It would seem not. First of all, the 1971 census and 1974 PEP survey showed that the proportion of self-employed amongst the Asian communities was lower than for the working population as a whole: 8 per cent of Asian working men, compared to 12 per cent of white men, were self-employed according to Smith (1977, p. 92). Secondly, the National Dwelling and Household Survey (NDHS) carried out for the Department of the Environment in 1977–8 showed that hardly any Asians were large employers (Ward and Reeves, 1980, pp. 12–14). In other words, the picture of commercial vigour drawn by Forester and others is largely illusory. In fact, while there has undoubtedly been a rapid rise in Asian-owned small businesses in Britain, particularly since the arrival in the late 1960s and early 1970s of Asian businessmen from East Africa, the typical self-employed Asian is to be found behind the counter of a small corner shop either selling general provisions, such as groceries or newspapers, or catering for the specialized needs of an Asian clientele.

The most systematic study of the Asian-owned small business sector in the UK has been carried out by Howard Aldrich and his colleagues (1981). It's worth focusing on their work not only because it provides an empirical rather than impressionistic account of this development but also because, by implication, it gives clues as to why there has not been a parallel growth in black businesses in this country.

Aldrich and his co-workers carried out their survey in those areas of Bradford, Leicester and Ealing where the highest proportion of Asians lived, and it was in these heavily segregated residential areas that the growth of Asian retailing was most striking. A number of writers, for instance, have identified the preservation of ethnic identity and the maintenance of cultural integrity as important goals for the Asian communities in the UK, and the growth of tight residential concentrations in particular cities can be seen as facilitating and ensuring this exclusiveness (Dahya, 1974; Saifullah Khan, 1976). In this context, as Aldrich *et al.* point out, the development of Asian-owned shops in these areas helps to 'reinforce the insulating effect of residential segregation' (1981, p. 176). By providing specialized goods and services to maintain cultural and dietary habits as well as other general goods such as newspapers and groceries, the shops allow for an even greater degree of independence from the wider society. In a related article, two of Aldrich's colleagues, John Cater and Trevor Jones, specified the functions of the Asian retailer in Bradford:

> With the exception of a few general stores, grocers, off-licences and restaurants, Asians retailers are rarely patronised by whites and apparently make little effort to attract white custom. As a whole they are geared to a predominantly Asian clientele, an ethnic exclusiveness which becomes most marked in the case of firms offering specialised goods or services. Thus Hilal butchers are totally Asian-orientated as are cinemas showing Punjabi films and travel agencies promoting trips to the subcontinent (1978, p. 81).

Because of the largely Asian clientele, this cultural independence from the mainstream is complemented by economic independence. As Aldrich *et al.* put it: 'the pattern is one of income earned in the white economy and spent in the Asian sub-economy' (1981, p. 178).

It's possible to infer from the work of Aldrich and his colleagues at least some of the reasons why there has been no parallel development of black businesses in the UK. Part of the reason, of course, is, as Robin Ward and Frank Reeves have pointed out: 'Asians have over generations occupied a world-wide role as middlemen trading communities... whereas most West Indians have gone into construction or areas of the service sector outside distribution' (1980, p. 33). A similar point was raised by Kazuka in his report on ethnic minority businesses in Hackney, East London (1982, p. 6). On top of this, however, we have also seen how important the emergence of segregated residential areas has been to the rise of Asian-owned shops in the UK, and the fact that blacks in Britain tend to be distributed, unlike the Asians, in modern council housing as well as the older working-class areas of public housing has also inhibited their entrepreneurial initiatives. Because they are not so tightly clustered, West Indian shopkeepers would be more likely to find themselves in competition with actual or budding white retailers for a largely white clientele. A related point concerns the distinctive needs of the submarket which Asian shopkeepers tend to cater for. The cultural and dietary habits amongst South Asians is sufficient to sustain specialist shops and services. Within the black community, however, there are far less distinctively different preferences, a factor which once again discourages entrepreneurial activity. Despite these various obstacles — which as Mike

Phillips (1978) and Ward and Reeves (1980) point out, also includes the reluctance of banks to lend black applicants capital to start their own businesses — there are indications that members of the black community are now starting up their own businesses. As Ward notes: 'The obstacles to the black entrepreneur are still formidable but you are now getting West Indians coming on to the labour market with some education. A business breakthrough is not going to happen overnight but it is now much more likely than ever before' (quoted in Barber, 1982, p. 55).

The ownership and control of businesses is conventionally viewed as an instrument for minority social mobility and despite our refinement of the exaggerated picture of commercial enterprise amongst the Asian communities in Britain drawn by journalists such as Forester and Roy, there is no denying that there has been a burgeoning of Asian-owned small businesses in the UK. Even so, Aldrich *et al.* suggest that this has not led to significant social or economic mobility. On the contrary, they conclude that the Asian shopkeeper has simply exchanged the status of second-class worker for that of second-class proprietor, and that self-employment has done nothing to minimize the persistence of racial disadvantage (1981). How do we account for this?

It is clear that racial discrimination in the white labour market has influenced the decision of many Asians to open their own businesses. Dilip Hiro has made the point that those of Asian origin in Britain have only 'minimally exposed themselves to situations where they might be discriminated against' and in this context any form of self-containment — whether in residential or occupational spheres — is an attractive strategy (1973, p. 113). Chera, for example, pinpointed racialism as the main factor in his decision to become self-employed when he told Forester: 'Nobody gives you a chance in this country. If it wasn't for the racial hatred, I wouldn't be here' (1978, p. 420). Because of the wish to avoid discrimination and to remain a self-contained community, Asian shops have generally opened up in those very areas vacated by whites; in this sense, therefore, they are not perceived as a threat to white retailers but are simply continuing their role as replacement labour in the UK. However, because the Asian-owned shops are concentrated almost entirely within their own specific communities, the potential for development remains severely restricted. Cater put this well when he wrote:

> Being largely dependent upon a numerically and financially limited clientele, their prospects for future expansion are severely limited without penetrating often discriminatory white markets, and such penetration seems highly unlikely at present. Just as Asians are restricted to residual residential space in provincial cities, they are predominantly restricted to economic opportunities voluntarily relinquished by the host community (1978, p. 565).

Appearances, then, are not always as they seem and the more conspicuous rags-to-riches experiences of migrant entrepreneurs are highly untypical. Although Alison Baker makes the point that many self-employed Asians are hopeful of 'considerable financial gains from their enterprises', it's clear that many fail to achieve this objective (1981/2, p. 481). For every Murjani jean company or Regines night club, there are thousands of other Asian businesses barely ticking over, and tens of thousands of other Asian workers struggling to make ends meet. As Andrew Sills and his colleagues commented in their descriptive summary of the circumstances of Asian households in Leicester's inner area: 'For this community as a whole the low ratio of wage earners to dependants, low earnings, high dependence on income maintenance, and high housing costs, combine to create widespread poverty.' They conclude: 'The glitter of Melton Road prosperity becomes on closer inspection a hollow façade, masking considerable disadvantage and deprivation' (1982, p. 5).

For the most part, Asian businesses remain marginal, relying on a limited, largely segregated market, and the number of shops is rapidly reaching the point when it is greater than this submarket can bear. 'At the most basic level, the ineffectiveness of Asian retailing is a problem of demography' is how Trevor Jones sums up the situation (1981/2, p. 473). In addition, because they are predominantly secondary rather than primary producers (like heavy manufacturing industries, automobile makers or oil producers) Asian entrepreneurs have only a finite chance of expansion and little exporting potential.

The vast majority of migrants and their children are not socially mobile in that they stay rooted at the cellar level of the labour market, and the chances are that they will remain in that position. Some would argue that only a wholesale destruction of the capitalist system which perpetuates exploitation and ensures splits in working-class loyalties will break the pattern. Other, more liberal, commentators have looked towards piecemeal strategies such as that one embodied in positive discrimination.

Positive discrimination

'At the beginning of the 1921 depression', wrote Herbert Northrup, 'a delegation, composed of Negroes employed at River Rouge and prominent members of the Detroit Negro community, approached Henry Ford and expressed their concern over discrimination in layoffs' (1944, p. 189). The response to the delegation was a sort of prototype of positive discrimination: 'Mr. Ford then adopted the policy of employing the same proportion of Negroes at River Rouge as the proportion of Negroes in the population of Greater

---

POSITIVE DISCRIMINATION
(Or affirmative action, as it's known in the USA.) A policy usually directed by central government in an attempt to reverse the historical trend that has consigned many minority groups to positions of occupational disadvantage. It involves actually encouraging employers, administrators, etc. to grant access to or promote members of disprivileged groups — even though, at times, white candidates may have commensurable qualifications.

Detroit . . . .Actually, the proportion of Negroes at River Rouge usually exceeded that' (1944, pp. 189–90).

Ford's motives were dubious, for, given the blacks' mistrust of trade unions, he was able to use them as a means of preventing organized labour's growth in his industries. The motor company had a sizeable part of its work force docile and anti-union. The modern equivalent of his strategy is not intended to produce similar results, but to redress the kinds of imbalances documented earlier in which minorities are underrepresented in many areas of employment, particularly in managerial and supervisory posts.

Positive, or reverse, discrimination is impelled by the wish to ensure equal opportunities for all; consequently, it provides opportunities for those who might be underprivileged in other spheres to 'catch up' in work. The idea, as put by the CRE, is that even if racial discrimination 'were stopped overnight', some groups would still not be able to compete for jobs because of the past effects of racialism and disadvantage (1980).

Ford's policy was inspired by a different motive, of course, but the end result was the same: giving preferential treatment to groups which are otherwise deprived, thus enabling their members to develop potential and to aspire to occupational equality. Since the Civil Rights Act, 1964, the USA has encouraged programmes implemented with this aim; their operation has been known as affirmative action which is geared both to the elimination of all types of discrimination and the provision of occupational training to members of disadvantaged groups to help them compete an equal terms with the rest of the population in all fields of employment. Blacks, migrants and women, were singled out for preferential treatment, though some, like Diane Robbins, express doubts about the success of the American policies (1981).

As expected, there were some controversial episodes involving positive discrimination, the most famous being when Alan Bakke, an applicant for a medical school place, was turned down as preference was given to minority group candidates. Bakke's qualifications were enough to gain him admission in normal circumstances and so he challenged the decision, having his claim upheld by the US Supreme Court, which took the view that the limits of positive discrimination should be set in such a way so as not to work against the interests of whites by requiring their discharge and replacement by blacks and others. Nor should it act as a bar to the advancement of white workers. Further, it should be recognized as a purely temporary measure en route to the ultimate objective of ensuring total equality of opportunity in society.

Technically, positive discrimination would seem to be an effective way of equalizing people's opportunities. But there is a big debate about whether it is morally justified. It's been articulated by Ronald Dworkin (1977) and Nathan Glazer (1975), the former defending positive discrimination, the latter opposing it. To summarize the first position, Dworkin contests that programmes aimed at the achievement of important social goals, such as equality of employment opportunities, should not be defeated by the interests of individuals. He concedes that rejected majority group members (like Bakke) who may possess greater qualifications than accepted minority groups are rendered disadvantaged but this is 'a cost that must be paid for a greater gain,' that is the gain to the community.

Dworkin distinguishes between equal treatment, by which he refers to the right of every citizen to some opportunity resource or burden (such as voting) and treatment as an equal, which is a right not to receive the same distribution of some benefit or burden, but to be treated with the same respect and concern as everyone else. So, for example, Bakke, in Dworkin's view, should not have had the right to equal treatment: he shouldn't have expected to receive a place just because others with similar qualifications had. Yet, he did have the right to treatment as an equal: he had the right to expect that his interests be treated as fully as anyone else's. This can happen when an institution gives a person's case full attention; but that institution might include several criteria for admission, including colour as well as qualifications. This is justified by the overall long-term gain to the society rather than to the individual and, in such instances, Dworkin believes that preferential admissions can help decrease differences in power and wealth and so make for a more equal society.

Against this, Glazer argues that positive discrimination is undesirable on three counts. First is the fact that improvements in the position of blacks (in the USA) have been made and, where differential treatment happens, it is problematic to assume racial discrimination (rather than, say, qualifications) is the operative factor; it does operate, but not in such a broad way as to be tackled by positive discrimination programmes. Second is the observation that such programmes tend to benefit the skilled and better qualified rather than the chronically poor.

But the third point is the most crucial: Glazer insists that, by establishing categories of people to be singled out for preferential treatment, governments formally divide populations into groups with different rights. This he sees as tantamount to George Orwell's *Animal Farm* situation in which 'all animals are equal, but some animals are more equal than others.' Further, the divisions, as well as being morally suspect, create new resentments and cultivate new angers, thus prompting the possibility of a white backlash.

The debate is moral rather than practical in tone and, certainly, there is no real hard evidence to support the arguments one way or the other. There is certainly a case for viewing the social benefits as outweighing individual costs and for emphasizing that positive discrimination is but a device for balancing out inequalities in other areas. Yet there is still the grave danger that, in creating categories for positive treatment, governments may be perpetuating them and, therefore, establishing conditions for a new brand of racism. And there is an even stronger case against positive discrimination. This says that it is merely a cosmetic device to cover up the gross inequalities so essential to the continuance of capitalism and that the condition of blacks and other minority groups can be improved only marginally (if at all) by such programmes, for their condition as a fraction of the working class is too advantageous to powerful group interests. It follows that discrimination in some form is functional for the total system and that divisions amongst the working class, whether existing before positive discrimination or exacerbated by it, are integrated elements of a system of control rather than emancipation.

To close this chapter, let us emphasize once more the important and manifold consequences of work on the life of the immigrant, in particular, and on race relations, in general.

(1) 'Push' of periphery or 'pull' of centre brings migrant to metropolis.
(2) Migrant has only limited range of employment opportunities available relative to native workers.
(3) Migrant takes low-level 'cellar job' unwanted by native population and so becomes suspicious of unions (and vice versa).
(4) Migrant earns less money than native workers and so has less spending capacity, leading to: (i) poor accommodation; (ii) inadequate education for children; (iii) poor diet and, therefore, health; (iv) a likelihood of being involved in crime or forms of insurgency.
(5) This has two effects: (i) he is judged by others as unsuccessful, capable of only cellar jobs, suited to poor living conditions, limited intellectually and is, in sum, inferior; (ii) he judges himself by his achievements and has self-doubts, maybe self-hates and sees himself as, in some senses, inferior.
(6) The two judgments of inferiority based on stereotypes become rationales for prejudice, racial discrimination and working-class divisions.

Further reading

One-way Ticket: Migration and Female Labour edited by Annie Phizacklea (1983) is a marxist analysis highlighting the significance of racism in the work experiences of ethnic minority women in Europe. Its case studies disclose the dual-sided disadvantage of female migrant labour.

Ethnic Communities in Business is edited by Robin Ward and Richard Jenkins (1984) and reports on developments primarily within Britain. The volume derives from a two-day workshop held in Birmingham in the early 1980s and is geared, above all, to the contribution which ethnic businesses are making to capitalist economies in industrialized societies such as the UK. Jenkins identifies three major explanations for the involvement of ethnic minorities in business: economic, cultural and reactive. He emphasizes that these may not be mutually exclusive predispositions.

Racism and Recruitment by Richard Jenkins (1986) is a study of the selection criteria used by managers in the recruitment of labour into manual and non-manual occupations. Jenkins distinguishes between 'suitability' criteria (i.e., the extent to which applicants' formal qualifications and training prepare them for the job at hand) and less specific, more subjective 'acceptability' criteria by which employers judge whether or not the applicant will 'fit in'. Jenkins found that acceptability criteria were often based on racist and culturally loaded perceptions of an applicant's ability. These 'gut reactions', then, facilitated the operation of indirect discrimination which systematically places 'many black job seekers at a disadvantage'.

'The black economy' by Malcolm Cross in **New Society** (24 July 1987) advances the claim that racial inequality in the labour market is best seen as a three-dimensional model. To begin with, racism is a barrier which black citizens searching for work must overcome. At the same time, Cross argues, there's a need to ensure that blacks have the requisite qualifications to get the new jobs springing up in the cities and that they have access to the labour markets in which these jobs are situated.

The Making of the Black Working Class in Britain by Ron Ramdin (1987) is a comprehensive history of minorities from New Commonwealth countries to Britain and the experiences that followed. Key events, such as the Courtaulds dispute of 1965 and the Grunwick dispute of 1976 are dealt with. These and other events revealed 'the entrenched positions adopted by white employers, white workers and the trade unions towards black workers'.

The Truly Disadvantaged by William J. Wilson (1987) is a provocative American text by the author of **The Declining Significance of Race** and extends the neo-conservative argument that racism is a less potent disadvantaging instrument than is popularly supposed. 'The social transformation of the inner city has resulted in a disproportionate concentration of the most disadvantaged segments of the urban black population, creating a social milieu significantly different from the environment that existed in these communities several decades ago', writes Wilson. The dislocation of the ghetto has contributed significantly to the disavantage of the black underclass and attributing this to racism alone is a simplification, according to the thesis.

Tackling Racism, produced and distributed by the Trades Union Council (1989) is essentially a guide for use by all trade unionists. It is a prescriptive document, spelling out the extent and nature of racial inequality and how practical efforts might be made by trade unionists to combat it in the workplace.

5
Cities — space — politics

- **What is the ghetto?**
- **Do blacks prefer to live together?**
- **What causes the problems of the inner cities?**
- **Is there an urban crisis?**
- **Can we choose between dispersing and herding?**

Living for the city

The Stevie Wonder song, *Living for the City*, tells of a young black visitor from the suburbs to the big city. In his naivety, he wanders into one of the less salubrious areas, the type strewn with stripped cars at the roadside and graffiti on the walls, where he encounters residents and soon becomes an innocent victim of police overzealousness. At one level, the song contains a story of a particular piece of injustice; at another, it makes a statement on the experience of life in specific areas of many modern cities — those areas popularly known as ghettos. In his way, the song's hero, who is ultimately wrongfully sentenced to imprisonment is forcibly made aware of the fact of inequality between blacks and whites.

The industrial city is a kind of mosaic that mirrors the divisions and inequalities of society as a whole. They are mirrored most vividly in the contrast between areas such as London's middle-class suburb, Hampstead, and its densely black-populated slum, Brixton. Birmingham has, at its one extreme Solihull and, at its other, Handsworth, Aston and Sparkbrook. These are the UK equivalents of New York's Long Island-Harlem, or Los Angeles' Bel-Air-Watts extremes and they highlight the ways in which nearly all cities have populations sifted, sorted and packaged in certain areas.

In the last two chapters, we detailed how the New Commonwealth migrants travelling to the UK headed, logically enough, to the places where they expected to find work. As in all industrial-capitalist societies, the areas most fertile in job opportunities were the cities; these were the more prosperous centres of industrial expansion which formed the foci for commerce and industry and so provided the majority of jobs. Migrants went to and settled in places like London, Birmingham and Manchester. We've noted how blacks and Asians became concentrated in specific types of occupations, often in textile and other manufacturing industries, and tended to remain in unskilled manual jobs, the wages for which were rather poor compared to earnings generally. On the whole, they settled for the residue of jobs left over by whites who originally sought better prospects. A pattern of work evolved and this repeated itself over the next three decades from 1950, with migrants, their sons and daughters experiencing little upward job mobility.

Where we work is our place of production; here we earn the resources to shelter, feed and clothe ourselves. Where we live, our residence, is where we relax and refresh ourselves for our labour. So there is a vital and intimate link between the two. Obviously, the amount we earn determines how much we can lay out on rent or house purchase, as well as on food and clothes. And proximity is also important: nearness to work means less money and time to spend on travelling to and fro. We try to shelter ourselves where we feel comfortable and can get to our work — within the limits of what we can afford.

So inequalities in employment have other dimensions and, in the case of New Commonwealth immigrants, these were brought out by their living, in the main, in deteriorated or deteriorating areas, where the quality of the dwelling was poor and the chances of improvement were limited: just as it was difficult for the immigrants to escape from their cellar jobs, it was difficult for them to get away from these areas, which were considered undesirable and unpleasant. The pattern of work in which migrants took jobs the whites didn't want was repeated in housing: they lived in dwellings the whites desired least. Deprivation in one sphere spilled over into deprivation in another and, over time, became a cycle out of which it was difficult to break.

We will document precisely the development of the housing cycle in the next section, but for the moment, let's note that, unlike in work, where a total concentration of migrant workers in particular trades or firms was not usual — although, by no means, rare — residential areas do have this characteristic. Places such as Harlem and Brixton are populated by vast numbers of black residents. The congregation of particular groups sharing common characteristics in a certain space of the city often takes the form of a segregated area and is described as a ghetto. The residents of a ghetto are usually poor relative to the rest of the population and they don't generally have the qualifications, income or other resources to get out. Physically, the environs are run-down and dilapidated. As a

GHETTO
This term was originally used to describe Jewish communities in European cities in the middle ages; these communities were concentrated in specific areas, were culturally homogeneous and were relatively insulated from the rest of the city. More recently, the term has been applied to sectors of modern cities occupied, principally, by blacks or immigrants. New York City's Harlem is a prime example.

consequence, the property is low status and lacks estate value. It is not a place for the affluent.

The solidification of the proverbial black ghetto comes after more and more migrants cram into the area to live in the most accessible quarters with the result that conditions become over-crowded. Rumours of falling property prices and lowerings of the tone of the area circulate and white residents continue to leave. Those who remain develop their own values and distinct cultural styles, thus discouraging prospective white residents and, effectively, putting up invisible walls around the segregated ghetto.

The word ghetto itself is an emotive one: it has come to symbolize all that's negative about city life, such as high crime rates, and disorders, poor quality housing, bad sanitation, noise, pollution, etc. Though, as a concept, ghetto is notoriously imprecise and often gives rise to more confusion than clarification, Charles Wagley and Marvin Harris trace the origins of the term back to Europe in the middle ages when it described 'a corporate city within-a-city established voluntarily by Jews for their own protection but gradually turning into an instrument for their oppression' (1958, p. 206).

Louis Wirth in his study of the Jewish settlement and social relations in Chicago provided more detail about the ghetto which:

> applies to those areas where the poorest and most backward group of the Jewish populations of the towns and cities reside. In our American cities the ghetto refers particularly to the area of first settlement, i.e. those sections of the cities where the immigrant finds his home shortly after arrival in America. Sometimes the area in which the Jews once lived but which is subsequently inhabited by other population groups, particularly immigrants, still retains the designation of ghetto (1969, p. 4).

Technically then, a ghetto should have a high degree of homogeneity, all residents sharing similar backgrounds, beliefs, and so on. They should also be living amidst poverty — relative to the rest of the city's population. More contentiously, they should segregate themselves into ghettos voluntarily. Wirth

---

SEGREGATION
A process whereby different groups have very restricted physical and social contact with each other either because of customs (*de facto* segregation) or by law (*de jure* segregation) as in South Africa. For example, in the inner cities of the USA and UK, there is a process of spatial segregation in which specific groups occupy some zones and other groups occupy other zones without frequently coming into contact with each other.

---

particularly noted the voluntaristic or unforced nature of the ghetto and, hence, its positive features. For him, it was a cultural community that expressed a 'common heritage, a store of common traditions and sentiments' (1969).

This rather romantic interpretation of the ghetto was subjected to something of a mauling by the Kerner report on the American black riots of the 1960s, which focused on the very negative dimensions of ghetto life with residents living under conditions of involuntary segregation (1968, p. 12). And Robert Blauner has gone so far as arguing that the USA's black ghettos are an 'expression of colonized status' because they have 'remained under colonial control: economic, political and administrative' (1972, p. 86). In other words, the ghetto is a means by which whites are able to prevent blacks dispersing and spreading discontent; they trap them in tight corners where they can keep blacks under surveillance and control.

Two questions of interest arise then: (1) How appropriate is it to call the concentrations of the UK's inner cities ghettos? (2) To what extent are those concentrations formed because the residents actually want to live together? These two questions will occupy the next section.

Voluntary segregation?

In the UK, it seems that, despite the concentration of colonial migrants and their children in certain districts within urban centres, the term, ghetto, is wholly inappropriate; there is nothing approaching all black areas on a large scale in any UK city. As Glass remarked in the early 1960s: 'The images of Notting Hill and Brixton as the "Harlems" of London are still far from reality' (1960, p. 41). More recently, Ratcliffe reported that whites continue to constitute the majority of residents in Handsworth (1981, p. 144). On analysis, these and other areas of colonial migrant settlement tend to be very mixed and the overwhelming presence of blacks and South Asians is generally confined to a few streets. Nevertheless, colonial migrants are not dispersed evenly throughout the country but are to be found outstandingly concentrated in the largest urban centres of the South East, West Midlands, Yorkshire and Lancashire with a secondary concentration, especially since the influx of migrants from East Africa, in the East Midlands (Leicester). Indeed, P. N. Jones calculated that of the 1,486,000 New Commonwealth migrants recorded in the 1971 census only 0.3 per cent lived in rural districts (1978, p. 516).

This overwhelming trend towards urban residence is not altogether surprising, since as we've emphasized in previous chapters, the infusion of colonial migrants into the UK was set in motion largely by the economic imperatives of the metropolitan society. Consequently, where they came to live was largely influenced by the availability of work and, more particularly, by the relative difficulty experienced by employers in inducing white workers to fill the gaps in certain local labour markets. In short, what Ceri Peach has called 'industrial attraction', that is, the demand for replacement labour, has been the primary control of minority group settlement patterns (1968, p. 63). Summarizing his analysis of the settlement trends of West Indians in the UK, Peach writes:

> Geographically, they have been drawn to those regions which, in spite of demand for labour, have not been able to attract much net population from other parts of the country. In towns they are proportionately twice as numerous in those that lost population between 1951 and 1961 as in those which increased. They have gone to the decreasing urban cores of expanding industrial regions (1968, p. 82).

This is an important point because it demonstrates that, contrary to popular belief, the colonial migrants were neither the cause of the white flight from particular areas of the UK, nor were they the main reason for the strain on housing resources. In fact, they were replacement residents just as they were replacement labour.

This national profile necessarily conceals important variations in residence patterns both between and within the Caribbean and South Asian communities. The 1974 PEP survey, for instance, revealed that the heaviest concentration of these groups was in the south east, an area which offered numerous and diverse employment opportunities in the 1950s and 1960s, and which has still the lowest level of unemployment in the UK. The survey also showed, however, that whereas 66 per cent of the Caribbean sample lived in the region, the corresponding proportion of South Asians was only 40 per cent, which is not much higher than the proportion of the general population living there (Smith, 1977, pp. 36–7).

The picture changes dramatically when we look at the West Midlands conurbation: 27 per cent of the South Asians lived there compared to 17 per cent and 10 per cent of the Caribbean and general populations, respectively. Again, these patterns are explicable in terms of employment opportunities and the availability of migrants as replacement labour. The heavy engineering industries, such as foundries and castings, in the constellation of towns west of Birmingham had vacancies for unskilled and semi-skilled workers prepared not only to do menial jobs but also willing to work shifts. Such work was not attractive to whites who, as we've already seen, could virtually pick and choose their jobs in the late 1950s and early 1960s. For South Asians, however, economic considerations were paramount and because of their lack of proficiency in English, they had a smaller range of jobs from which they could select. Heavy engineering, then, was relatively attractive to them because it promised full employment and provided a work setting which made few demands on their limited English skills. The same pattern holds true in the North of England where the textile towns attracted a large number of Pakistani workers (Allen *et al.*, 1977; Anwar, 1979).

The skewed regional distribution of colonial migrants is also reproduced in their residential location within cities. This is, at least partly, a reflection of their job status in the UK. 'Because they tend to occupy the bottom end of the labour market, black immigrants, like other immigrant groups before them, could only afford accommodation that was relatively inexpensive. The housing was therefore of a poorer quality and in less desirable areas,' is how the Runnymede Trust and Radical Statistics Race Group described this association (1980, pp. 83–4).

Wirth's romantic vision of what Robert Park, in the foreword to the study, called a 'mosaic of segregated peoples in the city' was based on the view that people of similar backgrounds with broadly similar outlooks, beliefs and circumstances from urban groups were 'each seeking to preserve its peculiar cultural form and unique conceptions of life' (1969, p. vii). Studies in the UK in the 1960s, in particular that of Joe Doherty, found that the colonial immigrants tended to replicate the pattern depicted by Wirth in much the same way as the Jews and the Irish before them had (1969). Elizabeth Burney described the conditions in which the immigrant settled:

> These are the areas of old, decaying private housing which often contain the only available accommodation for newcomers of limited means near the city centre. Very often the accommodation is in large, once middle class houses now sub-divided into ill-adapted furnished rooms and suffering from long-term neglect (1967, p. 16)

But this suggests a less than voluntary basis to the pattern of residence: low wages, the need to live near the workplace to reduce travelling expenses, the scarcity of other, realistically priced housing, and, as well, discriminatory practices in the housing market, combined to funnel the immigrants into areas such as Sparkbrook and Handsworth in Birmingham, Manningham in Bradford, Notting Hill in London and Highfields in Leicester. The continuing nature of such processes also ensures that for many migrant settlers these districts became areas of stagnation.

The infusion of migrants into the residual space willingly vacated by whites has inevitably led to their concentration in clearly demarcated enclaves in the city. A report by the Department of the Environment in 1976 showed that 70 per cent of the black and South Asian populations lived in 10 per cent of the census enumeration districts (quoted in Runnymede Trust, 1980, p. 83).

Racial discrimination in the allocation of housing is only one reason for the emergence of these small, segregated enclaves, but it's an important one. The 1967 PEP study had revealed widespread discrimination, both intentional and *de facto*, by private landlords, accommodation bureaux and estate agents, as well as by local authorities in their allocation of council property (Daniel, 1968). By the time of the second PEP survey, overt discrimination has decreased although there was still evidence of a 'colour tax' being operated — whereby minorities had to pay more than whites for the same housing — and systematic discouragement from estate agents and building societies for black and South Asians wishing to purchase property in designated 'respectable areas'. More covert, and insidious forms of discriminaiton have been found to operate in the public housing sector with the result that minorities are differentially worse off in their access to council housing. The studies by Hazel Flett (1977) in Birmingham and by John Parker and Keith Dugmore (1976) in London have shown not only that blacks and South Asians have been underrepresented in council property, but are also likley to be allocated inferior council housing in the least desirable areas. The persistence of these procedures verifies the claim of Derek Humphrey and Gus John that: 'Institutional racism — manipulating the bureaucratic system to outflank the unwanted — may not be as rampant in Britain as in America, but it appears vividly among the planning and housing regulations' (1971, p. 112).

From what we've said so far it would seem that the colonial migrants' residential location in the city has been largely predetermined in that the formation of small-scale immigrant areas in the major cities of the UK has been one of the inevitable consequences of migration to the metropolitan centre. According to this formulation, then, the colonial migrants were forced into the so-called ghettos: they had little say in the matter — an argument strongly put by sociologists such as John Rex and Robert Moore whose important study we will review in the next section.

Other writers, such as Badr Dahya, rejected the view that migrant concentrations in the areas derived solely from the constraints imposed by the metropolitan society (1974). Dahya's study of Pakistanis' settlement in Bradford led him to conclude that, whilst discrimination in the housing market is a contributory factor, it is neither the only, or indeed, most important determinant of the pattern of immigrant settlement. For Dahya: 'the immigrants' perception of the situation in the context of their socio-economic background, their motives for migration and their ideology or myth of return are essential for a meaningful understanding of their behaviour' (1974, p. 78). Dahya maintains in relation to South Asians:

> given their economic circumstances, their motive for migration and their predilection for living in their own homes rather than in rented accommodation, their choice is voluntary and rational, and irrespective of whether racial discrimination occurs or not (1974, p. 112).

Other studies have also suggested that choice is an important factor in clustering (Burney, 1967; Davies and Taylor, 1970; Jackson and Smith, 1981; Moynahan, 1976) and these provide a useful complement to the interpretation of Rex and Moore. Robinson has provided even greater support for the view that clustering derives largely from a matter of choice (1981). His study of South Asian settlement in various northern textile towns demonstrates not only a high level of segregation but also intra-Asian separation along national, religious and linguistic lines. So, East African Asians lived separately from those born on the subcontinent, Muslims distanced themselves from Hindus, and Gujerati speakers lived apart from Punjabi speakers. Peach and Susan Smith follow Wirth in highlighting the positive aspects of segregation:

> Clustering assists both the formal institutional arrangements of clubs, schools and churches, the crossing of commercial thresholds for specialised shops and the informal networks of friendships. Moreover, all of these personal and institutional networks are intertwined and mutually supportive (1981, p. 11).

However, there are others who see the process of 'ghettoization' in a different light: not as the voluntary residential movements of people seeking mutual support in segregated areas; but as a forced response to environmental circumstances. People are not seen to live their lives as they wish, so much as compelled to live them in specific ways. This is a much more deterministic account of the ghetto formation process and involves theories of the actual city itself rather than the people who live in it. The next two sections will deal with such theories of the city.

Urban ecology

Explaining the ghettoization, or, to be more precise, processes of spatial separation of distinctive groups, outlined in the last section would be simple to a racist. He or she would argue that humans, like animals and birds, have shared genetic features that produce a natural impulse to establish a home territory and defend it against intruders. In the cities, humans who possess common racial characteristics define their territories and exclude those with whom they wish no contact (see Ardrey, 1966).

This is fine if we accept the validity of race as an explanatory concept in the field of human behaviour. But we, for reasons listed earlier, do not, so we have to turn to alternative theories based on social processes rather than so-called natural ones. Perhaps the most influential theory is that of 'urban ecology' developed by Robert Park and Ernest Burgess with Roderick Mackenzie (1923). Writing in the 1920s and 1930s, mainly of Chicago, Park and Burgess argued that the spatial segregations of the city could be understood by taking the city itself as a physical unit for analysis and studying how human beings adapt to this environment. As Charles Darwin had theorized that competition for basic natural resources resulted in the adaptation of different species to each other and to the environment, so Park and Burgess theorized analogous processes happened amongst humans with competition being replaced by a form of mutual cooperation that necessitates a division of labour. And this, in turn, leads to a spatial distribuiton of the functions.

The resource sought after is land: urban space is necessarily limited and different groups have varying degrees of access to it, depending mainly on their income or wealth. In their studies, Park and Burgess identified clearly distinguishable parts of the city that were occupied by specific groups. They called them concentric zones and at their centre is a business district comprising shops and office blocks. This is ringed by a zone of transition where there are high crime rates, low rents, vice and general residential instability. Beyond this is a zone occupied by the working class, then two more zones where the more privileged classes dwell. The model reflects each group's capacity to compete for resources, the more powerful, 'the dominant species', in Darwin's theory, taking the more desired land at the periphery.

Burgess added to this model the concept of 'succession', referring to the fact that the concentric rings, built up one after another as the city evolves, are successively invaded from the inside. For example, when an inner zone which is occupied by wealthy residents begins to get run down, the dwellings are taken over more and more by poorer families who use them as rooming houses, prompting the original residents to move outward to suburban localities.

The Park-Burgess theory proved a most fruitful basis for studies in the

1920s, when many northern American cities were being 'invaded' by immigrants from Poland, Sweden, Germany and other European countries, closely followed by blacks who were fleeing from the south. The cycle of succession involved the European migrants' displacing middle-class inner-zone residents and having to tolerate overcrowded conditions and high rents before themselves being displaced by blacks. Eventually, the blacks were forced out by economically stronger competitors, businessmen, who moved in to concentrate in shops and offices in the centre. This accelerated the deterioration of the inner zones, which were the most mobile in the sense that most of the residents were continually coming and going. This constant flux led to 'social disorganization', characterized by property decline, crime and vice in what Burgess called the 'zone of transition'.

Changes in the city, then, are represented as an evolutionary process involving a disruption caused by the invasions of new groups, rapid inward and outward movements and an adaptation causing a new state of spatial development. The changes are orderly and almost a reflection of the 'natural' life of the city. Not that all the creatures of the city are in a continual unbridled competition for land: they develop patterns of consensus and mutual cooperation to assist ther survival. As Park put it: 'in human as contrasted with animal societies, competition and freedom of the individual is limited on every level . . . by custom and consensus' (1952, p. 156).

This observation was used as a general starting point for a study in the 1960s by Rex and Moore, who, whilst accepting the basic three-zone model, thought that the accent on the consensual, cooperating nature of it, in particular, the deteriorating inner zone was misleading as depicted by Burgess:

> What he did not see was that the inhabitants of ths zone did not simply enjoy a happy segregated community life of their own, but had their total situation defined by an urban value system in which they were at the back of the queue to move to the most desired style-of-life in the suburbs (1981, p. 9).

Basing their theory on research in the British city, Birmingham, specifically the inner Sparkbrook district, Rex and Moore argued that there are distinct types of residents corresponding to each spatial zone: the upper middle class, living in large houses away from the factories; the working class renting small terraced cottages and exhibiting a sense of collectivity, or social solidarity; and the lower middle class, renting their houses but aspiring to a better bourgeois way of life. The three groups all shared the 'urban value system' and aspired to the scarce resource of suburban housing. Hence there was the basis for at least a potential conflict between the groups wanting the same limited resource.

The period prior to the 1960s had seen massive infusions into cities like

TWILIGHT ZONE
Known also as the ZONE OF TRANSMISSION, this refers to that segment of the inner city which has been vacated by members of the better-off middle classes and left to go to ruin. Its value diminishes as it deteriorates physically and poorer people move in, particularly new immigrants, who, in turn, try to move out themselves. The zone eventually becomes run-down; it has a lot of crime, prostitution, vandalism and other undesirable features.

Birmingham and so competition for housing intensified in much the same way as it had done in Chicago in the 1920s. The white middle class was relatively advantaged and had sufficient income to secure the aid of building societies and gain ownership of dwellings. Access to good quality council housing was determined by the local authroities on two criteria: housing need and length of residence. As the Birmingham City Council stipulated a five-year residential qualification, the vast majority of recent migrants were excluded. Of those who were eligible. most were offered condemned housing in slum clearance areas. In short, the migrants occupied a residual zone of transition and were denied access to the more desirable housing tenures.

So, in early phases, new migrants had either to find rented private accommodation or buy the large deteriorating houses previously owned by middle classes, many of whom had fled the inner cities to the suburbs. Jokes about migrants sharing beds on shift bases were circulating at the time; like the one that went: there was a serious accident in Birmingham last night; a bed collapsed — 24 Pakistanis injured. These were not based on fiction, but on the fact of multi-occupied houses in places like Sparkbrook, an area that virtually had ghetto status conferred on it: 'The Council was clearly opposed to the spread of multi-occupation in the better areas of the city, but had classified Sparkbrook as an area where it had to exist and could, at best, only be kept under control' (Rex and Moore, 1981, p. 226).

Sparkbrook became a kind of exemplar for other inner city areas with authorities tending to neglect such 'twilight zones' (as Rex and Moore renamed the 'zones of transition') and leaving the multi-occupied houses to deteriorate. Inhabitants of the zones were lodging house landlords and their tenants, inhabitants of condemned property and occupiers of old, nineteenth-century working-class dwellings. All groups had only limited access to the better forms of accommodation they strove for and were in potential conflict with those who had more access and those who controlled that access.

In this sense, the city is a source of inequalities quite separate from other spheres, such as work. Rex and Moore theorized that, just as work produces

---

HOUSING CLASS
A term coined by Rex and Moore to depict the units of possible conflict in the inner cities. A more conventional view of class would be that conflicts over scarce resources originate in the work place (over issues of production). Housing classes are meant to convey the theory that one's place in the market place (in particular, the housing market) is an important determinant of one's potential for conflict (i.e. rather than one's relationship to the means of production). The view is influenced by the theories of the classical sociologist Max Weber.

---

certain conflicts, housing in the city produces its own unique conflicts with respect to the distribution of life chances. Like Park and Burgess, they saw the city as a more or less enclosed system with its own patterns and processes of inequality.

This was an interesting formulation in that it proposed that the city as an entity, in some degree, acted independently in maintaining inequalities. A person might occupy one position in the labour market but this did not necessarily affect his power in the housing market. For example, a Pakistani worker might be relatively well-qualified and have a position of seniority that pays well; but he may still be crushingly disadvantaged in his access to desirable housing. The opposite case may hold for a white labourer who has reasonable quality accommodation. In other words, Rex and Moore argued against the conventional marxian view that one's place in the division of labour (and ability to generate wealth and income) determines one's total life experiences and, instead, put forward the theory that one's position in the housing market is not directly derived from the labour market but from a separate housing market tiered in terms of housing classes.

The concept of housing classes has been called into question by, amongst others, Colin Bell who notes that, whereas social classes imply an exploitative relationship between more than one group (say owners of the means of production and workers), Rex and Moore never make clear who exploits whom in housing classes (1977). Peter Saunders argues for replacing the concept with 'consumption sectors' to prise it away from issues of ownership, which the notion of class suggests (1981, p. 145). Yet, Rex has been steadfast and, in another, more recent work argues that he was theorizing not about exploitative relations but the relative position of groups of individuals within a politically and bureaucratically organized allocative system: 'They are, however, in competition and in conflict with each other because resources are scarce and some get better treatment than others' (1981, p. 47; see Rex, 1973, pp. 32–42, for more detail on housing classes). In another study, again in Birmingham, this time with Sally

Tomlinson, Rex introduced some modifications to the early theory arguing that: 'the fact of discrimination in housing has given rise to partially segregated areas, and to locally based and relatively effective communal and ethnic organisations which are useful as a means of protecting the rights of minority groups' (1979, p. 157).

Saunders interprets this to mean that housing itself is not a cause of conflict but a shared basis on which to organize for struggle (1981, p. 143). So, the importance of housing as a source of inequality is diminished and the whole study, according to Saunders, shifts the explanation away from the earlier theory: 'The key factor, then, is not housing but race, and the focus of concern turns out not to be urban inequality but racial inequality' (1981, p. 143). This is quite a change from the position of the early study, which was summarized by Rex and Moore thus:

> Put simply, it is that there is a class struggle over the use of houses and that this struggle is a central process of the city as a social unit . . . class struggle was apt to emerge wherever people in a market situation enjoyed differential access to property . . . men in the same labour situation may come to have different degrees of access to housing and it is this which immediately determines the class conflicts of the city as distinct from those of the workplace (1981, p. 273–4).

With Tomlinson, Rex argued for a more general explanation of disadvantage not only in housing but also in work and education, with accommodation being a basis of race relations situations. It seemed that an underclass of migrants in the inner city had been created by concentrations of similarly disadvantaged groups in specific zones of the city and it was speculated that these groups will eventually mount serious struggle when they perceive the commonness of their position in relation to society generally.

Consumption, crisis and struggle

The Sparkbrook study followed Park and Burgess in isolating the city as the focus of analysis: it was regarded as a spatial area that created and perpetuated patterns of inequality. In particular, the Chicago pair made some strong assertions about the relationship between social behaviour and the physical space of the city. For example, the zone of transition contained a high amount of poverty, crime and prostitution and this was seen as no coincidence, but a reflection of the significant effects living conditions can have on the way people behave.

We still think in these terms when we talk of inner city problems, or, more specifically, the possible solutions to them. A ground assumption seems to be that, if we improve the physical conditions of zones of transition, we can reintegrate disaffected groups and so quell tension, reduce street crime, limit vice and so on. Such an assumption was also implicit in the Rex-Moore model: that social problems could be averted, or alleviated, by providing new forms of space to live in though, of course, wider political influences were also considered important in this model and Rex acknowledged the significance of the decisions of 'planners, estate agents, private developers, builders, councillors or housing officers' in shaping the city (1973, p. 66). A great deal of urban research is organized around the notion of space as a determinant.

From a different vantage point, however, such views are little more than justifications for capitalism in that they locate the causes of various kinds of behaviour in cities themselves; this serves to keep the focus narrowly on cities rather than on the broad economic and political processes underlying the creation and maintenance of those cities.

For Manuel Castells, the city equates to a unit of collective consumption. This requires elaboration. Under a capitalist system, production (work) involves the application of human labour to the environment and the products themselves are commodities. The exchange process means that these commodities are distributed for consumption, in the course of which the owners of the means of production make a profit. Consumption has a twofold purpose: (1) Supplying profit to the dominant capitalist classes; (2) Sustaining, refreshing and reproducing the labour force (workers) which needs food, shelter, recreation, education and so on in order to live and work and, therefore, contribute to the production of new commodities. So, this reproduction of labour means a physiological replenishment and a process of turning out a labour force with skills and motivations appropriate for modern, industrial society.

Units of production (basically, industries) are dispersed on regional, naitonal or even international bases to suit the requirements of capitalism. Units of consumption are not: they are situated in concentrated areas of space so that houses, shops, schools, libraries, leisure facilities, etc. are bound together in small units — again to suit the needs of the system. So, urban concentration clusters markets and lowers costs for businesses (by bringing consumers together, thus minimizing the exchange network and cutting down on the expenses of distributing commodities).

Whereas for Burgess and the others, the city was an enclosed area of space, a grouping of people each sharing aims about where they wanted to live, for Castells, it is a convenient unit linked very firmly with the powerful needs of capitalism to perpetuate itself. As a consequence, Castells understands the so-called problems of the inner city rather differently. He sees them not as a result

INFRASTRUCTURE
This is the network of shops, buildings, roads, etc. and other physical artefacts of society.

of spatial organization, but as the outcome of what he calls a fundamental dislocation between the city and the state.

Briefly stated, the burden of the cities is borne by the workers who live in them. Urban growth is advantageous to owners of businesses, but land prices and rents rise and health and welfare provisions have to be increased to cope with the bigger populations; so too do educational and leisure services; roads also have to be maintained. On top of these, there are environmental costs in terms of pollution and general decay. Taxing profits takes care of some of the costs, but this in itself is not sufficient to meet the mounting price of keeping the cities going.

The solution? The state intervenes by providing the revenue to fund public services like housing; and this revenue has become increasingly necessary in modern society. Castells calls this a 'dislocation between the private control of labour-power and of the means of production and the collective character of the production of these two elements' (1977, p. 279). And the result of this is that the state pays the increasing costs of keeping the working population fit, refreshed, educated and skilled while private enterprise takes away the profit derived from labour for further private investment. So the state pays the cost of maintaining a working population, but, it doesn't appropriate any profit from it, because the population works for private industries which extract the profit and keep it circulating in the private sector. This leads to a fiscal gap.

Closing the gap by increasing taxation on profits would undermine the private industry on which the capitalist system depends and increasing taxation on workers' wages would cut down on their spending capacity, reduce demand for commodities and, eventually, prompt working-class action for more wages. The dilemma is resolved by the state's cutting levels of expenditure for working-class facilities. It stops pumping cash into the inner cities and uses it to prop up ailing private industries. Collective consumption areas (cities) are left with a basic infrastructure of houses, shops, roads and the rest, and without enough money to maintain them. These services are initially provided by the state, but, as their financial life blood is drained away, like a cadaver, they degenerate and the state's role becomes less like a nursemaid, more like a mortician.

The end result: a massive decline in urban social services and an 'urban crisis'. Dire housing shortages and the persistence of sub-standard accommodation, fewer hospitals and clinics, inadequate schooling and other educational facilities; these were the basic maladies of the city the state originally sought to remedy through what amounted to central political management. But they return in a politicized form, for the state, having once assumed responsibility for solving the problems of the city, remains responsible when they manifest themselves in a different form.

Castells speculates that this urban crisis will produce more and more struggle over issues of housing, welfare services and other items of consumption. A traditional marxian view would be that conflict between labour and capital is likely to take the form of workers against bosses; in other words, the conflict revolves around wages, conditions or other elements of work. For Castells, workers (labour) are affected by the city's deterioration and want to preserve their standard of living and so engage themselves in conflicts not directly related to work, but to their environment.

For example, high rents, housing construction costs, the siting of factories emitting noxious chemicals or fumes, the planning of roads in awkward places, the closing of schools are potential issues about which inner city dwellers could mobilize to form what Castells terms an 'urban social movement'. It has to be stressed that such a movement is defined as a class conflict with the working class struggling over the use of facilities in the city rather than over the more conventional issues of working conditions and money. In other words, the struggle is about issues of consumption not issues of work (production). The collectivization of consumption in concentrated areas brings people together in circumstances conducive to their becoming aware of their common position and problems. In sum, being in close proximity and sharing the same facilities breeds a consciousness that can be galvanized into a coherent political movement and this, in turn, can force bureaucratic changes, for example in housing departments' policies, to make the quality of life in the cities more tolerable. For an organization to qualify as an urban social movement (in Castells's terms, at least) it has to go beyond a mere protest group and successfully implement change.

Approaching an urban social movement was the Sparkbrook Association which was mobilized in the mid-1960s because, as Rex and Moore put it: 'The people of Sparkbrook then were conscious of a physical decline in the area' (1981, p. 214). The authors describe the association as 'the fightback of the community against demoralization'. As well as gaining improvement and other types of grants from several sources, including the city council, it created new alignments between the various groups, including Caribbeans and South Asians in the area, according to Rex and Moore, who suggest: 'It more than any other organization, was capable of finding some degree of consensus and defining common interests amongst the conflicting sub-groups' (1981, p. 228).

This example of a movement in action can be understood in terms of

STRUGGLE
In social science, this does not necessarily refer to an open physical
confrontation, but means a situation in which two or more groups have
basically different sets of interests and clash when pursuing these
interests. The struggle may, very occasionally, erupt in violence, but more
usually, it takes the form of negotiation, protest and consolidation.

Castells's model, for, according to this, the state is quite responsive to struggle and various working-class developments. It arbitrates the demands made of it and reconciles them with the requirements of capitalism. The working class can be successful in prompting improvements, but those improvements are always so small that they never undermine the actual structure of relations.

It follows from Castells that what we conventionally regard as problems of the inner city are secondary problems in the sense that our attempts to solve them through state aid, in the form of housing action areas and urban renewal programmes, never challenge directly the political structure in which some groups dominate others. Urban social movements are few and far between and even these are but stages in widening the eventual struggle to include many diverse groups.

The state is not simply an instrument of the ruling, dominant classes, but reflects patterns in which some groups have power over others; patterns, therefore, of inequality. In view of the fact that, for four centuries, white colonialists have dominated the nonwhite populations they colonized and incorporated into their empire, it is to be expected that the basic trends in the UK's state institutions and operations will express the interests of whites; in particular, those of the white ruling class. The state will express also the interests of blacks (through, for example, anti-discrimination laws and franchise extensions) and this explains why there are political reforms to accommodate blacks' interests. But ultimately, those more limited interests will be subservient, or, more precisely, incorporated into the interests of dominant groups.

This is a totally different view of the city to that offered by theorists of the ecological tradition in which the city is depicted as a self-contained system replete with its own 'natural' processes, patterns of spatial distribution and levels of organic evolution. The blunt difference is that Burgess *et al.* saw the city in spatial terms, Castells sees it in political terms — the city isn't about houses, shops, offices, skyscrapers and roads, but about the political management of the interests of capital.

So, Castells is not particularly concerned about the issues of race relations and housing and the formation of ghettos or the twilight zones as phenomena of the city: he understands them only as expressions of the political system. The conditions that lead to conflict in the cities are aspects of the wider urban crisis, leading eventually to misguided attributions of blame, such as: 'The area's gone to ruin since the blacks moved in.' Such divisions lead to a segmentation of the working class (through racialism) and this suits the requirements of capitalists to 'over-exploit' workers, to use one of Castells's terms (1980, p. 184).

Castells shares with Burgess, Rex and the others a view of the city in which the residents have little say in their own destiny: they are subject to forces beyond their immediate control. Ghettoization is not a process propelled by people who freely will it. But whatever view we take on the creation of the ghetto and its problems, there can be no denying its importance as a feature of many modern cities. Some political moves have been made to dissolve it, others designed to modify it. We will consider their effectiveness next.

A no-win moral game

'Our nation is moving toward two societies, one black, one white — separate and unequal' is how the Kerner Commission summarized its basic conclusion to its report on the 1967 civil disorders in the US (1968, p. 1). The commission had been set up by the then president, Lyndon B. Johnson, who in his address to the nation on 27 July 1967, outlined the urgency with which the conditions which contributed to the disorders had to be attacked:

> All of us know what those conditions are: ignorance, discrimination, slums, poverty, disease, not enough jobs. We should attack these conditions — not because we are frightened by conflict, but because we are fired by conscience. We should attack them because there is simply no other way to achieve a decent and orderly society in America (quoted in Kerner, 1968).

The commission's brief was to identify the most productive way of attacking these conditions; or, put differently, it was asked to pinpoint strategies which would avert the possibility of further disorders such as those witnessed at Watts, Newark and Detroit. It was unequivocal in its identification of the most fundamental of the 'underlying forces' which had precipitated the disorders: it was 'the accelerating segregation of low-income, disadvantaged Negroes within the largest American cities' (1968, p. 389). For the members of the commission, there were three paths along which ameliorative policies could proceed. The first they characterized as the 'present policies choice' which, according to Otto Kerner and his colleagues, carried the 'highest ultimate price' of an even greater likelihood of major civil disorders, possibly even surpassing the scale of the 1967 incidents. An 'enrichment' policy, or 'gilding the ghetto', constituted the second strategy. This recognized the positive characteristics of ghetto life — the notion of maintaining the value of ethnic, cultural and community life to the identity and happiness of America's black population — and was premised on the idea of separate but equal communities. This strategy paralleled the demands of some of the Black Power movements in the US, but, as the commissioners pointed out, any enrichment strategy would require the allocation of a substantially greater share of national resources into the black ghettos; only then would the prospect of future civil disorders be diminished.

The third, and, for the commissioners, preferred course of action was 'the integration choice' which combined enrichment with 'programs designed to encourage integration of substantial members of Negroes into the society outside the ghetto' (1968, p. 406). The enrichment constituent of this strategy would only be an interim measure, 'a means toward the goal' rather than the goal itself. In short, they came down heavily in favour of dispersal as the course most likely to improve the material and educational standards of blacks, to facilitate social integration and, ultimately, to secure social stability. The attempt to resolve incipient conflict in the USA resulted in what amounts to dispersal policies; they were a move towards crisis-management in that they tried to avert confrontations between .blacks and whites by preventing the formation of concentrated areas of blacks. By scattering blacks throughout areas rather than leaving them in concentrated zones, or ghettos, the chances of mass action were, it was thought, minimized.

As we saw in chapter 3, the US disorders of the 1960s also had a profound impact on public conceptions and policy responses to race relations in the UK. After the 1967 Detroit riots, Norman St John Stevas had implored the Labour government and his Conservative party colleagues to 'learn cheaply and vicariously from the experience of others' in the drafting of future policies on race (quoted in Ward, 1977/8, p. 170). Clearly, his advice was taken and, in the late 1960s, the advocacy of dispersal policies in the UK gained momentum. As Hazel Flett has put it: 'the fear was racial conflict, the solution integration, the means dispersal' (1979, p. 189). Flett demonstrates this by analysing the practice of the dispersal of blacks and South Asians in Birmingham between 1969-75. In an article with Jeff Henderson and Bill Brown, Flett points out that the decision of Birmingham's Housing Department to adopt the policy was precipitated by a threatened rent strike by nine white tenants in a block of council maisonettes in the Ladywood area of the city against the allocation of one of the twelve maisonettes to a second black family (1979, p. 191). The chairman of the housing committee rejected the petition but received all-party support for the (covert) introduction of a set-ratio policy for black council property tenants. Flett's discussions with members of the committee show the extent to which they perceived spatial integration as the prerequisite for social integration and hence the maintenance of harmony in the city. According to the housing officer:

> Birmingham was in a position to say that there has been no racial trouble in the city. There has been trouble in Leicester, trouble in Notting Hill Gate and elsewhere in London; there had been no difficulties in the city. Well, surely this was not all accidental but in part was due to the policies followed by the City Council (quoted in Flett, 1981, p. 28).

Birmingham initiated its policy, but not its method, of dispersal in 1969 and, in the same year, the government's Central Housing Advisory Committee under the chairmanship of J. B. Cullingworth endorsed the principle. So did Rose and his colleagues in their survey for the Institute of Race Relations. However, both reports pointed out the potential problem of reconciling dispersal with the preferences of black tenants and applicants. For this reason, both were more circumspect in their support for dispersal than had been the Birmingham Housing Committee:

> Dispersal is a laudable aim of policy, but this policy needs pursuing with full respect for the wishes of the people concerned. Dispersal of immigrant concentrations should be regarded as a desirable consequence, but not the overriding purpose, of housing immigrant families on council estates. The criterion of full, informed, individual choices comes first (CHAC, 1969, p. 136).

Central government's belated pronouncement on housing dispersal policies in 1975 seemed, by implication at least, to adhere to Cullingworth's recommendation. It devolved responsibility to individual local housing authorities and required them to 'formulate a balanced view on it' (DOE, 1975, p. 9).

In the end, therefore, the decision about whether or not to introduce dispersal policies boils down to whether one subscribes to the 'choice' or 'constraint' explanation of minority group concentration in the city. If these concentrations are largely voluntaristic then dispersal policies are likely to contravene individual and group preferences. If, on the other hand, one accepts the view that concentration derives mainly from discrimination, allocation procedures or unseen processes of the city and that minority group members don't wish to reside in their present areas, then dispersal policies would seem to have much to commend them. 'The difficulty', as Deakin and Cohen see it, 'is to strike a balance between the benefits which would undoubtedly flow from a measure of voluntary dispersal of minorities and the countervailing advantages of communal solidarity (1970, p. 195).

According to Flett, this issue was largely circumvented in Birmingham because the Corporation had only very limited consultation with black community 'representatives' (1981, pp. 14–15). Although the evidence is patchy, there are indications from surveys carried out by Trevor Lee in London (1977), Martin Plant in Birmingham (1970) and the Community Relations Commission in Lambeth, Bradford and Leicester (1977) that dispersal would be resisted by minority communities in the inner city, particularly by those of South Asian origin. Despite the fact that black people live in areas which contain the least desirable housing, both public and private, they offer residents the opportunity to maintain contact and affinity to other members of their ethnic community (Field *et al.*, 1981; Smith, 1977). As Peach and Shah put it: 'poorer housing conditions are part of a trade-off between housing in isolation and poorer housing with contact' (1980, p. 340).

The increasing incidence of racialist harassment, particularly on isolated housing estates has also acted as a daunting prospect to moving away from inner city estates, according to the report of the London Race and Housing Forum (1981). Indeed, it was largely because of the protection from racialist violence and intimidation afforded by the Bengali community in the Brick Lane area of East London that many families returned to the area from outlying housing estates in the late 1970s (Bethnal Green and Stepney Trades Council, 1978; CRE, 1979). In response, the then Conservative-controlled Greater London Council (GLC) announced in June 1978, its proposal for a 'racially segregated' area for Bengalis in the Tower Hamlets borough. This artificial creation of ghettos by the GLC attracted considerable criticism both from the media and from the Labour opposition on the GLC: it was seen as divisive, discriminatory and an avoidance of the fundamental issue, that of eradicating racialism. As Angela Singer wrote in *The Guardian*:

> The 'ghetto' policy is in a sense an easy way out — easier to 'live with our own people' and easier for local authorities perhaps to herd people together and submit to people's fears and prejudices than to encourage the spread of language and reason, and much, much easier than solving the problems of unemployment and poor housing which nurture the need for a scapegoat (1978, p. 17).

It is indeed easier 'to herd people together' than to address the deeper problems and to close this chapter we want to consider one exceptional, but exemplary, case of such herding by city planners.

In the early 1950s, the city of St. Louis planned a large-scale housing project consisting of large, high-rise slabs sited on grounds intentionally left open for the use of both the resident population and the surrounding community. Play and seating areas were provided and buildings were left unguarded in a spirit of architectural innovation.

Originally, the idea was to segregate the area into two distinct areas, Pruitt for blacks and Igoe for whites, but, after the US Supreme Court ruled this unconstitutional, the whole housing area became occupied by some 10,000 blacks. The first families moved in during 1954. By 1959, the project had become a total scandal not only because of the unusual architectural designs, but because of the high incidence of crime, vandalism and prostitution. Its unattractiveness was indicated by a vacancy rate exceeding that of any housing complex in the States. Pruitt-Igoe became a totally manufactured 57-acre black ghetto.

The basic philosophy behind the project was to concentrate 'problem' families, those for which there were no other places to live. As Lee Rainwater, in his study of life *Behind Ghetto Walls*, noted:

> The original tenants were drawn very heavily from several land clearance areas in the inner city.... Only those Negoes who are desperate for housing are willing to live in Pruitt-Igoe — over half the households are headed by women; over half derive their principal income from public assistance of one kind or another; and many families are so large they cannot find housing elsewhere (1973, p. 3).

For the 'average' families with two parents and a small number of children, life in Pruitt-Igoe proved 'particularly unappealing', as Rainwater put it; it was more or less a 'dumping ground' for poor blacks. The residents became victims of what Herbert Gans calls 'a no-win moral game' in which they were forced together with people from similar backgrounds and sharing similar problems and expected suddenly to display patterns of behaviour quite different from those they had left behind in their previous areas (1972, p. 302). In the event, they became caught up in one huge nightmare in which street violence was an everyday occurrence, robbery was common-place and the buildings were allowed to deteriorate horribly. Eventually, the only strategy left for the families was: get out.

Rainwater argues that poor residents such as those in Pruitt-Igoe had broadly similar expectations and aspirations to the rest of society, but, knew they coudn't live up to them and so developed styles of life to fit the conditions in which they found themselves. Eventually, what emerged equated to Oscar Lewis's 'culture of poverty': the dwellers cultivated attitudes and expectations that were limited to their own internal way of life and were not geared to those of the 'wider society' (1967). In effect, the residents perpetuated their own conditions by adapting to them rather than trying to improve them. And, significantly, as Rainwater argued, they knew it: 'The physical evidence of trash, poor plumbing and the stink that goes with it, rats and other vermin, deepens their feeling of being moral outcasts. Their physical world is telling them that they are inferior and bad just as effectively perhaps as do their human interactions' (1966, p. 29). But, Oscar Newman noted, 'in a short time most residents rebelled and simply moved out; the remaining few got together to insist on administrative and physical changes' (1972, p. 207).

The vacancy rate of 65 per cent attested to the ultimate failure of the project and, twelve years after the first families moved in, Pruitt-Igoe was quite literally blown up. This 'public housing monstrosity', as Newman calls it, serves as a sharp reminder of the negative effects of projects based on *de facto* segregation. It poses the other half of the dilemma to housing policy issues: if you don't deliberately disperse and integrate blacks and other minorities, you can bring them together in public housing — possibly with dire consequences.

Obviously, we have simplified a most complex issue in the effort to present the stark alternatives. Forced dispersal and segregation are equally unacceptable as solutions to the problem of the inner city ghetto and one is also compelled to concede that dissolving the ghetto is technically and administratively easy, but not wholly satisfactory to the former residents of that ghetto.

Indeed, Birmingham City Council's Housing Committees as good as acknowledged this in 1982, when it approved the rehousing of black and Asian residents (who might have been dispersed) on the sole grounds that they were victims of 'racial harassment' either from whites or other ethnic groups (*Birmingham Post*, 18 June 1982). Equally, facilitating the continuation (or even the creation) of the ghetto can be catastrophic — as Pruitt-Igoe demonstrates.

Perhaps, the problems seen as emanating from the environment are best tackled totally away from that environment — by educating blacks, Asians and others how to adjust more satisfactorily to society, how to benefit from the full range of possibilities it offers and how to wrench oneself away from the wretched ghetto existences of ones' parents. Idealistic it may sound, but there are those who place great faith in the importance of education as the instrument that may bring a diminution of inequality. In the next chapter we will see how this is not strictly the case.

Further reading

Urban Social Movements by Stuart Lowe (1986) is a review and evaluation of Castell's work and of others' attempts to develop an overarching theory of political struggle in cities. Of particular interest is the chapter, 'The mobilisation process'.

Living in Terror was produced by the Commission for Racial Equality in 1987 and reports on the nature and extent of racial harassment in housing. Typical cases included verbal abuse, racist graffiti and physical attacks on black residents. The CRE recommended that all local authorities adopt policies and procedures for dealing with incidents of racial harassment. These included action to support victims; use of the law against perpetrators and arrangements to liaise with local community groups such as the police and other local authority departments.

'Languages of racism' is a section of the book, **Maps of Meaning: An introduction to cultural geography** by Peter Jackson (1989). The author examines the 'spatial basis' of the 'social construction of race', using a geographical approach.

Ethnic Minority Housing: Explanations and policies by Philip Sarre, Deborah Phillips and Richard Skellington was published in 1989. Drawing on an eclectic range of theories — including human geography and sociology — which emphasize both 'individual choice' and 'structural constraint' explanations, the authors explore the pattern of ethnic minority housing experiences, and conditions in a single 'multi-racial' town: Bedford.

The Politics of 'Race' and Residence by Susan J. Smith (1989) is seen as a contribution to the development of an anti-racist social science. The author rejects the reality of 'race' as an explanatory concept and considers racial inequality in the UK as being constituted through economic, political and social activity. The author develops her argument from a social geographical perspective.

6
Education — culture — disadvantage

- Do schools provide educational equality?
- How do blacks and South Asians fare at school?
- Is there a genetic link between race and IQ?
- How have we tried to improve the educational performance of young blacks?
- Can MRE 'compensate' for society?

The one good thing about Britain?

It's difficult to think in terms of a modern society without some means of formally educating its population. We unquestioningly accept the value of education; it's socially necessary and encouraged politically. The reasons for our acceptance of the benefits of education are many, but are premised on at least three assumptions. First, that education equips us to be aware, sensitive and contributing members of society. Second, that we can improve ourselves socially by being educated and gaining the qualifications that are likely to lead to well-paid and prestigious jobs. Third, that through learning from and about others, we can liberate ourselves from the ignorance and prejudices of those before us. Underpinning these is the conviction that every member of society should be given the opportunity to develop their intellectual potential to the full through unimpaired access to educational institutions and the credentials they offer.

Indeed, it's this doctrine of equality of educational opportunity, originally enshrined in the 1944 Education Act, which remains the philosophical lynchpin of the UK's educational system. The 1944 Act provided universal secondary education till age 15 (now 16), free of charge, and ended the distinction between the elementary and secondary educational systems. What has changed since this legislation was enacted are the views concerning how equality of educational opportunity can best be achieved. The 1944 Act laid the basis for a tripartite system of secondary education comprising technical, secondary and grammar schools. Pupils were tested at eleven and assigned to the type of school considered most appropriate to their intellectual ability. However, although it was intended that the three-tier system should enjoy 'parity of esteem' it soon became clear that the grammar schools were seen as the most prestigious because they provided the most direct route to higher education and the best-paid occupations. It also became clear that children from middle-class backgrounds tended to be disproportionately represented in the grammar schools while pupils from working-class homes found themselves the recipients of an 'inferior' education (O. Banks, 1955, 1968; Halsey, Heath and Ridge, 1980; Halsey, Floud and Anderson, 1961; Tyler, 1977).

Now, in an ideal world, children's background would not interfere with their intellectual development and everything they received in terms of educational qualifications would reflect their ability rather than their parents' class or status. But the available evidence suggests the opposite: the social position of parents has an important bearing on what their children achieve at schools. Even with the inception of comprehensive secondary education — which has now replaced the previous tripartite system in most Local Educational Authorities (LEA) — the pattern of results produces a picture in which children of higher social class families consistently progress further in education and attain more valuable qualifications than children from poorer backgrounds (Halsey, Heath and Ridge, 1980; Mortimore and Blackstone, 1982). So, in fact, education does not so much put into practice the philosophy of educational opportunity, as reflect basic inequalities of wealth and status in the rest of society.

In fact, some would argue that education actually perpetuates and re-affirms general inequalities. The contention here is that educational institutions are established and run by groups in power who wish to preserve their class positions rather than have them disrupted by the next generation with their heads full of ideas about human equality. Interests are best served if people are educated to accept the trends of inequalities that permeate society, and not question them at every turn. Samuel Bowles and Herbert Gintis, two American marxian economists, are important contributors to this debate (1976). They argue that 'educational meritocracy is largely symbolic' and that 'beneath the façade of meritocracy lies the reality of an educational system geared toward the reproduction of economic relations only partially explicable in terms of technical requirements and efficiency standards' (1976, p. 103). For them, the link between the process of schooling and the hierarchical division of labour is both causal and direct:

Schools foster legitimate inequality through the ostensibly meritocratic

---

MERITOCRACY
In Michael Young's speculative novel, *The Rise of the Meritocracy*,
IQ + effort = Merit; and this is the sole criterion of educational and
occupational success in the society known as a Meritocracy, where there
are no barriers between ability and achievement and the class origins of
one's parents are irrelevant to success. As Young's cover blurb puts it: 'It
is no longer enough to be somebody's nephew . . .'; attainments are based
on individuals' capacities and application.

---

manner by which they reward and promote students, and allocate them to distinct positions in the occupational hierarchy. They create and reinforce patterns of social class, racial and sexual identification among students which allow them to relate 'properly' to their eventual standing in the hierarchy of authority and standing in the production process. Schools foster types of personal development compatible with the relationships of dominance and subordinacy in the economic sphere (1976, p. 11).

This process is what Pink Floyd allude to in *The Wall* with its reference to 'thought control' which inhibits critical and independent judgment (Harvest Records, 1979; see also Ogbu, 1978, p. 358).

Far from being great levellers of opportunity, then, schools, in this perspective, actively contribute to the continuance of inequalities; as Anthony Heath has put it:

Education has come to play an increasing role in the transmission of status (loosely defined) from father to son; the *direct* influence of social origins — whether through patronage, nepotism, inheritance or some other mechanism — on occupational attainment has declined, but simultaneously its *indirect* influence via the educational system has increased as family background has become more closely linked to educational success and failure (1981, p. 191).

And the research of Christopher Jencks, in particular, supports this by emphasizing that family background has a more profound effect than education in the determination of future life chances (1972).

Quite logically, we should expect the children of immigrants, coming, as we've seen, mainly from working-class families, to undergo similar experiences to the rest of that class and not make astounding educational progress. And, given our argument about the self-generation of ideologies regarding inequalities, we should expect immigrant groups to believe in the value of education, the equal chances it's supposed to provide everyone with and the eventual opportunities for social and material advancement it apparently offers. Monica Taylor informs us that 'the evidence of research on parental aspirations (among Afro-Caribbean communities in the UK) is somewhat scant' and the same is true for parents of South Asian origin (1981, p. 144). Nevertheless, if the few relevant studies are to be taken seriously, a great number of migrants from both the Caribbean and South Asia accept the dominant ideological notion of schooling as a good thing and tend to value education instrumentally: that is, in terms of providing social mobility and job opportunities for their children. They therefore have high expectations for their children to succeed in the UK educational system (Ballard, 1979; CRE, 1977; F. Taylor, 1974, pp. 111–13; M. Taylor, 1981, pp. 142–7). Pryce, for instance, claims that Caribbean migrants have 'great academic aspirations for their children' and they believe that 'ultimately education is the most reliable means whereby their group, as a whole, through their children, can achieve recognition and status on an equal footing with others in society.' He goes on to say that these parents feel that 'despite the injustices meted out to them, there is "one good thing" about Britain and that is that the chances offered by the society to improve one's education are almost limitless' (1979, p. 120).

One could try and justify these convictions by identifying black and South Asian lawyers, civil servants, executives and teachers and insist that these examples show that it's possible to 'make it' on merit alone. Possible, perhaps, but not probable. For the statistics tell us that the chances of success on this scale are minimal. Although it's true that pupils of Asian origin are tending to perform at a level comparable to, and in some cases exceeding that of their white counterparts in school there is currently considerable cause for concern about the academic performance of Bengali pupils in Inner London schools. There is also disquiet about the low school performance of black pupils and this has persisted since the 1960s, particularly after Alan Little and his colleagues of the Inner London Educational Authority (ILEA) had revealed that the relatively poor performance of black pupils in the authority's primary schools stretched across the curriculum: passive and active vocabulary, verbal reasoning, reading, English, mathematics and study skills (Little, 1975a). Black pupils, then, are conventionally typified as 'underachievers' in the British educational system. The Committee of Inquiry into the Education of Children from Ethnic Minority Groups (The Rampton Committee) described the notion of 'underachievement' thus: 'While we accept that there will perhaps always be some children who will underachieve and for various reasons will fail to reach their full potential, our concern is that West Indian children *as a group* are underachieving in our education system' (1981, p. 10, para. 10). The committee adduced evidence for this claim from data for school-leavers from six LEAs in 1978–9. According to

---

EDUCATIONAL ACHIEVEMENT
The level a student reaches as measured by scores on various tests and examinations, as different from EDUCATIONAL ATTAINMENT which is the number of years of education completed by a student. Black children in the UK are known for their persistent UNDERACHIEVEMENT for they tend as a group to score less in examinations relative to white and South Asian pupils.

---

these statistics black pupils performed consistently worse than 'Asian' or white school-leavers in public examinations and were less represented amongst those pupils who went on to university. For example, only 3 per cent of the black school-leavers obtained five or more higher grades in 'O' level and CSE examinations (i.e. grades A–C) compared to 18 per cent of Asian and 16 per cent of other leavers. There was a similar trend in the pattern of 'A' level results; only 2 per cent of the black pupils gained one or more 'A' level passes compared to 13 per cent of Asian and 12 per cent of other leavers (1981, pp. 7–8).

Certainly, these data seem to support the conclusions of previous studies of black educational attainment which have been extensively reviewed by Peter and Jo Mortimore (1981), Monica Taylor (1981) and Sally Tomlinson who, in her review article on this subject, concluded: 'Of the 33 studies of West Indian educational performance reported here, 26 show the children to score lower than white children on individual or group tests or to be over-represented in ESN schools and under-represented in higher school streams' (1980, p. 227).

Nevertheless, the almost uniformly bleak picture presented by Tomlinson and others has to be treated with some caution. In the first place, as Tomlinson recognizes, assessment of educational performance has generally been carried out either through conventional, individual psychometric tests, aimed at measuring 'ability', or through group tests to measure performance; however, 'in both types of test situation it is rare for test conditions adequate for examing ethnic minority groups to be developed,' according to Christopher Bagley (1979, p. 78). Secondly, researchers have been so overwhelmingly concerned with differences (or otherwise) in educational attainment along ethnic lines that they have tended to overlook the important influence of social class background on performance levels. In other words, they may not have been comparing like with like. Frank Reeves and Mel Chevannes, for instance, have pointed out that the data presented by the Rampton Committee do not constitute reliable evidence of black underachievement precisely because they were not standardized to take into account class backgrounds (1981). We know that black pupils come largely from working-class families and that family background has a profound moderating effect on levels of school performance. Well, according to Reeves and Chevannes, if the data had been analysed along class as well as ethnic lines the results would have shown that black pupils were performing no better or worse than other working-class school-leavers.

Another hole in the research is that few studies have looked at the relative performance of black and white pupils in public examinations; those that have, produce contradictory results, which is not really surprising considering the highly localized focus of the research. Sheila Allen and Christopher Smith interviewed over 600 school-leavers in Sheffield and Bradford in 1972 and found that very few of the black pupils in the sample had gained 'O' level or CSE passes and that none had obtained 'A' levels (1975). In 1975, Rex and Tomlinson interviewed twenty-five young blacks (aged between 16–21) in Handsworth, none of whom had passed 'O' or 'A' level examinations (1979). Now, this is a depressing picture but it must be pointed out that, in both studies, a large number of the youngsters had received a sizeable proportion of their education overseas and that other studies have shown that length of education in the UK has a crucial impact on educational attainment (Little, 1975b).

Another study of differential achievement based on public examination results was carried out by Geoffrey Driver in five multiethnic schools up and down the country (1980a; 1980b). His results contrasted sharply with the previous research by suggesting that black pupils, especially girls, were performing at least as well, and in some cases better in 'O' level and CSE examinations that their white classmates. Partly because of the sensational way in which Driver initially presented his findings in *New Society*, but principally because these findings went against the grain, his study, *Beyond Under-achievement*, has been carefully and systematically scrutinized by researchers and educationists. The result? Driver's study has been found to be methodologically flawed and it has been claimed that he drew 'educational conclusions on the basis of statistical evidence which in many cases is found wanting in statistical terms' (Taylor, 1981, p. 121). But, as we've seen, similar criticisms should, and have been, justifiably directed at the statistics presented by the Rampton Committee. It's more than a little ironic then that Monica Taylor, who had been commissioned by Rampton to write an evaluative review on the education of West Indian pupils and who, as part of the review vigorously attacked Driver's research, should then go on to say: 'If such a detailed analysis [of Driver's study] had been undertaken with respect to other research studies it is quite possible that some similar deficiencies would have been found' (1981, p. 122).

Let's make our position clear: we're not denying that black pupils, as a social group, tend to perform at a relatively lower level at school than white pupils or those of South Asian origin. Despite the fact that the social class origins of many black pupils are likely to depress their level of educational attainment and that in some cases this critical factor has been overlooked, it's been established in at least one study that even when pupils are matched for social class the performance in examinations of black pupils was lower than all other groups (Craft and Craft, 1981). However, that the research evidence for this trend is not as clear-cut as much conventional wisdom would have us believe and that many of the studies have inherent methodological and conceptual weaknesses are the points we want to stress.

What the specific causes are of this trend towards black underachievement in UK and American schools is a question which has tantalized educationists for many years and the answer remains elusive. The Rampton Committee, for instance, could be no more precise than suggesting that there were 'many causes, both within the educational system and outside it' (1981, p. 11, para. 1). Monica Taylor was only a little more specific when she wrote that low performance derived from 'factors such as quality of schooling, teachers' attitudes, pupils' home backgrounds and pupils' motivation' (1981, p. 122). However, some educationists eschew social and cultural explanations for this trend and prefer instead to argue for the lower innate intellectual ability of black people. Before looking at the social and cultural factors which have been adduced to explain this phenomenon, let's consider what has been termed by Michael Syer as 'the racist aspects of the debate' (1982).

IQ: the lethal label

Human characteristics are products of genetic features and environmental influences. This is widely acknowledged; we are shaped by two types of factors, one the result of nature, the other, the result of nurture (or upbringing). But the precise amount of influence each has is a matter of some conjecture. Many would argue that genetic qualities have only a limited effect on our eventual human character and that the decisive factors lie in our experience with the physical and social environment. In sharp disagreement with this, other theorists would propose that what we are born with has the most decisive impact and that environmental influences have only a marginal effect in modifying the human being.

The issue is of central importance to education for, if the nurture view is favoured, then significant steps can be taken to improve a child's learning by rearranging his or her educational environment. A nature view would tend to lay less emphasis on the effectiveness of educational reforms: if people are intellectually dull, it's because they're born that way and no amount of outside influence can change that biological fact. The relevance of the latter view to the question of educational performance is very apparent, for, if you believe that natural qualities are the crucial determinants in education (or educability), then the question of why blacks achieve less in education than whites is quite simple: they are not genetically equipped to achieve. Crudely stated, black people are intellectually thick and this thickness is a product of genetic differences between groups — differences that are quite beyond the power of any manipulations of the environment to change.

This particular argument has a reasonably vigorous tradition beginning in the first quarter of this century, with the argument over whether intelligence is inherited (a contention put forward by Sir Cyril Burt) or learned, continuing through the 1950s when more stress was given to environmental factors (by UNESCO, amongst others) and coming back to life in the 1960s with the publication of an article in the *Harvard Educational Review* which argued very forcefully that whites' intellectual superiority over blacks was related to genetic factors. In this article, Arthur Jensen, an American psychologist, reported on a series of experiments on the IQ score of different groups; his results suggested that intelligence was about 80 per cent genetically determined and that blacks consistently score 15 points below whites (1969). Conclusion: whites were naturally superior to blacks.

A parallel series of studies by Jensen's mentor, Hans Eysenck (1971) in England and Richard Herrnstein (1973) in the USA, followed, with the results corroborating the Jensen theory, which Nobel Prize winner William Shockley used to support his argument that blacks be sterilized to prevent their transmitting inferior genes. Even if Jensen's motives were, as he stressed, pure and unaffected by racism, the implications of his research ensured him a place in the tradition of Gobineau *et al.* in giving scientific credibility to the belief in race. Jensen argued that: (a) the hereditability of IQ is the same *within* the white and black population as *between* the populations, and (b) the genetic variance involved in IQ is about one-fifth less in the black than in the white population (1972, p. 10).

One obvious reaction to his theory would be to segregate educational facilities, isolating whites from blacks so as to allow them to progress unhindered and develop their superior intellects. (Note: Jensen's results were published in the aftermath of controversial attempts to desegregate not only schools but all other social institutions.) We've already expressed profound reservations about the viability of race as a concept for dividing up human populations and so Jensen's assumption that in the USA, blacks belong to one genetic grouping and whites to another, is highly questionable. Even if it was technically possible to trace back black Americans to their slave ancestors on the African coastline and isolate a genetically comixed group of people, it would be absurd to suggest that present day blacks collectively share a common genetic make up — if only because of the miscegenation, or interbreeding of blacks and

---

CULTURE
A notoriously vague concept, this, in its broadest sense, refers to the experiences of the human being that are social as opposed to biological; put another way, our culture is what we learn through our contacts with other humans and as such it is transmitted in a very specific way. For example, we experience speech through a particular language, we are educated in a particular curriculum; these are cultural elements picked up in our later lives rather than things we are born with.

---

whites. By the same reasoning, whites could not plausibly be viewed as a genetically pure race.

But equally, Jensen's, other main concept, IQ (intelligence quotient) is rather nebulous as a profile of intellectual ability. IQ tests are groups of tasks measuring a number of intellectual abilities, given to large groups of people from a variety of backgrounds. Efforts are made to minimize the importance of background and culture so as to obtain a score based on individual capabilities freed of environmental influences — social and geographical. Such methods of measuring intellects have many critics, who regard them as too crude in trying to capture intellectual processes on a single scale, too one-dimensional in disallowing creativity and innovation and, despite attempts to be 'culture-free', insensitive to influences on the individuals' upbringing, particularly in early childhood. For example, Sandra Scarr conducted a study in which she measured the IQs of black children adopted and raised by white families (Scarr and Weinberg, 1976). The younger the children were at the time of adoption, the closer they approached the equivalent whites' IQ averages, thus suggesting that a child's background, experience and culture will to a great extent influence the child's knowledge and thought processing as measured by an intelligence test. (Other psychological evidence on how environment can affect IQ is summarized by Dworetzky, 1982, pp. 384–91, Evans and Wates, 1981; Kamin, 1977 and Richardson and Spears, 1972).

That the environment plays some part in the development of intelligence is beyond doubt. What the studies don't indicate precisely are how and to what extent it aids the development. Steven Rose has explained how mentally stimulating environments can actually elicit bio-chemical changes in the brains of animals and, conversely, how deprivation can retard the growth of intelligence (1970). Yet, in human populations, no totally convincing evidence has been turned up to establish the exact degree and kind of influence nurture bears.

Peter Watson has gathered together evidence in favour of the view that enriching one's environment can have a positive, uplifting effect on the IQ performance, though, significantly, the effects on blacks, as opposed to other minority groups, were in some doubt (1973b). All of these arguments were, of course, totally rejected by Jensen and his followers, who held the view that intelligence is fixed from birth and cannot be boosted (or depressed) by changes in the environment.

Certainly, the research of Jensen and the others reinforces the nature view and provides evidence that whites do in fact consistently outscore blacks in IQ tests. But there are alternative explanations of why whites come out on top. One is offered by Irwin Katz whose research indicated that the colour of the person administering the tests can bear a significant influence on the person being tested (1968). Blacks feel more secure in the presence of a black tester and so improve on their equivalent performance with a white tester. Watson replicated the research with similar results (1972).

The point is that any intelligence test is likely to be biased in some sense. Even if we could eliminate the problem of the colour of the tester, the very fact that language is used introduces the possibility of bias, as Jane Mercer found in her research with white, black and children of Mexican origin (Chicanos). She found that the black and Chicano children, having been raised in different circumstances to the whites, were unfamiliar with the kinds of words, objects and strategies required by the tests' questions. Mercer's studies led her to call IQ 'the lethal label' because its attribution could lead to the child's being treated as retarded when he was simply unfamiliar with particular words and vernaculars (1972).

As well as the conceptual difficulties, the 'race and IQ studies' suffer from several problems of method which tend to undermine some of the larger claims about the inferior intelligence of all blacks (Kamin, 1977; Ogbu, 1978, pp. 55–9). Plus, as Douglas Ekberg spells out, such studies rest on four tenuous theoretical assumptions about the 'measurement', 'structure', 'social importance' and 'inheritance' of intelligence, all of which suggest that 'it must be possible to stratify people on a simple hierarchy of mental abilities' (1979, p. 8). Because of the insurmountable ethical problems connected with experiments designed to ascertain the relative influences of heredity and environment on intellect, the issue is likely to remain divided and the 'race and intelligence' debate will continue as long as the nature vs nurture discussion carries on.

Research on the subject is still in progress. Yet this doesn't prevent us from reflecting on the reasons behind such research; why do we want to know about the contributory factors in different groups' intellectual capacities? It could be because we can use the evidence to provide children of inferior intelligence with maximum scope for the expansion of their intellectual horizons. Or it could be to give scientific credibility to the belief in racial inequality and so justify the kinds of extreme political stances taken by such organizations as the National Front (NF), one member of which provides a logical and coherent defence of his position by employing Jensen's data in James Flynn's book, *Race, IQ and Jensen* (1980, pp. 8–14). It's certainly difficult to overestimate the impact of Jensen's work on the growth of organizations such as the NF; as Martin Webster, National Activities Organizer of the party wrote in 1973: 'The most important factor in the build-up of self-confidence among "racists" and the collapse of morale among multi-racialists was the publication in 1969 by Professor Arthur Jensen' (quoted in Walker, 1977, p. 169; see also Billig, 1978, pp. 143–52). The outrage Jensen and company generated was not so much because they were right or wrong in their work — although as we've shown much of it has subsequently been discredited — but because of the uses their results could be put to in the areas of immigration controls, special educational provision (which Jensen advocated for blacks), and, as Shockley indicated, compulsory sterilization.

The electoral advances of the NF during the 1970s ensured increasing prominence for 'scientific racism' and fears for its application into educational contexts. This prompted the National Union of Teachers (NUT), the largest teacher union in the UK, to commission Rose to produce a critique of the Eysenck/Jensen position. The document, which was produced in 1978 and distributed free to union members, was a vigorous attack on 'scientific racism' and alerted teachers to the dangers of being duped by its apparently respectable presentation:

> Racism dressed up in pseudo-scientific clothes, even when it attempts to look respectable by quoting apparent 'scientific authority', remains racism and should be combatted today in schools. Teachers, especially those in schools with significant numbers of ethnic minority children but also those in largely 'white schools', have a particular role and responsibility in this context (NUT, 1978, p. 15).

The reasons why blacks do not do well at school may well have something to do with fixed inherited features. We are not convinced, if only because the contrary evidence from environmentalist studies, uncertain as it is, suggests other avenues worth investigation. As social scientists, our view is that biological and associated explanations should not be cavilled about simply because they are nonsocial, but that alternative possible explanatory avenues should be thoroughly investigated. Jensen's case may be a powerful one, but we should not accept his reasons without exhausting all other factors, historical and social, which may play parts in disadvantaging the black child. Philip Green points to some of them in arguing that Jensen's work was 'ultimately unnecessary': 'Indeed, given the history of race in the United States, what needed to be explained was not why the gap is so large but why it is not even larger' (1981, p. 55).

Repairing the child

For many educationists and policy makers both in the UK and USA the problems which black pupils experience in school, and which are highlighted by their relatively low level of educational attainment, derive not from their genetic make-up but from the mismatch between the cultural background of the children and the school culture. This is not a new phenomenon, of course, but one which has its antecedents in the relationship between pupils from working-class backgrounds and the mainstream, middle-class values embodied in the educational system. For that reason, middle-class parents have tended to regard the school 'as an extension of the home, extolling the same virtues, upholding the same values and having the same objectives. Middle-class children fit nicely into the school system and have little alternative' (Stone, 1981, p. 10). The infusion of a large number of black and South Asian pupils into British schools in the 1950s and 1960s has, according to Maureen Stone, merely 'heightened and thrown into relief many inherent problems which have been a feature of the British educational system since its inception' (1981, p. 35). Now, if the root of the problem lies in the fact that the culture of black, working-class pupils is at variance with the school's culture, there seem to be at least two ways of tackling it: the first is to recognize the two cultures as being of equal worth and to acknowledge and integrate the pupils' culture into the school setting. Part of this process could see a move towards making teachers and their schools more bicultural (or multi-cultural), literally competent in two (or more) cultures; that of the (middle-class) school and that of their pupils. The second approach is premised on a conception of the pupils' culture not only as different but deficient; the problems of educability, according to this view, emanate from the 'culturally deprived' background of the pupil. Simply, their failure at school is located in the home and in the pre-school environment where mainstream middle-class values do not prevail. It is this second interpretation which has conventionally been used to explain and rationalize the persistently poorer academic performance of working-class pupils compared to those from middle-class backgrounds. As the authors of *Unpopular Education* demonstrate, sociologists of education in the 1950s and 1960s repeatedly assessed working-class practices 'according to their approximation to a social ideal which was in fact that of the ideal middle-class parent: familiarity with the school, relative ease with the teacher, an unambiguous recognition of the individual advantages of certification, valuing also of education "for its own sake" and hence a wholehearted encouragement of the child.' Consequently, 'any discrepancy provided the explanatory ground for failure in terms of either psychic or cultural deficiences or rationalizations for such deficiencies' (Baron, *et al.*, 1981, p. 141). It's not difficult to see how, or why, this 'cultural deficit' model has been extended to include explanations for black educational failure: it hasn't even required much amendment. Inadequate child-rearing practices, single-parent families, family structure and organization, over-crowding and depressing living conditions which have habitually been invoked to sustain the 'deficit' model of working-class failure are now readily applied to the black family as the following extract from the Rampton Committee's chapter on 'The factors contributing to underachievement' exemplifies:

> A disproportionate number of West Indian women are forced to go out to work because of their economic circumstances.... The percentage of West Indian men employed on night shift is almost double that of white males and the incidence of one parent families is higher for West Indians that for whites. West Indian parents may therefore face particular pressures affecting their children in the vital pre-school formative years ... While it is now generally accepted that young children need to form a stable and consistent relationship with only a limited number of adults we are faced with a situation where West Indian parents are stretched in ways which make steady, relaxed care of their children hard to achieve ...

> Many West Indian parents may not be aware of the pre-school facilities that are available and may not fully appreciate the contribution that they can make to the progress of their child before he enters school. They may not recognise the importance to a child of an unstrained, patient and quiet individual dialogue with an adult (1981, pp. 15–16, paras 2–3).

Now, we are not necessarily questioning the Rampton Committee's observations; the point that we wish to stress is that such observations have generally assumed an important influence on subsequent policy initiatives. In other words, the cultural deficit/deprivation explanation provides the rationale for educational strategies and programmes designed to alleviate the problems of the 'disadvantaged' black working-class pupils. So, the provision of relevant educational experiences to 'compensate' the culturally deprived child becomes the priority for action.

As we've said already, neither this formulation of the issue nor the policy initiatives it gave rise to, are new. During the 1960s, two influential reports in the USA gave legitimacy to the view that it was the child rather than the educational system which should be the focus of attention and these led to the growth of 'compensatory education' programmes. The first of these reports was written in March 1965 by Daniel P. Moynihan, Assistant Secretary of Labor. His report promoted a pathological conception of the black family in the USA

MATRIARCHY
This refers to a condition in a culture in which women play a dominant role in kinship systems. Matriarchal insitutions are those in which women play the influential parts.

suggesting, amongst other things, that its main weaknesses were its instability, proclivity for producing illegitimate children, and its matriarchal structure and that it was this disintegrating family structure which was keeping blacks from social, economic and political parity with whites. The implications for policy initiatives, including education, were clearly spelled out by Moynihan: 'In a word, a national effort towards the problem of Negro Americans must be directed towards the question of the family structure. The object should be to strengthen the Negro family so as to enable it to raise and support its members as do other families' (quoted in Rainwater and Yancey, 1967, p. 93). The following year saw the publication of James Coleman's report on the achievement of over 640,000 students in 4,000 American elementary and secondary schools (1966). His conclusion was that educational attainment was largely independent of the schooling a pupil received and that working-class and black educational failure derived ultimately from bad family background and poor self-concept. Both reports, then, were exercises in 'victimology', that is blaming the victims for their oppression rather than the society. Coleman's report reaffirmed President Johnson's commitment to set up Project Headstart as part of his administration's 'war on poverty' campaign. The project was conceived as a 'comprehensive programme for pre-school children from economically and culturally disadvantaged backgrounds in an attempt to "break the cycle of poverty",' according to Julia Evetts (1973, p. 63). Whatever the efficacy, or otherwise, of Project Headstart, it aroused the objects not only of leading educationists such as William Labov (1973) but also of the US Commission on Civil Rights (1967), both of which criticized the underlying assumptions of compensatory education programmes. As Labov put it: 'Operation Headstart is designed to repair the child, rather than the school; to the extent that it is based upon this inverted logic it is bound to fail' (1973, p. 55).

In the UK, parallel developments took place in the 1960s and these were prompted by roughly the same concerns: first, to enhance the educability of 'disadvantaged pupils' (who were either working class, or of immigrant origin, or both) through compensatory education strategies; second, more generally, to break the cycle of poverty which persisted at a depressingly high level despite the 'swinging sixties' image (see Abel-Smith and Townsend, 1965). The 1967 Plowden report on primary schools adhered closely to American conceptions of

---

EDUCATIONAL COMPENSATION
Programmes designed to give intensive help to students who might be
disadvantaged in other areas such as family life, residence, poverty, etc.

---

this issue by openly embracing a deficit model of working-class and black pupils. Plowden saw one way of alleviating the problems of these children through the designation of Educational Priority Areas (EPA) which were to receive positive discrimination. Needless to say, one of the criteria of an EPA was a district with 'a high concentration of immigrants', and the rationale for this social policy response was strikingly similar to the principles which had underpinned compensatory education programmes in the USA:

> Schools in deprived areas should be given priority in many respects. The first step must be to raise the schools with low standards to the national average; the second, quite deliberately to make them better. The justification is that the homes and neighbourhoods from which many of their children come provide little support and stimulus for learning. The schools must supply a compensating environment (1967, para. 151).

From what we've said so far two characteristics of the way educational policy in this area was defined should have become clear. First, attempts to enhance the educability of working-class and minority group pupils and to facilitate their absorption into the mainstream, middle-class culture of the school were predicated on the belief that 'changing attitudes' was the name of the game. Put simply, it was thought that if the disjuncture between the schools' culture and that of the pupils could be reduced either through changing the children's attitudes (as the Newsom report had suggested in 1963), or parental attitudes (which Plowden had emphasized) then compliance with the system and higher performance would ensue. As Stone has remarked: 'in the educational game of attitude change, certain groups are "most likely" targets: the groups who are "problems" the truants, disrupters, educational failures for whom nothing appears to work.' In other words, 'change the attitudes of lower class parents and children and all will be well' (1981, p. 26). As we shall soon see, this commitment to the goal of attitude change has endured and constitutes one of the main cornerstones in the support for multiracial education (MRE).

The second feature of educational policy in this area has been called by David Kirp its 'racially inexplicit' nature (1979). That is to say, the needs of minority group children have, with the conspicuous exception of language provision for pupils whose mother tongue is not English, been seen by policy makers as largely indistinguishable from those of their white classmates.

However, as Michael Rutter and Nicola Madge have documented, the disadvantages which minority group children suffer are over and above those of the disadvantaged white children (1976). Even so, it is under the broader categories of educational disadvantage, urban and cultural deprivation and so on, that these needs have been tackled (Dorn and Troyna, 1982; Kirp, 1979; Troyna, 1982a).

The one exception to this pattern was the UK central government's endorsement of busing — the dispersal of immigrant pupils from their concentrated presence in selected schools and areas. Busing marked the only occasion in which race was placed explicitly on the educational policy agenda and this was as much for reasons of political expediency as for educational purposes (Troyna, 1982a). Again, the rationale for government sanction of this policy had its roots in the USA.

Busing

In 1954, in the Brown v. Board of Education case, the US Supreme Court ruled that segregated education was unconstitutional, and in violation of the 14th Amendment. So schools had to be desegregated.

The parallel with housing dispersal policies is almost exact: instead of breaking up the ghettos by dispersing concentrated populations of minority groups and, to put it strongly, forcing them to live with whites, black school children were quite literally taken out of their previous schools and made to go to schools with white children. Along with Chicano and other Latin American children, black pupils were transported to schools in the suburbs by specially laid-on buses. This legally sanctioned process of desegregation caused a furore in several states in the 1960s and 1970s with white parents protesting vehemently against their children being made to share facilities with black children. 'Because of forced busing,' wrote Louise Day Hicks, president of the Boston City Council in 1976, 'the public school system has lost close to 40,000 white students, leading to a predominantly black enrolment' (*New York Times*, 3 May 1976). Coleman, whose 1966 report had highlighted the benefits of desegregation on the educational standards of low-income black children, nevertheless agreed that its value was largely negated by the fact that it accelerated white flight. His view was captured in the title of the article 'Integration, yes: busing, no', in which he was interviewed by Walter Goodman (1975).

In Britain the controversy over busing arose in 1963 when a group of white parents in the Southall district of London complained to the Minister of Education, Sir Edward Boyle, that the educational progress of their children was being inhibited in those schools containing large numbers of immigrant pupils.

Boyle was receptive to these complaints and recommended to the government that the proportion of nonwhite immigrant children in any one school should not exceed 30 per cent. In 1965, 'Boyle's Law', as it came to be called, received official backing from the DES and dispersal policies, which had already begun in Southall and West Bromwich, were adopted by more than a handful of LEAs (see Killian, 1979; Kirp, 1979, for discussion).

Despite these similarities with the USA experience there were also profound differences, not the least of which were the attitudes of the black people themselves to the policy. According to a Gallup Poll in 1981 (February), 60 per cent of the black Americans interviewed supported busing and, as Kirp (1979) points out, the initiative for the policy derived largely from the demands of the American blacks. Malik Miah explained the basis of this support:

> the 1954 decision only outlawed de jure, or legal segregation — not de facto segregation, the type that exists in most Northern and Western cities. De facto segregation is not accidental. It is consciously fostered by banks, real estate agencies, and zoning boards. Blacks are forced into neighbourhoods with the worst housing and the worst schools. On top of that, school district lines are gerrymandered to create even more glaring segregation.
>
> Schools in Black areas, like the housing, are usually old and run-down to start with. Under racist school boards they are the last repaired, the worst funded, the most understaffed. The only way to force school authorities to equalize education is to end the system of segregated schools. And the only short-term way to do that is to bus students across district lines, as in Boston, or across city and council lines, as in Louisville (1976, pp. 17–18).

In contrast, there is little evidence to suggest that the UK's black communities favoured the busing of their children. On the contrary, Farrukh Dhondy and other members of the Race Today Collective (1982), Lewis Killian (1979) and Kirp (1979) report that in the London borough of Ealing, which includes Southall, there was unanimous condemnation of the policy by representatives of the leading black community groups. This is understandable; neither the DES nor Boyle had presented an adequate educational justification for the policy and it was difficult to find one. The research evidence collected by Little in the ILEA, for example, demonstrated that the ethnic mix of a school had a minimal influence in the level of reading ability attained by primary school pupils. 'Compared with parental occupation and the index of multiple deprivation', wrote Little, 'the factor of immigrant concentration would appear to be of small and inconsistent importance' (1975a). No, the main objectives of busing in the UK had been: (1) To facilitate the absorption of minority group children into the mainstream culture through enforced contact with white pupils; and (2) To assuage the anxieties of white parents (see DES, 1965). Which pupils were dispersed was defined by one sole criterion: skin colour. As David Milner puts it, in those LEAs which adopted busing, pupils of Caribbean and South Asian origin were dispersed 'irrespective of whether they had language difficulties or not, including among them some West Indian children, who, in contrast to what we now know, were then thought not to have language difficulties of the same order as the Asians' (1975, p. 201). As he goes on to say, racially explicit policies such as busing which are premised on such divisive grounds effectively 'institutionalize the recognition of the disparity between the races' and 'confirm the immigrants' second-class status' (1975, p. 202).

MRE: life styles, life chances

Compensatory education programmes and busing policies in the 1960s and 1970s were related to the extent that they exemplified dominant, assimilationist views of the position of blacks and South Asians in the metropolitan society. Simply, the aim was to assimilate these pupils into the mainstream culture of the school as quickly and with as little fuss as possible. School-based surveys of this period reflected just how far those at the 'chalk face' shared and endorsed this idea. In Sparkbrook, for instance, Jenny Williams found that teachers conceived of their role as 'putting over a certain set of values (Christian), a code of behaviour (middle class), and a set of academic and job aspirations in which white collar jobs have higher prestige than manual, clean jobs than dirty . . . ' (1967, p. 237). In their national survey of multiracial education initiatives in the early 1970s, H. E. R. Townsend and Elaine Brittan found that the following view, expressed by one headteacher, was common: 'I do not consider it the responsibility of an English State School to cater for the development of cultures and customs of a foreign nature. I believe our duty is to prepare children for citizenship in a free, democratic society according to British standards and customs' (quoted in Townsend and Brittan, 1973, p. 13).

In other words, the educational system was sacrosanct, the cultural values and assumptions which underpin it and the society in general were non-negotiable. If minority group children wanted to succeed within that system and gain the qualifications which their teachers and parents informed them were necessary to get a good job, indeed any job, they were compelled to reject their own cultural identity. Assimilation, that is the total absorption of a minority ethnic group so that it is no longer seen as a discrete group, was the goal. To facilitate 'equality of opportunity' in the competition for educational credentials

---

MRE
Multiracial Education as a possible method of combating the apparent
cultural deficit of immigrants' children grew out of the 1970s. It has been
defined in a bewildering variety of ways, but the basic impulse behind it is
to balance out the alleged white bias in western educational curricula. This
is thought to benefit both the minority pupils, who will gain self-respect
through seeing their cultures recognized and celebrated in school, but also
the white children whose educational experience will be more extensive.
In all, it is seen as a means of averting conflict between different ethnic
groups.

---

the LEAs and schools affected would prescribe language tuition (English as a Second Language, or E2L) for those pupils whose mother tongue was not English. Apart from this recognition of the 'special needs' of minority group children, especially those of South Asian origin, the 'colour-blind' approach to teaching in multiracial schools prevailed. As we shall show in chapter 8, school texts and library books presenting negative images of black people remained on classroom and library shelves and teachers adhered rigidly to the ethnocentric bias of the curriculum (Dixon, 1977; Townsend and Brittan, 1973).

But, by the mid-1970s, the coercive strategy of assimilation, which rested on the total suppression of cultural differences, was plainly not succeeding either in enforcing the compliance of minority group children, particularly those of Caribbean origin, or in improving their academic performance. In one of the most influential educational pamphlets on this issue during the 1970s, Bernard Coard, himself black, drew the attention of Caribbean parents to the disproportionately large numbers of their children in schools for the educationally subnormal (ESN). He argued that the school system, both deliberately and unwittingly, contributed to this trend. In other words, he laid the blame for the academic failure of black pupils fairly and squarely at the door of the schools:

> The Black child acquires two fundamental attitudes or beliefs as a
> result of his experiencing the British school system: a low self-image,
> and consequently low self-expectations in life. These are obtained
> through streaming, banding, busing, ESN schools, racist news media,
> and a white middle-classs curriculum; by totally ignoring the Black
> child's language, history, culture, identity. Through the choice of
> teaching materials, the society emphasizes who and what it thinks is
> important — and by implication, by omission, who and what it thinks
> is unimportant, infinitesimal, irrelevant. Through the belittling,
> ignoring or denial of a person's identity, one can destroy perhaps the
> most important aspect of a person's personality — his sense of identity,
> of who he is. Without this, he will get nowhere (Coard, 1971, p. 31).

On the face of it, Coard's observation that black pupils were rejecting their group and self-identity, was empirically correct, at least according to social psychologists such as Gajendra Verma and Christopher Bagley (1975), and David Milner (1975). They argued that schools had failed to nourish positive self-images in black pupils, that this had contributed to loss in self-confidence and, consequentially, to their poor academic performance. Black educationists such as Raymond Giles (1977) and parent groups, including the Black Peoples' Progressive Association (1979) went along with this interpretation. So did the Afro-Caribbean Educational Resources (ACER) project team which had been set up in the ILEA in 1976 with the expressed aim of producing curricular and teaching materials to counteract the alleged 'white bias' in the educational system. 'The identity of a child or what he inherits', wrote the ACER team in their first annual report, 'is important to his or her self-esteem; to deny this is to deprive the individual of a basic human right. The school should become an enriched inter-cultural learning environment for the non-racist society that we all hope for' (1977, p. 4). In the face of increasing anxiety about the lack of educational progress gained by black pupils, the DES and a handful of LEAs and their schools abandoned assimilationist conceptions of education. After a brief flirtation with 'Black Studies' — which had been piloted in the UK by the London Borough of Lambeth and which had comprised lessons on black history, reggae, Indian culture, and so on, as appendages to the established curriculum — LEAs and their schools have set about reappraising curricular, pedagogic and organizational procedures to ensure that they take into account the changing complexion of UK society. Hence MRE, multiracial education.

Now, MRE is a diffuse and complex conception of educational reform: it means all things to all people. James Banks (1981) and Margaret Gibson (1976) in the USA and Jenny Williams (1979) in Britain have shown how MRE can be based on a number of different and sometimes contradictory premises, and therefore assumes various trajectories. In both countries, however, the most common response derives from the view that, if self-image is the key to achievement and the poor performance of black pupils derives from their negative self-images, then the education system should set about recognizing and celebrating cultural differences and ethnic life styles, rather than trying to suppress them. Clearly, this conception of MRE owes much to social psychological approaches; changing attitudes once again becomes the priority for action. As Madan Sarup puts it:

> The educational 'solution', then, is a cultural one of changing attitudes and promoting 'inter-ethnic respect'. The main strategy now being employed is that of changing the *content* of the curriculum, of replacing the monoethnic, ethnocentric curriculum with a multicultural one.

ETHNOCENTRIC
A view of the world in which oneself or one's group is at the centre of things; a failure to take into account the perspectives of others. So, for example, teachers have been accused of being ethnocentric for tending to ignore such things as the language difficulties of some immigrant children and using teaching materials linked too closely to white or European culture.

This kind of approach has led to a stress on multiculturalism (the focusing on life styles and beliefs of minority groups); the dissemination of information to counteract racialist myths; and the demolition of racialist stereotypes in books and teaching materials (1982, p. 106).

Since the 1981 riots, a growing number of LEAs have enthusiastically produced policy statements declaring their commitment to MRE and have urged their schools to reflect cultural diversity in their habitual practices and procedures (Little and Willey, 1981; Dorn, 1982). Only by adopting this approach, they argue, will the life chances of black pupils be enhanced. This is a compelling argument and has attracted considerable support from black educationists, parents and community groups. But it has also invoked criticism and here, Stone has been amongst the most vociferous (1981). She has argued that current conceptions of MRE are based on erroneous assumptions: black pupils do not suffer from low self-esteem and strategies predicated on this ground are diversionary, likely to increase educational inequality rather than enhance the academic performance, and hence the life chances, of these youngsters. She insisted that schools should not focus on changing attitudes, or adopt 'mental health' goals, as she put it, but should be concerned with 'teaching methods associated with mastery of skills and knowledge and the development of abilities' (1981, p. 254). A similar point has also been argued by Brian Bullivant who reviewed the development of MRE initiatives in six countries during the 1970s (1981). Bullivant writes that proponents of these initiatives, which commonly take the form of those we've sketched out here, often assume that there is a direct relationship between the improvement of minority group children's identities, knowledge of their cultural backgrounds and enhancement of their life chances. Despite the absence of any hard evidence to support this view, and the fact that children of Jewish, Armenian and Chinese origin have succeeded academically without learning in school about their respective cultural backgrounds, it is an assumption which, according to Bullivant, has 'become part of the rhetoric and conventional wisdom of multicultural education' (1981,

p. 237). Tanya Birrell's cautionary comment clearly has some relevance to those LEAs and schools which are considering the adoption of MRE initiatives along those lines already established in the UK, USA and elsewhere:

> The time and effort required to learn and maintain ethnic languages and customs could inhibit the acquisition of skills and knowledge which, while in absolute terms are no better than ethnically valued ones, are nevertheless more useful in securing jobs, promotion, influence and the like (1978, p. 107).

By and large, then, the thrust of these initiatives and the common sense assumptions on which they are based have fogged the most critical factors which face minority group children in Britain.

Whether the initiatives taken in schools are compensatory, aimed at changing the attitudes of the pupils either towards the education system or toward themselves, or whether they respond to Stone's injunction for more academically oriented provision, neither are likely to enhance radically the life chances of those children in a society suffused with racism and racialism (Jenkins and Troyna, 1983). As Basil Bernstein wrote in the early 1970s, 'education cannot compensate for society' (1970); schooling simply does not have the capacity to eliminate inequalities. Those inequalities seem to endure from one generation to another regardless of steps taken to reduce them via education. But different generations do not necessarily respond in the same ways to what are its basically similar conditions — as we will see next.

Further reading

'Learning to resist: black women and education' is by Beverley Bryan, Stella Dadzie and Suzanne Scafe and features in **Gender under Scrutiny** edited by Gaby Weiner and Madeleine Arnot (1987). It is based on their experiences as black pupils in British schools — an experience which was informed primarily by racism: 'it is *racism* which has determined the schools we can attend and the quality of the education we receive in them'. Returning to education as mature students enabled a critical re-examination of these experiences and the opportunity to develop both collective and individual strategies in opposition to the education system's expectations.

' ''Race'' and education: two perspectives for change' by Richard Hatcher appears in Troyna's edited volume, **Racial Inequality in Education** (1987). Hatcher insists that, despite the ostensibly radical complexion of the 'new' multiculturalist paradigm within which writers such as Lynch, Banks and Parekh embed their arguments, there remain irreconcilable differences with antiracist conceptions of education reform.

Education, Justice and Cultural Diversity by Mark Halstead (1988) is a detailed and careful analysis of the controversy surrounding the refusal of the then headteacher,

Raymond Honeyford, to support his Local Education Authority's antiracist and multicultural education policies. Written in the perspective of social philosophy, Halstead teases out from 'the Honeyford Affair', as it came to be known, a number of salient issues: racism, free speech, teacher accountability and multicultural education. His analysis might usefully be compared to Olivia Foster-Carter's chapter on the same issue which appears in **Racial Inequality in Education** (1987).

Education for All: A Landmark in Pluralism and **Race and Culture in Education** are edited by Gajendra Verma (1989) and T. Chivers (1986) respectively. They contain a range of critical appraisals of the Swann report, *Education for All*, including contributions from the USA, Australia and Canada. They give a flavour of the way in which parts of the report have been exploited to further anti-racist education in a range of educational settings.

Right Turn by Ken Jones (1989) traces what he terms 'the Conservative revolution in education'. It identifies the anti-egalitarian premises on which the 1988 Education Reform Act (ERA) is based. It also illuminates how the vilification of antiracist education in areas such as Brent and Haringey provided a rationale for the centralization of political power, secured through the ERA.

7
Ethnicity — youth — resistance

- What is ethnicity?
- How did early migrants try to make themselves invisible?
- Do many migrants really want to go home?
- Why are Asians 'two different peoples'?
- Why did blacks riot in the streets in 1981?

People united

Summer 1981 was a turning point in the development of modern UK race relations in much the same way as 1966 was in the USA. 'Burnin' and lootin' ' was the phrase most favoured by the media to sum up the sequence of events which affected virtually every major city in Britain. Gangs of predominantly black youths rampaged through cities like London, Birmingham and Liverpool splitting their communities asunder: they burnt their properties, attacked police and emptied shops. It was an expression of rage, of hostility. But against what or whom?

Against the police perhaps? Well, certainly the incidents precipitating the events involved altercations with police officers in much the same way that the events that spurred the Watts riots in Los Angeles were prompted by skirmishes with the police. In the States, the outbreaks were not simply the spontaneous uprisings of a bunch of angry black malcontents: they were the cumulative result of decades — some would say centuries — of white domination.

In the early 1960s, Martin Luther King's civil rights movement signalled the first politically coherent protest against the ill-treatment of blacks. But, dismayed at the lack of meaningful progress made by King, the Watts rioters eclipsed anything that had preceded them. They responded violently to what Glasgow in his study of the Watts ghettos colourfully described as:

MARTIN LUTHER KING
Reverend Dr Martin Luther King, Jr (1929–68), born in Atlanta, Georgia,
emerged as the leader of the civil rights movement which gained millions
of black adherents in the 1960s. The movement was the most successful
of its kind in achieving legal and civil advancement for US blacks. After
King was assassinated in April 1968, 125 cities erupted in violence that
required 70,000 troops to quell.

> Being broke, hustling, jiving, stealing, rapping, balling; a fight; a
> bust, some time; no job, a no-paying job; a lady, a baby, some weight,
> some wine, some grass, a pill; no ride, lost pride, man going down,
> slipping fast, can't see where to make it; I've tried, almost died, ready
> now for almost anything (1980, p. 104).

Consciousness has been a central theme of this book: part of the argument is that underprivileged groups themselves cannot remain untouched by ideologies, particularly racial ones, and that they have, to a large degree, accepted them. In this way, they have contributed to their own subordination in a system of what Blauner calls 'internal colonialism' where the colonial relationship affects both the dominant and subordinate groups' self-conceptions (1972).

Now, it is very evident that groups designated racial do not always passively accept subordinate positions. The Watts outbreaks teach us that groups change their consciousness both of themselves and their status in society. So ideologies about race are not always self-maintaining: sometimes they are punctured and movements emerge which either reject the notion of racial inequality — as, say, King's organization — or seek major modifications in it — like the black power that proliferated after Watts.

The 1981 UK disturbances were symptoms of such a rejection and, although they weren't the first, they were certainly the most volatile. They issued a challenge against old ideas without necessarily offering alternative new ones. It was as if the youths involved were, in a nihilistic frenzy, trying to wipe out the existing situation, but didn't have a vision of a new situation to replace it. The rioters in Miami's Liberty City in 1980, showed almost the same nihilism, randomly attacking whites and destroying hundreds of millions of dollars in property. The Miami riots left eighteen people dead, but brought about no new society.

Much of the book thus far has concerned the principal institutions contributing to race relations; laws, work, housing and education are all areas of society of central importance to anyone's life today and we've tried to show how in each of these areas, racism operates as a factor disadvantaging certain minority

---

BLACK POWER
The collective name for a series of movements which emerged in the US during the 1960s. The movements, such as the Black Panthers led by Huey P. Newton, signified an assertion of black consciousness, demanding radical improvements in the material, social and political conditions for US blacks. In the UK, similar movements sprang up under the leadership of Michael Abdul Malik and Obi Egbuna.

---

groups. Part of our argument is that groups can, however unwittingly, contribute to or even compound their own disadvantage by believing in ideas about fundamental divisions and stratifications. Situations of racial inequality are not just the result of impositions of groups holding power and wishing to preserve that power, but also the acceptance of those situations by the groups that are adversely affected.

Now, obviously, this account is incomplete. The two examples of Watts and the 'burnin' and lootin' ' episodes alone tell us that there are periods when group perceptions of situations of inequality are repulsed, even if only momentarily. Less dramatic, but equally as important are instances of disapproval such as King's rallies.

It's important to appreciate race relations as a two-way process implicating advantaged and disadvantaged groups. Power, as we've shown, has a decisive influence on the shape of the relationship, but it's still important to investigate the responses of the subordinated groups. Otherwise, we run the risk of leaving our view as one-sided and insensitive to the roles and contributions of disadvantaged groups.

The term ethnic is derived from the Greek word referring to a people or naiton and has undergone several mutations without losing its basic meaning: members of ethnic groups are people who are conscious of themselves as in some way united or at least related because of a common origin and a shared destiny. Usually, though not always, they are descendants of immigrants who left their lands either to seek improvements elsewhere or were forcibly taken from their lands, as were African slaves. Conversely they might be original inhabitants of lands alienated from them by invaders — like North American Indians or Australian aborigines. Whatever the circumstances, the ethnic group reveals a response of disadvantaged peoples who believe themselves to be participants in a common plight but who also feel that they can find comfort, stability and perhaps further their interests, by emphasizing the features of life, past and present, they share. Banton contrasts ethnicity with race, 'so that the former reflects the positive tendencies of identification and inclusion where the latter reflects the negative tendencies of dissociation and exclusion' (1977, p. 136).

INTERNAL COLONIALISM
Term from Robert Blauner (1972) who contrasted it with classic
colonialism in which a country's native population is subjugated by a
minority of colonizers from another country. In internal colonialism, the
colonized group are minorities in the white bureaucratic control, have their
culture depreciated or destroyed and are confined to low-status social
positions. This in turn affects their self-conceptions and they tend to view
themselves as inferior — in much the same way as whites view them.

Beyond this basic definition, there is no meaningful, detailed way of capturing the concept of ethnicity, for the forms it takes are varied: Puerto Ricans in New York, Aboriginals in Australia, Surinamese in Holland — the list is almost endless. Some are more severely disadvantaged than others; some overcome their material disadvantages and aspire to elites, like Irish Catholics and Jews in the USA (Greely, 1974). Sometimes the ethnic impulse spills over into political realms and political organizations are created to represent minority interests, such as the IWA and the Lewisham Black People's Alliance; sometimes it enters occupational spheres, like the formation of the Black Media Workers' Association and the black lawyers' and teachers' groups in the UK in the early 1980s — attempts to create elites within elites. But always the group begins from a position of marginality.

Ethnicity, then, is the way we try to encapsulate the various types of responses of certain groups. The ethnic group doesn't have to be racial in the sense that it is seen as somehow naturally inferior, though there is a very strong overlap and most groups which align themselves ethnically and perceive common interests are often regarded by others as racial. And where a group is disprivileged because the rest of society perceives it as racially inferior, there is usually at least a minimal ethnicity. But we stress there is no necessary relationship between the two.

The mystique of whiteness

What is socially distinctive about blacks and Asians in the UK, it could be argued, is not their colour, but their exploited positions in the division of labour. We agree. But, whilst acknowledging and, over the past few chapters, confirming that they can be seen as a particularly disadvantaged class, both groups have developed unique customs, practices, beliefs, languages, diets, leisure activities. And these are ethnic responses.

They are, in part, responses to marginal social positions and, in part,

---

MARGINALITY
Expresses the condition that individual groups are, in some sense,
peripheral to the mainstream society; the marginality may take an
economic form (if the groups are habitually poor), or a physical form (if the
individuals or groups are physically handicapped, say); with reference to
black youths, it expresses their social marginality, meaning that they are
not fully participating culturally or economically in society.

---

initiatives to define and assert a sense of human selfhood — who you are, whom you belong to and who are your allies and enemies. In the post-war UK, this response has always been present amongst immigrant groups and their offspring, though not always readily identifiable. Now, while Sheila Allen points out that there is a 'lack of research-based evidence of the lives of the generation who came in the 1950s and 1960s,' the indications are that, for example, the first wave of immigrants from the West Indies were not recognizably assertive: they organized their response so as to arouse little interest, less still antagonism, from the rest of society (1982, p. 146).

To understand this response, which we take to be illustrative of a great deal of first generation immigrants whatever the country of origin or destiny, we must try to appreciate the expectations of the immigrants on arrival in the UK in the early 1950s. The very act of emigration from the Caribbean to the UK was itself an optimistic move. But, what the studies also show was that the West Indians were generally disappointed at their experiences in the changed environment and went through unpleasant periods they could not have anticipated prior to or on their arrival. As Daniel Lawrence was told: 'I was not expecting at all any prejudice or discrimination. As a matter of fact I did not know I was a coloured man until the English told me so. Somebody referred to me as a coloured person on the bus once, and that was the first time I knew who I was' (1974, p. 40). We've been over the reception of the immigrants and noted how racialism grew to such a pitch that legislative action had to be taken. So it comes as no surprise to learn that the migrants, who had by all accounts, identified quite positively with the 'British way of life,' were both shocked and dismayed at their rebuttal.

In the 1950s and 1960s, research dug up evidence of blatant racialism in employment, housing, education and social services and, of course, in the everyday face-to-face circumstances. Now, there's no reason to suppose that the conditions first generation Caribbeans lived through were any easier than those experienced by their sons and daughters. Yet they didn't go burnin' and looting and prompting the likes of Lord Scarman to mount large inquiries. So what did they do? On the surface: nothing visible. But what was happening was a social involution, a turning inwards at the edges to form a rough community. As we've seen, this was assisted by employment markets which more or less determined which part of the country the migrants could settle in and housing policies consigning them to specific zones of the cities. These, plus the immigrants' obvious desire to avoid feeling estranged and different, combined to produce a ghettoization of the inner cities.

Inside the zones, distinct immigrant communities developed. It gave Caribbeans a feeling of separateness which they perhaps didn't crave when they first set foot in the UK. The hostile reception would have promoted experiences of isolation; grouping together with others who had undergone similar experiences would have served to assuage this. At the same time, this provided emotional support, a feeling of group solidarity or togetherness and a sense of community.

If any phenomenon symbolizes this involution it was Pentecostalism, a sectarian movement that had old roots in the Caribbean and USA, but grew amongst West Indian migrants in Britain. Wolverhampton 1954 were the place and the year of the first Pentecostal assemblies, according to Malcolm Calley (1965). At first, the services were conducted at private homes with only a small number of followers and no organization of note. Within thirteen years, it was revealed by Clifford Hill that one branch of the movement alone had a following of 10,861 congregations, employed fifteen full-time ministers and owned several buildings, including its own theological college (1970).

The attraction of Pentecostalism is, at first sight, puzzling. Members, or saints as they are called, were not allowed to drink alcohol, wear jewellery, use cosmetics, practise extra-marital sex or speak foul language. They were compelled to adhere to a strict ethical code reserved for them as 'chosen people'. As God's elect, they awaited the Day of the Pentecost, written in Acts 11:1–2, when they could receive their salvation. In the interim, they were supposed to maintain as much distance as possible from the outside world they thought was 'contaminated.' Hence a kind of withdrawal from the mundane world and the cultivation of a special relationship with God.

Hill asked whether the 'Pentecostalist growth' was the 'result of racialism?' and answered on the basis of his research, 'there is a definite link between the experience of deprivation and membership of the all-black immigrant religious sects in Britain' (1971, p. 189). His argument is that, although they were materially better-off in the UK than they were in the Caribbean, they suffered status deprivations because they were discriminated against on the basis of their colour. 'Deprivation has the effect of driving together in social solidarity members of the pariah group' (1971, p. 189).

While most of the immigrants were materially better-off compared to the life they had left behind, they encountered a racialism they had not anticipated

---

PENTECOSTALISM
A term embracing a range of religious movements which proliferated in the USA, West Indies and, in recent times, the UK, attracting mainly black followers. Malcolm Calley's book, *God's People* (1965), is a careful piece of research on the growth of the churches in the UK. Essentially, a passive, withdrawing movement that contrasts very sharply with the later RASTAFARIAN MOVEMENT whose members adopt a far more active and volatile posture in relation to what they see as a racialist and oppressive society, known as BABYLON.

---

and so felt unexpectedly excluded. This had the effect of 'driving them together' and the Pentecostal movement was one result.

The Pentecostalist posture was not designed to elicit volatile reactions from the rest of society; the typical saint was, for the most part, passive, withdrawn and, interestingly, as Hill pointed out: 'He still has his traditional strong regard for the "British way of life" and desire for acceptance into British society' (1970, p. 39). The attempt to gain acceptance was made by lowering profiles rather than heightening them as the next generation was to do.

The 'strong regard' the Pentecostalists had for the so-called British way of life would seem to indicate a basic acceptance and approval of the existing order of things. Racialism was, according to reports of the time, fairly common and the general ideology, as we have seen, was racist. Blacks were employed overwhelmingly in lower grade, manual jobs and their chances of advancement were limited, even with qualifications. They were allocated and lived in the worst housing. These were the elements of the British way of life they supposedly had a regard for. It seems they accepted the inequality that pervaded life in the UK and, of course, by accepting it, they perpetuated it, albeit in an unknowing way.

The first generation immigrants by and large did not reject the racially structured roles that were cast for them and so their actions confirmed the prejudices of others, prejudices they often recognized yet did nothing about; as one of Foner's respondents captured it: 'I don't push myself because insult is not a good invitation. I have English neighbours and we say hello. But if we meet on the high road, they look the other way' (1977, pp. 133–4). On the broader level, the Pentecostalists' tolerance of immediate material conditions because of the assurance of salvation had the further effect of dampening their enthusiasm for doing anything practical about improving what were by all accounts rather miserable existences.

Pentecostalism fits almost perfectly into Marx's theory of religion as the 'opiate of the people': like a narcotic, it worked to dull the believers' senses and led them to seek salvation in an other-worldly realm which was disconnected from their material existences. Thus it was a political convenience serving the needs of a capitalist system which relied, at that stage, on a ready, compliant and undemanding reserve labour force, available to occupy jobs that the native labour force didn't want, living at the bottom of the social ladder and, at the same time, respecting the established order of things that institutionalized the inferiority of black people.

Under conditions such as existed in the UK at that time, no automatic challenge was made to inequality. Racism was more or less accepted as a fact of life in the new country and West Indians were in awe of what Foner calls 'the mystique of whiteness'.

Asian myth

'The myth of return' is how some writers describe the motivating vision of many South Asians in the UK. For early settlers from India and Pakistan, it may have been a possibility, in some cases a probability, though, as Roger and Catherine Ballard detected: 'From its original status as a realistic short-term goal, the idea of a return has gradually become a myth which, although increasingly unrealistic, has important social consequences' (1977, p. 40).

As we've pointed out, there were a few Asian residents in England as early as the mid-1800s, though, as in the case of West Indians, the migration after World War II surpassed everything. The general position of Asians was simply stated by the Ballards: 'They sought high wages and were prepared to do tedious and unpleasant jobs for very long hours — often twelve hour shifts six days a week' (1977, pp. 29–30).

So the main goal of Asians was to earn as much money as possible in quick time and return home. Like the West Indians who preceded them, they withstood hostile receptions and were quite prepared to do so in the quixotic pursuit of the return. Some did go back; but, for the most part, the return to Asia was a myth, albeit an enduring one.

The research of people like Stuart Philpott (1973), Lawrence (1974) and Miles and Phizacklea (1981) suggests that the desire to return to the native land was also entertained by West Indians and this would have had consequences on their postures too, though, as we've indicated, their links with the UK were, in a sense, stronger than that of the Asians. This strikes us as interesting for, on the one hand, we have Caribbean migrants roughly attuned to the British way of life, speaking English, believing in Christian religions, dressing in English styles and geared to an education system based on the UK model. On the other, we have Asians, oriented to the UK only instrumentally, using a totally different set of languages, adhering to nonChristian beliefs and different modes of dress and less familiar with the western concept of education. The odds against Asians integrating more smoothly than the Caribbeans would have been enormous in 1958. Yet, in the early 1980s, the sons and daughters of West Indians were rioting in the streets while those of Asians were sedulously working their ways through the education system, acquiring qualifications and aspiring to professions.

This rather unexpected pattern of development is the result of different postures taken by the first generation migrants. Superficially, the Asians, despite their variety of backgrounds, all seemed to take a stance similar to the West Indians: passive, withdrawn, resigned with only limited contacts with whites. But their reasons were different. Returning to the homeland was an ambition shared by both groups. But, whereas West Indians felt more strongly a desire to be part of British society, Asians felt no compulsion to establish social relationships with the British; for their aim was to save money and flee. Dilip Hiro puts it like this:

> Outside the economic field, the average Asian had no aspiration or expectation. He had come to Britain knowing full well that white people were culturally alien in his eyes. And he had neither the inclination nor the intention to participate in 'their' life (1973, p. 113).

The tensions of the late 1950s no doubt reinforced their ambitions. Reacting to what was interpreted as a rejection, Asians sought to make life as comfortable as permissible by restoring their former cultures in the new setting of the UK. They set about recreating as many institutions of their former societies as possible, particularly in the 1960s when more and more families were reunited, thus bringing more stability to the whole Asian community. Whatever part of South Asia they came from, the migrants were part of some rich cultures based on the Sikh, Hindu or Islamic religions (a few were Christians). These were centuries-old traditions having their own rules, rites and ceremonies pertaining to, for example, marriage, child birth, worship, even business. The cultures recreated by the Asians were different and distinct and made visible by the appearance of turbans, saris and traditional elements of dress, new temples of worship, particularly mosques, and an infrastructure of Asian services and businesses, like shops, travel agencies, warehouses and cinemas — the type of enterprises we considered in chapter 4.

The Asians became a highly recognizable ethnic presence; their ethnicity was further strengthened by the fact that their migration was based on purely economic considerations. Simply put, as they were only temporarily in the UK, they saw no particular need to assimilate to British culture and thought it more imperative to adhere to their homeland values. Inside ethnic boundaries, traditions were upheld and this afforded them the feeling of uniqueness.

Ostensibly, the Asians were similar to their West Indian equivalents in that they were undemanding, largely inactive and, for the most part, sequacious. Once detail is added to the outlines, however, we see several distinguishing features of the utmost importance, particularly in relation to the second generations.

Like West Indians, Asians were the objects of hostility; in fact, during the 1970s, the almost ritualistic paki-bashing made life treacherous to Asians living in the big British cities. They were employed mainly in working-class occupations though, as we saw in chapter 4, some made progress in commercial spheres. But the ability to sustain ethnicity provided Asians with an alternative to this world encountered in the working day. The alternative lying inside the ethnic boundary was in sharp contrast to what must have been an unsatisfactory, if necessary, existence. Traditions and values which seemingly had no relevance in the British context were kept alive and were used to support morale and identity and, on occasion, prompt action.

The ethnic preserve gave Asians an added dimension in their lives: it gave them the consciousness of belonging to an elite. They belonged to groups that were essentially their own: whites didn't have access. In those groups, they were able to embrace principles of some significance not only to them but to white society: stability of community, centrality of family, firm internal controls leading to strict morality, self-discipline and respect for seniority. All of these were regarded as virtuous.

Materially, they were struggling, yet this didn't do harm to their feelings of elitism if only because, coming from South Asia, they would have been familiar with stratification systems based on cultural criteria rather than the move obvious power, wealth and race. In effect, Asians may have been stuck amongst the working class in material terms, but they thought of themselves as detached or removed from that class by virtue of their ethnicity. West Indians didn't have a comparable facility: the culture they brought with them lacked the firmness, depth and history of the Asian equivalent; and the reasons for this stem from the slave days when the original African culture was denuded to the bone in the effort to reduce slaves to the status of chattels. The West Indian culture was one pieced together from remnants.

Our argument is that Indians and Pakistanis by no means completely accepted the ideology of inequality. The images they held of themselves had two dimensions: (1) The immigrant working in somewhat unpleasant conditions forced into austerity because of the need to save; (2) The ethnic group member sustaining centuries-old traditions and preserving unfaded cultures.

The Asians' pronounced ethnicity sparked occasional issues, such as the bus conductors' insistence on wearing turbans instead of regulation head gear (Beetham, 1970). In contradiction to the law pertaining to crash helmets, many Sikhs wore turbans on motor cycles. The Muslim practice of polygamous marriage was tantamount to bigamy in the UK. These small episodes indicated the growing confidence of Asians and their willingness to stand fast for their ethnicity, a willingness which surfaced once again in 1982 after Lord Denning's endorsement of a headteacher's refusal to admit a Sikh child wearing a turban to his school. Before this, as we've seen, during the 1970s, there were a number of disputes in industry in which Asians protested, often vigorously, against racialism. In these instances, they showed that Asian ethnicity had practical value when needed.

Two different people

Now, this reassertion of Asian ethnicity amongst first generation immigrants meant that their sons and daughters would be brought up in two quite different worlds, one based in the home, one in the school. The pressures at school were to conform to the standards of British education and, generally, become Anglicized. But, those at home were to retain the ethnic impulse. Often, the two sets of demands were contradictory. For example, the conformity, discipline and authority learned at home were quite different from the values of peers and even teachers at school, who encouraged self-expression, freedom and independence. Even fashions in clothes could provoke conflict when the parents favoured the more traditional turbans for Sikh boys or the salwar kamiz outfits for girls when the children felt more inclined to dress in the mode of their contemporaries — and were strongly encouraged by teachers to so so.

Asian parents didn't want their children to become British in a cultural sense, but were forced to reckon with the fact that the second generation grew up in a world in which the ethnic way of life had less relevance than it had in the early phases of migration and settlement. They were educated, some born, in the UK and, quite logically, made associations with people of their own age group, some Asian, some white, some black. Yet, on returning to their homes they would be expected to enter a totally different set of relationships amongst families. As a way of coping with these situations, the youths brought new skills to bear; as one of the boys in the Ballard study put it:

> I've learned to be two different people. I'm quite different when I'm away at college with English people than when I'm here with my family and my Punjabi friends. I'm so used to switching over that I don't even notice (1977, p. 46).

This is not meant to convey that all youths were able to effect such smooth transitions: tales of runaway Asian girls and homes split between generations were commonplace in the late 1970s and early 1980s. In some areas, hostels especially for Asian runaways were set up — much to the anger of many Asian parents (see Waind, 1981). What's certain is that enough were able to handle the switching well enough to maintain reasonable family lives and still do well in education without too much apparent conflict.

Asian parents tended to have a strong regard for British education and encouraged their children to work assiduously in the effort to gain qualifications — yet without losing their ethnic identity or allegiance. Often, this meant dissociating themselves to a great degree from their white and black peers and complying with the families' wishes to work academically. The improving examination results gained by Asians at the turn of the decade suggests that this was a most effective policy.

Despite the generally low profile of Asian youth and the image of the studious, earnest scholar they presented, there were occasional episodes of violence in the 1970s and 1980s in which Asians featured prominently. Southall in West London, an area of significant Asian settlement has been the location for a number of these episodes. In June 1976, for example, Gurdip Singh Chaggar was killed by a gang of white youths and violence flared in the aftermath. The police response was to call in reinforcements and systematically stop and search Asian youths. This, in turn, 'strengthened the feeling that the police were more concerned with policing the Asian community than with arresting those responsible for the murder' according to one account of the incident (Campaign against Racism and Fascism, Southall Rights, 1981, p. 51). The police response solidified the resistance of young Asian to police practices and led directly to the formation of the Southall Youth Movement.

Three years later, in April 1979, Southall was again the scene of violence as the whole community turned out to protest against the provocative decision of the National Front to hold a pre-General Election meeting at the town hall. The ensuing disturbances saw the death of an anti-NF demonstrator, Blair Peach, and, as the Campaign Against Racism and Fascism put it: 'For the black community in Southall, life will never be the same again. April 23 was the culmination of struggle and, at the same time, the beginning of a new stage of community action and resistance' (1981, p. 62).

The resistance came to light again in July 1981, in Walthamstow, East London, where a Pakistani woman and her three children were killed after their house was maliciously set on fire. The day after, there was a concert in Southall, with the 4 Skins, a band that made reference to Nazi slogans and attracted a great following of skinheads. Around the concert venue, hundreds of Asian youths assembled, and the whole scene erupted when they attacked the concert hall, which was eventually petrol-bombed and gutted. Under the circumstances, it seems the Asians were responders to rather than initiators of action and the combination of apparently racialist arson, plus the Nazi-style skinhead concert spurred them to fight. Despite these incidents, Asian youths, for the most part, have not engaged themselves in any disturbances on the same scale or same frequency of black youths, whom we will now consider.

Babylon's burnin'

The weeks either side of the Southall episode were packed with events that made 1981 an *annus mirabilis* of UK race relations. In fact, in the previous year, the St Paul's district of Bristol had provided the setting for a disturbance after police had entered the premises of a cafe used mainly by black locals. A crowd assailed the police, who were eventually forced to withdraw, leaving St Paul's effectively a 'no go area' for some four hours, while vehicles were destroyed, shops looted and property devastated. Twelve months passed before the next serious disturbance and that was in Brixton, South London, when an exercise in saturation policing, codenamed Swamp 81, resulted in a total of 1,000 people being stopped with 100 arrested in four days. This served to exacerbate an already tense relationship between police and blacks in the area and it needed only an incident involving a certain Michael Bailey and a group of police officers trying to apprehend him, to trigger what turned into a literally explosive scene. Sporadic fighting led to petrol-bomb attacks on police cars and buildings and, for two days, a three-mile area of Brixton ringed by 1,000 police with a further 3,000 on call, was the scene of the first spate of 'burnin' and 'lootin', resulting in damages estimated in millions of pounds.

Throughout the summer, similar disturbances took place first in Liverpool and, then, in virtually every major British city. The 'copycat riots' was how the media and several politicians described the outbreaks in July, suggesting that the youths involved were merely mimicking the events at Brixton rather than articulating any protest against conditions (we consider the suggestion in chapter 9). It was, of course, easy to disguise the underlying causes by arguing that the later outbreaks were the results only of imitation, though the Scarman inquiry on the Brixton riot did acknowledge: 'The common strands in many of the major disorders for which there is much evidence, are to be found in shared social conditions, in economic insecurity and perceived deprivation, in enforced idleness because of unemployment, and in the hostility of at least a section of young people to the police' (1981, p. 14).

'Shared social conditions' they are, but shared also by white working-class youth. Blacks may have been disproportionately affected by feelings of economic insecurity and the 'enforced idleness' unemployment brings, and we have ample evidence to suggest that police practices do not work in the best interests of blacks (IRR, 1981). But young whites are also affected in some measure by all these conditions. Certainly, the nationwide so-called copycat riots which climaxed on 11–12 July 1981, involved substantial numbers of white youths. But, there again, the Bristol and Brixton episodes were exclusively blacks vs police confrontations. Or were they?

The first episodes were not just blacks rioting against police malpractice, the refusal to protect blacks from racial attacks and the propensity to subject blacks to harassment. In both episodes, conflicts with the police provided catalysts setting in motion the larger affairs — in much the same way as in the Watts riots. But the black anger was not so much directed at police officers, but at the system they personified.

Black youth destroyed the houses in which they lived, the shops on which they depended for provisions, the environment in which they lived. They attacked the people whom they saw as their controllers. These didn't seem politically intelligible targets. But the rioting was directed at symbols: the properties and instituitons the youths attacked were symbols of the system they saw exploiting them. So they burnt and looted the actual community in which they lived, a community which stood as testament to the impoverishment of their lives. Simon Field makes a similar point in drawing out the parallels with the US riots: 'rioting has not occurred for the lack of an inside toilet, or even for the lack of a job. More likely it has occurred because certain groups have lost faith in the capacity and will of establishment institutions to take their interests into account and to provide them with the means of achieving social acceptance and material success' (1982, p. 33).

The kind of consciousness informing this action was greatly stimulated by the growth in popularity of the Rastafarian movement amongst young blacks. The movement has origins in Jamaica where it began in the early 1930s just after the demise of Marcus Garvey whose slogan 'Africa for the Africans' early Rastas used as their inspiration. Although never consciously acknowledging the movement, Garvey, with his insistence on black pride and the restoration of African culture, was regarded as akin to a prophet. Rastas adopted Haile Selassie, the one-time emperor of Ethiopia, as a messiah and made their goal a return to a united Africa.

During the mid-1970s, the Rastafarian movement surfaced, at first, in London and Birmingham and, later, in all the major UK cities. Black youths adorned themselves with the national colours of Ethiopia, coiled their hair into long dreadlocks, cultivated an esoteric langauge and, generally attempted to detach themselves from the society they regarded as inherently evil and exploitative of black peoples. The system that had ensured the early enslavement

---

BABYLON
The concept first used by members of the Rastafarian movement to describe the system of European colonialism which they felt had not only worked to enslave Africans in the Imperial expansion, but also worked to inhibit the consciousness of modern-day blacks (by providing 'white men's religions' and notions about the inherent inferiority of black people). Babylon is seen as operated by whites in a vast conspiracy to keep blacks suppressed and prevent them from realizing their true worth and organizing into a collective movement.

---

of Africans and cemented the continued oppression of blacks Rastas called Babylon and only when this system was obliterated would black people achieve total emancipation of the mind as well as the body. They would realize themselves as Africans.

The central insight of the movement was that it was not so much whites who were evil and oppressive as the system of Babylon of which they were part. Liberal or even radical whites who were concerned to improve the conditions of blacks were trapped in the system of Babylon. It followed that all blacks who had not gained this insight were involuntarily contributing to their own subordination. In this respect, Rastafarian theory was a critique of colonialism, and a rather sophisticated one at that in its depiction of the all-pervasive nature of imperialist ideologies and their penetration into the minds of subordinate groups. Christian religions were strategies implemented, at first, by missionaries and, later, by denominations, to distract blacks' attentions from their deprived material conditions and locate their salvation in an intangible after-life. But Rastas saw this working as a sponge to soak up blacks' energies. In the words of one of the great Rasta heroes, Bob Marley:

> We're sick and tired of your easing kissing game
> to die and go to heaven in Jesus' name.
> We know and understand
> Almighty God is a living man

The message delivered here in the track *Get Up, Stand Up* (Tuff Gong, 1973) is that black people should abandon thoughts of ultimate salvation and think of their destinies as controlled not by an imposing God but by themselves. Salvation was not to be waited for: 'you will look for yours on earth.' Rastas used the expression 'I and I' to signify that the spirit of God can be conceived of as within people not outside them. So when people act either to show dissatisfaction with present conditions or to improve them, they can still feel God as the motivating force behind their actions.

TWO-TONE
The name given to the movement beginning in the Midlands city of
Coventry which grew up in the late 1970s and early 1980s. Musical bands
such as the Specials, the Selecter and Madness all acquired a following of
youths committed to promoting harmony in relationships between blacks
and whites. Many of the two-tone concerts were disrupted by the racist
youth movement of SKINHEADS (see chapter 8).

The blossoming of the Rastafarian movement in the 1970s had a strong bearing on the outbreaks in 1981. Rastas brought a fresh and critical consciousness; theirs was an acerbic, anti-colonialist ideology. Their ultimate aim was the dissolution of the total system of control, Babylon. But this concept of Babylon had relevance not only for Rastas but for all black youth and, indeed many whites in the early 1980s. Young people, black and white, grew up in a world in which their prospects were limited by circumstances external to them. Their understanding of the world was wrought out of everyday material existences. In particular, blacks felt their chances of improvement restricted by, amongst other things, their blackness, so shared a conception of common destiny. As Rasta musician Peter Tosh expressed it in his song *African*, 'Don't care where you come from, as long as you're a black man, you're an African (ATV, 1977).

These views were cemented with every successive round of school-leavers armed with ideas about unemployment and the double disadvantage of being black and working class. Hence the upsurge in Rasta ideas; specifically the concept of a system geared to suppress black peoples gained enormous credibility. Babylon for many youths was not a rather bizarre way of describing the world: it was their world. The attraction of Rasta ideas to white as well as black youths suggested that, in the early 1980s, the movement began to speak to a general condition, the most important feature of which was a widespread loss of confidence in the future.

This shone through the copycat riots, but it was also evident in a more stylized form in two-tone, the predominantly musical movement decrying racism and insisting that blacks and white youths were united in a web of hopelessness.

So, although the events were precipitated by blacks in the very high immigrant districts of Bristol and Brixton, later, the disturbances involved blacks and whites. They were all seeming to run amok, aimlessly destructive and bent on wreaking havoc. But, in a way, they were expressing anger, rage, fury at the system they felt as constraining them — Babylon. They burnt and pillaged their own communities because those communities only reminded them of the squalor in which they lived and the hopelessness they faced.

In the 1950s and 1960s, we had barely visible groups of migrants posturing in such a way as to diminish their presence and quite prepared to accept the often harsh conditions amidst which they lived. In the early 1980s, their sons and daughters were rioting in the streets. How do we make sense of this difference? We can start by noticing the very obvious differences in the life experiences of the two generations: the first had the 'benefit' of an alternative they had left behind and, maybe, wanted to return to at a future, unspecified time; the second, for the most part, were educated and brought up in a society in which they expected to play a full part and draw full benefits. Their orientations to their society were quite different.

But there were constants: the evidence suggests that, for all the legislation enacted, racialism still remained in many of the dominant spheres of society and this undoubtedly had a lot to do with the fact that the class position of the two generations stayed the same. There was little or no upward social mobility and the youths stayed in almost the same spot at the bottom of the class pile. This was one of the series of contradictions in which the youths lived: made to work at school for qualifications which were to have little meaning in a context of proliferating unemployment; taught to regard work as central to one's life interests and intrinsically meaningful when in actuality it was dull and monotonous; made to aim for educational and occupational ideals the overwhelming majority were destined never to achieve; persuaded to ignore the colour of one's own and other's skin when it became increasingly clear that this could be the single biggest disadvantaging factor facing one and inhibiting one's progress.

Sarup put this series of contradictions into its proper perspective when he wrote: 'If after ''fifteen thousand hours'' at school there is no job, the usefulness of schooling and the nature of society will be increasingly questioned' (1982, p. 31). In fact, this comment has an even sharper edge when we take into account Cross's analysis which shows that in terms of their chances of getting a job, 'the *relative* position of young blacks is better at lower rather than higher levels of skills' (1982b, p. 25).

Out of these contradictions grew a fresh consciousness quite unlike the first generation's. The ideology of inequality was shattered; in fact, it was displaced by the theory of Babylon which offered a far more plausible and satisfactory view of reality. It also fuelled the postures of defiance and the actions of rejection. There emerged a new brand of ethnicity: blacks felt united; they shared a common low class position compounded by skin colour that was devalued. But this was no passive ethnicity: it was ethnicity forged in action. The awareness of shared interests and common futures did not prompt a withdrawal and the effort to establish ethnic enclaves as sources of comfort and support as they did when the basic inequality was in some degree accepted. The present situation was repulsed in a dramatic display of mutual identification and mass action. The action was that of a disadvantaged working-class subgroup which attracted the interests and supports of other groups, and of people designated racial and inferior — and beginning to feel it and wanting to get rid of that feeling. Youths' expectations had changed from those of their parents, but there had been no corresponding change in conditions.

We stated earlier that there is no meaningful way of defining ethnicity apart from its being a reflection of 'the positive tendencies of identification and inclusion' and the various forms it has taken in the UK bears this out. In the instances we have chosen, the ethnic responses were related to working-class groups without any power over their immediate material circumstances. For all the changes occurring over a 35-year span, that basic class position of blacks and Asians was the same.

But it's insufficient to see ethnicity as only related to class. We've tried to locate the different forms of ethnicity to changes in group conciousness and social condition. Early conditions as experienced by migrants permitted postures of only limited visibility. The ethnic forms were designed more for promoting cohesion, solidarity and comfort, though the later industrial disputes, particularly amongst Asians, and the very brief and ill-fated spurt of American-style black power in the 1960s, attests to their potential in providing bases for action. The more pronounced actions came in the mid-1970s and 1980s, when the Rasta phenomenon erupted and the 1981 riots signalled the complete rejection of society and its values by the second generation, which was eventually abetted by similarly disposed white working-class youth.

This is not to argue that all white working-class youths were inclined to join blacks: a great many were avowedly anti black. They were the modern equivalent of a centuries-old racist tradition. In the next chapter, we will investigate this tradition.

Further reading

Shattering Illusions: West Indians in British Politics is by Trevor Carter (1986), formerly chair of the Caribbean Teachers' Association and member of Lord Swann's committee. It chronicles in the most vivid way the black struggle in the UK since the 1950s and points to an alliance between the black community and the labour movement as the most viable strategy to combat inequalities. Carter insists, however, that 'Socialism as our goal must underwrite that alliance'.

There Ain't No Black in the Union Jack by Paul Gilroy (1987) is a collection of arguments on the class position of black youth in modern Britain. One of the key theses is that 'orthodox' Marxist accounts are inadequate and that a more fluid conception of the relationship between 'race' and class is needed — neither being a fixed category. The author links this to an analysis of young blacks, who, he argues, have been 'criminalized' and depicted as lawless. The book's central chapter is a long, detailed account of reggae.

Multi-Racist Britain is edited by Philip Cohen and Harwant Bains (1988) and includes somewhat dated contributions from John Solomos, Paul Gilroy, Errol Lawrence and Tuku Mukherjee. However, reflections on the political activism of Asian youth in Southall, West London in response to racist attacks and murders, and Trevor Griffiths' appraisal of the antiracist orientation of his play, *Oi! for England* are of particular historical interest. Without doubt, the volume is dominated by Cohen's analysis of what he calls the 'multidimensionality' of racism in the UK. In this detailed and complex exploration of various modern-day expressions of racism, Cohen suggests that education from the perspective of cultural studies offers some hope for the realization of antiracist goals.

Black Culture, White Youth by Simon Jones (1988) focuses on 'the impact of Jamaican popular culture and music on the lives of young white people'. Based on interviews with young whites in inner-city Birmingham this book's argument is that there is a growing 'convergence of experience between black and white youth in certain — particularly inner city — areas of urban Britain'. Reggae and rasta provide young whites with a language and 'symbolism of rebellion', according to the author.

A Pakistani Community in Britain by Alison Shaw (1988) illustrates the 'marked continuity' between life in Britain and life in Pakistan for a small section of Oxford's Pakistani population. This continuity has particular relevance for young women who get less access to training and employment opportunities and to whom marriage is central. Continuities are also apparent in **The Puerto Ricans: Born in the USA** by Clara Rodriguez (1989) which also takes a qualitative approach to the study of ethnicity, whilst paying due attention to the history and heritage of the minority group of its title.

8
Massacres — conspiracies — fascists

- How does racism blend with a vision of a perfect future?
- What organizations are based on the principle of white supremacy?
- Is there a Jewish conspiracy to rule the world?
- What is the meaning of 'Oi'?
- What does the burning cross symbolize?

The fascist revival

Bologna, Italy, 1 August 1980. It starts with a bomb explosion in a railway station waiting room: eighty-five people are killed, over 260 injured. Eight weeks later, another bomb blast, this time at the entrance of the Munich beer festival in Germany: thirteen people are killed and 300 others are injured. The following week sees another bomb go off outside a Parisian synagogue: four people die, a further twenty are injured. All three are massacres and follow a pattern which warns of an intensification of fascist activity. In the Bologna and Paris cases, fascist groups claim responsibility. But the pattern does not apply only to Europe.

Two years before the Bologna explosion in Greensboro, USA, there was a monstrous episode at an anti-Ku Klux Klan rally. A group of adults and children listened as a guitarist sang freedom songs, before the arrival of a nine-car cavalcade of white Klansmen and American Nazi Party members. The intruders unloaded their weapons from the boot of one of the cars and coolly advanced on the rally. They opened fire for 88 seconds and left as calmly as they arrived. Four white men and a black woman, all members of the Communist Workers Party, were left dead. Interestingly, 35 per cent of the population of Greensboro are black; when six people were brought to trial for murder, every jury member was white.

FASCISM
A political doctrine based, in part, on the belief in the racial superiority of white peoples. Its influences in the nineteenth century are varied: Darwin, Gobineau, Chamberlain, Spengler; but the philosopher Nietzsche was most important in promoting the idea of an elite group of men destined to rule; his basic anti-Christian tenet was: 'men are not equal'. He saw a reign of violence and terror which was to come true with the advent of Hitler, whose Nazism was an embodiment of fascist doctrines. One of the political visions of fascism is the complete totalitarian state with every facet of society tightly controlled. (See chapter 1, section on 'All great civilizations . . . ')

'A few years ago', wrote Michael Billig in 1978, 'one could be forgiven for thinking that fascism was essentially a historical problem' (1987, p. 1). The growth of fascist organizations throughout Europe, the USA, Australia, parts of Latin America and Southern Africa, even Japan, demonstrates, however, that fascism is no longer a curious relic of the past. Despite the enormous setback which fascists received with the defeat of Hitler and Nazism at the end of World War II, fascism has re-emerged in the 1970s and 1980s on an international scale and with regenerated vigour (Wilkinson, 1981).

Nor has the UK been immune from this recent fascist revival. The growth in popularity of organizations such as the National Front (NF) in the 1970s and, more recently, the British Movement (BM), has presaged a dramatic escalation in the physical intimidation particularly of the black and South Asian communities in Britain but also of Jews and left wing groups and their sympathizers. After discussions with the All-party Joint Committee against Racialism in February 1981, the Home Secretary, William Whitelaw, called for a Home Office investigation into the incidence of 'racial attacks' in selected areas of England and Wales (1981). On the basis of evidence submitted by the relevant police forces the Home Office reported that the propaganda of fascist groups 'is a crucial element in creating the climate in which a minority of people find it fashionable to engage in overt displays of violent racialism, or overt displays which could lead to racial conflict'. Nevertheless, 'the study has not found unequivocally that right wing extremist groups have played the primary role in organising racial attacks' (1981, pp. 30–1).

The Home Office's conclusions about the role of fascist groups in orchestrating violence in the UK differs, however, from those offered by other sources. In January 1982, for instance, the anti-fascist magazine, *Searchlight*, detailed the rise of convictions for violence among members and supporters of the NF and BM between 1979–81 while certain TV programmes and

PROPAGANDA
Information and similar materials to be disseminated amongst a general population which are designed to influence that populations' views and ideas. Usually, most effective when administered through a system of communication under the control of a single dictator, who is most able to impose his own ideas on his populace. Hitler's consolidation of power in Nazi Germany was facilitated by Goebbels's brilliant use of often false or bizarre information to influence his followers and change their ideas to suit his own.

newspapers have exposed the paramilitary activities of these organizations. A more realistic appraisal of the situation then, would seem to be that of Francesca Klug who, on behalf of the Runnymede Trust, submitted evidence on this subject to the Greater London Council Police Committee.

> There is clear evidence of links between fascist and neo-fascist organisations in Britain and racial and political violence, whether it is through direct involvement in gun-trafficking (sic) and paramilitary training, or through the publishing of overtly racist material liable to incite acts of violence, including the listing of names and addresses of 'enemies' who are later attacked. Furthermore members and supporters of such groups have been convicted of serious acts of racist violence (1982, p. 20).

Of course, violence of this nature is not a peculiarly recent phenomenon in the UK but can be traced back at least as far as the eleventh century when, as a consequence of the Norman invasion in 1066, a relatively large Jewish community came to settle in Britain (Nicholson, 1974). This was soon followed by their harassment, intimidation and, in some notable cases, mass murder. For instance, after the coronation of Richard I in 1189, thirty Jews were massacred in a riot in London. Seventy-three years later, 700 London Jews were said to have been killed and their property plundered by rioters. But 'Jew-baiting' as it came to be called culminated in Britain in 1290 when Edward I 'confiscated their bonds and most of their other belongings and banished them', according to Kiernan (1978, p. 27). Jew-baiting is only one facet of the anti-immigrant feelings which have persisted throughout British history however. As Josiah Wedgewood MP put it in a parliamentary speech in 1919:

> Generally speaking, aliens are always hated by the people of this country. Usually speaking, there has been a mob which has been opposed to them, but that mob has always had leaders in high places. The Flemings were persecuted and hunted, and the Lombards were

hunted down by the London mob. Then it was the turn of the French protestants. I think the same feeling holds good on the subject today. You always have a mob of entirely uneducated people who will hunt down foreigners, and you will always have people who will make use of the passion of the mob in order to get their own ends politically (quoted in Foot, 1965, p. 106).

The occasion of his speech was the proposed extension of the 1914 Aliens Restriction Act which he saw as an appeasement to an openly anti-alien campaign which had raged in Britain since the 1890s. There were a number of dimensions to the campaign: the bulk of the working class feared that migrant labour would be used to depress wage levels and be employed as blacklegs during strikes. There were also fears, which had been exacerbated by the Great War and its spy mania, that an unrestrained entry of foreigners would threaten the security of the country. But, there was also a definite anti-Jewish bias to the campaign with frequent allusions to an alleged Jewish conspiracy (Holmes, 1979). Intimidating immigrants and resenting their presence when your own livelihood is threatened is, in some senses, quite a rational response. These practices and feelings were often ill-defined and without a plan. On occasion, however, they can acquire a shape and clarity and become augmented to a vision of the future in which social conditions will be appreciably improved. Movements based upon a determination to rid societies of what their members consider to be outsiders and to restore some solidity and structure to society prosper under the type of conditions that existed in the first two decades of the twentieth century.

The ideas of race as interpreted by such figures as Gobineau, Chamberlain and Spengler had swept across Europe: the myth of a race of supreme white beings was gaining currency and policies for purifying that race by removing or even eliminating perceived outsiders were being seriously entertained — particularly in Germany, as we saw in Chapter 2. It was in this climate that one of the first significant UK fascist groups sprang up: the organization called 'The Britons' was founded in July 1919 by Henry Hamilton Beamish as 'a society to protect the birthright of Britons and to eradicate Alien influences from our politics and industries' (quoted in Lebzeiter, 1980, p. 41). The organization was openly anti-Semitic and like many of its more notable successors invoked the bogus *Protocols of the Learned Elders of Zion* to sustain and lend credibility to accusations of an international Jewish conspiracy.

The Britons' bizarre conception of reality could be reduced to this obsessive belief in the Jewish conspiracy, and one of its main functions was to disseminate anti-Semitic literature, including the notorious *Protocols*, a role which one of its offshoots, the Britons Publishing Society, continues today.

PROTOCOLS OF THE LEARNED ELDERS OF ZION
A mythical text which has consistently sustained and lent credibility to the fascist belief in an international Jewish conspiracy. It purports to be the minutes of a secret meeting of Jews held in the early years of the twentieth century in which plans for world domination are outlined. It was first published in Russia in 1903 and appeared in Britain about fifteen years later under the title *The Jewish Peril*. It remains the classic anti-Semitic text.

All in all, however, neither Beamish nor the Britons played a particularly important role in the development of British fascism. Far more influential in this context were Oswald Mosley who, having switched from Conservative to the Labour party in the 1920s, then formed the British Union of Fascists (BUF) in 1932, and Arnold Leese whose crude ideas about 'racial fascism' were embodied in the Imperial Fascist League (IFL) which he formed in 1929. In their different ways, Mosley and Leese provided the ideological inspiration and training ground for the organizations and personalities which came to dominate post-war British fascism.

Until fairly recently, the influence of Leese on British fascism has been largely overlooked and attention has been focused instead on Mosley and the BUF (see for example Benewick, 1972; Cross, 1961; Skidelsky, 1981). This is understandable: Mosley was a much more charismatic leader than Leese, his theories of fascism were more palatable to the British public and therefore made a much greater impact on public consciousness in the 1930s; and, consequently, he attracted considerably greater support. Although he never revealed the precise number of members in the BUF, Robert Benewick mentions a number of sources which estimate that, at its peak in the mid-1930s, it attracted between 20–40,000 (1972, p. 110). Like the NF and, even more so, the BM, Mosley's BUF tended to attract young people of all social classes. Why? Well, part of the reason may have been the attraction of the BUF uniform — black shirts — and the organization's frequent and violent confrontations, such as the one which took place in Cable Street in London's East End in October 1936, when anti-fascists prevented Mosley and a contingent of around 3,000 Blackshirts from marching through this area containing a significant Jewish population (Deakin, 1978). Important as these factors may have been in attracting youngsters to the BUF, Mosley's biographer, Robert Skidelsky, suggests that the appeal to youth went much deeper; fascism:

> claimed to stand for the new world against the old, for the future against the past. The division of politics between the pre-war and the post-war was central to Mosley's appeal. *Theirs* was the generation

that had muddled the nation into war and depression; *theirs* was the world of mediocrity and respectability, of the pot-belly and the bowler hat. Arise and come into your own was Mosley's message to the youth of England and it evoked a response (1981, p. 318).

Compared to the BUF, Leese's IFL was small fry in terms of the membership and publicity it attracted and, throughout its life, it remained confined to the fringes of British politics. Indeed, one of the reasons why Leese was so hostile to Mosley was because he suspected, probably rightly, that Mosley had attracted many potential IFL followers. But there were other reasons for this animosity: some were personal — Leese believed, for instance, that Mosley was 'a political adventurer', an assessment he made of Mosley when the New Party (the precursor of the BUF) was founded in 1931, suggests John Morell (1980, p. 58).

Much more important to this rivalry were the profound intellectual differences between Leese and Mosley. Leese was much closer to Beamish in his detestations of Jews and dependence on the *Protocols*; as Robert Gorman explains, to say that Leese hated the Jews 'is understating the case; he despised, loathed and feared them with pathological intensity' (1977, p. 67). The following extract from an undated IFL handout distributed in the mid-1930s demonstrates the veracity of this point. Under the sub-heading 'The Jewish Evil', it says:

> Owing to lack of statesmanship in the past and to the ignorance of our politicians on racial realities, our civilisation has become Judaised; in every strategic position we find a Jew, Bolshevism, the League of Nations and the Gold Standard are his weapons, and Democracy his stupid victims. The power of Jewish Money has been able to maintain a conspiracy of silence on this subject which the Imperial Fascist League is breaking down.

Further, Leese insisted that race was the basis of all politics and maintained that the races were placed in a strict hierarchical order in which the Aryan race was superior: 'the sole creators of civilization' who 'were chiefly responsible for the progress of mankind'. In this respect, he was clearly influenced by the theories of Chamberlain, who we discussed in chapter 2. As Britain was the most Aryan according to Leese, it was superior to all other European nations and the sole objective of British politics 'should be the preservation and expansion of the dominance of the white Aryan race at home and in the Empire . . . racial mixing was to be avoided at all costs' (Gorman, 1977, pp. 66–7).

Few commentators would now contest the view that anti-Semitism was an important, if often disguised feature of the BUF from the party's inception; this,

ANTI-SEMITISM
The ideology in which the Jew is seen as a demon. This entered the folklore and literature of Europe around the eleventh century. Images of the Jews as the 'devil incarnate' who used Christian blood for ritual purposes led to trials and mass expulsions from countries in the thirteenth and fourteenth centuries. In 1492, nearly 150,000 Jews were expelled from Spain. Later, this image was transformed into the Jews as controllers of a vast commercial empire: they were seen as the organizers of an intricate conspiracy — see PROTOCOLS. Anti-Semitic, or anti-Jew, theories take on a racist dimension when the Jews are depicted as a separate race who have to be exterminated (Nazism is the most obvious example of this).

despite Mosley's claim in his autobiography that: 'Anti-semitism was not our policy, for I never attacked the Jews as people' (1968, p. 336). Even so, it was not until 1934, when Mosley's popularity was receding and the party was rapidly losing the support of people such as newspaper magnate Lord Rothermere, who had used several publications to promote the BUF, that he elevated anti-Semitism to a significant position in the party's politics (Holmes, 1979, 1980). But, Leese regarded Mosley's earlier ambiguous and hesitant attitude to anti-Semitism as further proof of his contention that he was a puppet of the Jews. He dubbed Mosley's politics as 'Kosher Fascism' and nicknamed the party, the 'British Jewnion of Fascists'. He went further in April 1933 claiming that Mosley's wife, Cynthia, was the granddaughter of an American Jew!

There were also differences in their attitudes to the idea of racial purity; as we've seen, this was the organizing principle for Leese's political views while, according to Richard Thurlow, Mosley 'ridiculed the concept of a pure race' (1980, p. 109). Despite this allegation, Mosley, at one phase in the 1930s, actually championed the concept: 'We have created the Empire without race mixture or pollution . . . It should only be necessary by education and propaganda to teach the British that racial mixtures are bad' (quoted in Hayes, 1973, p. 30). However, in the next decade Mosley advocated the idea of a politically united Europe with no mention of racial purity. The vehicle for this was his Union Movement which was formally constituted in February 1948 (Mosley, 1968, pp. 432–46).

It is clear that 1934 had been the watershed for Mosley's political ambitions: on 7 June 1934 he had attracted the largest audience yet to a BUF demonstration in Olympia, London, but from then on in it was all downhill. The withdrawal of support, the escalation of violence between the Blackshirts and anti-fascists, the 'Battle of Cable Street' and subsequent passing of the Public Order Act 1936 which severely restricted the activities of the BUF, all effectively pushed Mosley into the twilight zone of British politics. By the onset of World War II, he was thoroughly discredited, a position underlined by the government's decision to intern him during the war under Defence Regulation 18b because of his anti-war propaganda and his anti-Semitism.

His final attempt to re-enter parliament came with the 1959 General Election. He chose the North Kensington constituency, which contained Notting Hill, and offered the white electorate a policy 'to repatriate immigrants to their homeland with fares paid and to fulfil the Government's pledge to buy sugar from Jamaica' (1968, p. 449). Despite his high hopes of success, Mosley gained only 8.1% of the total vote and, for the first time in his political career, forfeited his deposit.

But while Mosley's political ideas failed to attract public support after the war, his influence on the development of British fascism in the 1950s and 1960s persisted, albeit in an indirect way, via the activities of his ex-BUF colleague, A. K. Chesterton who, in 1967, was elected first chairman of the NF. The legacy of Leese's brand of fascism — 'racial fascism' — was, however, even more influential in the latest fascist revival in the UK; as Billig and Bell put it: 'Leese was supplanting Mosley as the mentor of British Fascism' (1980, p. 5).

Tilling the soil of prejudice

In chapter 3, we traced the growing importance of race as an issue in political and public debate once the British economy took a downward turn in the mid-late 1950s. By the mid-1960s, Richard Crossman, then Home Secretary in the Labour government, was recording in his diary that race had become 'the hottest political potato in Britain' (1975). We have also seen the common response of both main political parties to this dilemma, expressed simply in the phrase: keeping numbers down is good for race relations. But while this ideological and policy response may have appeased some of the 'lunatic fringes' in the House of Commons, it failed to satisfy them all; nor did it assuage the anxieties of those outside the House who had flirted with the ideas of fascism. 'The acceptance of the welfare state', writes Martin Walker, 'and the loss of India by the Conservative party, the liberal Toryism of R. A. Butler and the gathering speed with which liberal Tories were accepting a diminished British role in world affairs and a renunciation of the Empire, created something of a vacuum on the right wing of British politics' and this was filled by the League of Empire Loyalists (LEL) which was formed by A. K. Chesterton in 1954 (1977, p. 29). For the LEL the controversy over black immigration into the UK provided a focus for its activities: disrupting party political meetings throughout the 1950s. But the LEL could not legitimately be defined as a fascist organization nor did it ever seriously entertain the idea of winning mass electoral support although, at its peak in 1957, it had attracted somewhere in the region of 3,000 supporters. No, the LEL, as Neil Nugent points out, was never more than 'an adventurist, right wing, Conservative pressure group' (1980, p. 213). Its significance in the fascist revival was as a training ground for some of the personalities who were later to emerge as leading lights of the NF and other fascist groups: John Tyndall, Martin Webster, John Bean, Colin Jordan and Chesterton himself.

What gave the incipient fascist revival its greatest boost in the 1950s was the violence which erupted in Nottingham and Notting Hill in 1958. Popularly referred to as 'race riots' by the media and politicians alike, the violence was presented by fascists as a foretest of the future. In fact, it's likely that the fascists, themselves, played an important role in exacerbating the tension between white and black residents and in stirring up trouble, at least in Notting Hill. On the one hand there were the activities of the National Labour Party (NLP) formed in 1958 by two dissident members of the LEL, John Tyndall and John Bean; on the other, was the White Defence League (WDL) formed a year earlier by Colin Jordan, based in Arnold Leese's House in Notting Hill and supported financially by Leese's widow. Both organizations flooded the district with anti-black, racial nationalist leaflets and pamphlets. One of the WDL's most widely distributed leaflets read:

> The National Assistance Board pays the children's allowances to the blacks for the coffee coloured monstrosities they father, regardless of whether they are legitimate or illegitimate. Material rewards are given to enable semi-savages to mate with the women of one of the leading civilized nations of the world (quoted in Walker, 1977, pp. 33–4).

The amalgamation of the NLP and the WDL and the formation of the British National Party (BNP) under the leadership of Jordan in 1960 effectively marked the start of the fascist revival in post-war Britain. The largest and most significant of the fascist groups 'tilling the soil of prejudice throughout the 1960s' prior to the NF's formation in 1967 were all offshoots of the BNP (Hall *et al.*, 1978, p. 334; for a diagrammatic simplification of all British fascist parties, see Troyna, 1982b, p. 263). The BNP's ideology and that of many of its more auspicious successors, owed much to the racial fascism of Leese. It accepted the basic fascist principle of white supremacy and geared itself up to the future restoration of the white race as unassailable leaders of the world. The lyrics of the BNP's favourite song, 'Britain Awake', illustrate these points well:

> We are the front fighters of the BNP,
> True to our soil and people we will be.
> Red Front and Jewry will finally fall;

Our race and nation will smash them all.
(Quoted in Walker, 1977, p. 36).

But the BNP wasn't to last very long, at least in its originally constituted form. Both Jordan and Tyndall's infatuation with Hitler's National Socialist brand of fascism intensified and a paramilitary organization called 'Spearhead' was formed within the organization while members dressed up in uniforms and engaged in 'field exercises'. On 19 June 1962, Tyndall told *The Guardian* that the BNP aimed to 'get power with whatever means are favourable' and that 'we are recruiting the best types to be trained as leaders and are not after an elusive mass following'. The move towards explicit Nazism precipitated a split with Bean and Andrew Fountaine and on 20 April 1962 — Hitler's birthday — Jordan and Tyndall formed the National Socialist Movement; within two years Tyndall had left to form the Greater Britain Movement, another neo-Nazi group which aimed to make National Socialism 'more British'.

Now, none of these organizations really made much impact on public consciousness; in fact, as we've seen, some of them never really intended to. Both independently and collectively they were no more than pimples on the body politic appealing to very few people and vilified by both the media and politicians. The rejection of these parties is understandable: despite the growing anti-black feelings in the UK in the late 1950s and 1960s and the disullusion which many people felt over the way the main parties were dealing with immigration, few people were willing to join an organization which, through the parties' own propaganda and through exposés in various newspapers, embraced the ideas and tactics of Nazism. After all, it was these very ideas which had plunged the UK into a world war and led to the deaths of millions of people less than a generation before. Essentially, it was the failure of fascism to secure a toe-hold in UK politics which precipitated the decision of its leading ideologues to unify their individual organizations into a coherent, and electorally acceptable, party: in early 1967 the NF was born. But, although the initial merger of disparate groups had deliberately excluded John Tyndall's Greater Britain Movement because of the latter's extremism, the resistance was short-lived and the GBM was incorporated as one of the constituent groups of the nascent party in November 1967. 'The merging of the few genuine patriotic organisations in this country into the National Front', announced David Fraser-Harris, chairman of the NF National Council at the party's inaugural meeting, 'is in my opinion the most encouraging and significant event of the past decade' (*Spearhead*, no. 17, p. 5). It was an opinion echoed by the NF's first chairman, A. K. Chesterton, at the same meeting: 'The true motive is to ensure that the National Front is taken seriously as an acceptable challenge to the political parties that have brought the once proud name of Britain into the mire to be spat upon from one end of the world to the other. It is my determination and that of my colleagues that the National Front shall be taken seriously' (*Spearhead*, no. 17, p. 6).

On the face of it, however, Chesterton's ambitions for the insurgent party were irreconcilable with the brand of racial fascism and National Socialism which some of his leading members, especially Tyndall and Webster, had been espousing in the past: and Chesterton recognized this from the beginning, hence his initial reluctance to invite the GBM contingent to amalgamate with the NF. In one of the earlier planning meetings in 1966, Chesterton had insisted that there was no question of bringing into the merger 'those who wanted to relive the Nazi daydream' and Bean of the BNP had agreed; he assure the BNP Council in 1966 that 'Mr. Tyndall's group would not be coming into the new movement and that their past utterances on anti-semitism and pro-Nazism would most certainly not be part of NF policy' (quoted in Walker, 1977, p. 65). But Tyndall and Webster and the rest of the GBM were 'in' and from the outset it became clear that something had to give. Within four years, Chesterton had been forced to resign and his successor as chairman, John O'Brien, went the same way a year later. Their views on the party's development during its first five years are revealing. As Chesterton put it:

> I had had more than enough, after four years of stamping out nonsense such as plots to set fire to synagogues. Two per cent of the members of the National Front are really evil men — so evil that I placed intelligence agents to work exploring their backgrounds, with results so appalling that I felt obliged to entrust the documents to the vaults of a bank. Some of these men are at present placed close to the centre of things (quoted in Cockerell, 1972, p. 88).

O'Brien's version was substantially the same:

> There is a small caucus working within the National Front attracted by the trappings and ideologies of foreign nationalisms from the past. These persons see Britain's future best served by her becoming a rigidly administered, authoritarian police state. They sought to use me as a docile puppet behind whose respectability they could operate from the shadows (ibid.).

The resignation of O'Brien in 1972 left the way open for Tyndall to assume the chairmanship of the NF and with Webster as its National Activities Organizer — a position that he'd held since 1969 — it meant that the two leading lights of the neo-Nazi GBM had within five years effectively assumed control of the party. Under Tyndall and Webster, the NF made a sustained effort at impression management; that is, to present a respectable, and therefore

---

REACTIONARY
The political reflex that opposes change and harkens back to some past stage of society when things were supposedly better. The antagonism against immigrants and the wish to have social conditions restored to what they were before the 'alien presence' typifies this.

---

acceptable, alternative political programme to the British electorate. After all, Tyndall had not entirely eschewed the notion of parliamentary democracy as a means of securing power and, in his public writings and speeches, he emphasized that this was the only legitimate path to follow. What's more, both Tyndall and Webster repeatedly explained their earlier involvement in the NSM and GBM as an ephemeral and youthful phase of their lives. 'Fresh-faced exuberance' is how Tyndall put it in an interview in the *Sunday Telegraph* (2 October, 1977). But could they do otherwise when the party was entering candidates in local, by- and General Elections? A more serious investigation into Tyndall's ideology as shown by his lesser known writings and speeches reveals that he saw parliamentary democracy only as an option, and not necessarily the best option: 'Good government', he wrote in 1976, 'can sometimes take a democratic and sometimes an authoritarian form' (quoted in Troyna, 1982b, p.264. See also Billig, 1978 and Fielding, 1981).

Nor, as a number of commentators have conclusively shown, did Tyndall, or the NF under his leadership, radically depart from Leese's ideology: the ideas of racial nationalism, the international Jewish/Zionist conspiracy, the doctrine of biological determinism all became part of the ideological armoury of the NF (Billig, 1978; Edgar, 1977; Taylor, 1982). It's true that these beliefs were not often revealed in the party literature distributed to passers-by on street corners; in publications such as *Britain First* such ideas were veiled, if only thinly (Billig, 1978, pp. 172–80). But more systematic evaluations of the party's ideology and a detailed scrutiny of its literature and propaganda revealed the enduring influence of Leese and corroborated Morell's claim that: 'Modern racialists have been able to draw on Leese's theories and use them with only minor modifications for the more topical problem of black immigration' (1980, p. 71).

In common with the National Socialist Party in Germany in the 1920s and 1930s the NF adopted a 'two track' strategy to ensure publicity and hence public awareness of its existence. On the one hand, this involved electoral intervention; only very occasionally, however, did this reap rewards. In the West Bromwich by-election in May 1973, for example, Webster became the party's first, and so far only, candidate to retain his electoral deposit by obtaining 16.2 per cent of the votes. In all, 4,789 people voted for him. The NF was ecstatic: 'once and for all' read the special supplement in *Spearhead* in July 1973, it 'put an end to any doubts about the potential of the National Front as a political force in Britain'. In fact, it didn't: the party failed to capture either the imagination or the votes of the electorate in the two 1974 General Elections and the nearest it came to repeating the West Bromwich 'success' was in the May 1976 Leicester district council elections, when it came within sixty-two votes of having its first city councillor. Election results simply did not support the NF's claim to being the 'fastest growing party in Britain', a point well illustrated by its disastrous performance in the 1979 General Elections when all its 303 candidates lost their deposits and its share of the total vote in seats contested was only 1.3 per cent. Perhaps the best indication of the party's false optimism of the mid-1970s came in the Dover and Deal constituency where it received less votes than the joke entry from the Silly Party!

But if electoral intervention didn't have much of a pay-off, the NF's decision to organize public meetings and demonstrations did, at least in terms of attracting media and public attention. These were often volatile occasions: during the NF's demonstration in Red Lion Square in June 1974, for example, Kevin Gately, a Warwick University Student and anti-NF protestor became 'the first man to be killed in any political demonstation in England, Scotland or Wales since 1919', according to Richard Clutterbuck (1980, p. 158; see also Gilbert, 1975). A little less than five years later, on 23 April 1979, a London teacher, Blair Peach, was killed as anti-fascists tried to break up a pre-General Election meeting of the NF in Southall. The provocative intrusions of the NF into areas containing large black, South Asian and Jewish populations during the 1970s had similarly spectacular, if not fatal consequences: Haringey and Lewisham in London, the Ladywood district of Birmingham and Manningham Lane in Bradford all provided the settings for violent and bloody clashes between the NF, police and anti-fascists. The imperative for the party in staging these events was clear as Webster noted in *Spearhead* in March 1977. Under the heading 'ACTIVISM — The spirit that built the National Front', Webster insisted: 'Our marches and the increasingly viscous Red counter-demonstrations created yet more publicity, and every march resulted in new Branches, new members'. He continued: 'As a result of the constant publicity achieved by our Activists the NF grew to be a mass movement which is now able to put more emphasis on the real work of any genuine political party: *elections*'.

As we've seen, this complementary aspect of the Front's 'two-track' strategy failed dismally and, by the end of the 1970s, the party was in complete disarray. The 1979 General Election results had led to the surfacing of bitter internal recriminations which, in turn, provoked a series of breakaway movements including the New National Front formed by Tyndall in June 1980, after he had failed to secure support from the NF's directorate for the autocratic powers he demanded. By then, party leaders had drastically re-thought their recruitment campaign strategy: 'Now that the General Election has come and gone, we in the National Front have entered a new phase — a new situation', claimed Tyndall in his final speech as chairman to the NF's Annual General Meeting in 1979 (*Spearhead*, November 1979). What the new phase entailed we come on to next.

Young bulldogs

The 'new phase' was spelled out in the NF Members' Bulletin (July 1980):

> If it is true that the National Front has no hope of gaining power under conditions that are stable — economically, socially and politically — we should not be preoccupied with making ourselves more 'respectable' under present conditions. We must appreciate that the 'image' that we have been given by the media and which may well lose us some potential support today, will be a positive asset when the streets are beset by riots, when unemployment soars, and when inflation gets beyond the present degree of minimal control.

In other words: 'Having failed in the long haul to credibility, the obvious option was to concentrate on the more immediate politics of intimidation and agitation' (Murdock and Troyna, 1981, p. 9). The target for this new strategy was youth, especially young working-class males and the settings were the traditional leisure-time arenas for these youngsters: football grounds, rock concerts, inner city streets and so on.

This attempt to mobilize youth was not a totally new venture for the NF, however. In June 1977, the party launched its youth wing, the Young National Front (YNF), and teenage-orientated newspaper, *Bulldog*. The following year saw the start of the party's schools campaign and the publication of *How to Spot a Red Teacher* and *How to Combat a Red Teacher*. The party seemed to be on strong ground in this strategy with survey after survey in the late 1970s showing that actual and potential support for the NF was extensive amongst youth; for example, Martin Harrop and his colleagues had shown that by 1977–8, just over half of its supporters were under 34 years old and 21 per cent were aged between 15 and 20 (Harrop, England and Husbands, 1980. See also, Taylor, 1978; Weir, 1978). 'Young, ungifted and white' is how Harrop and Zimmerman (1977) described the 'ideal-typical' NF supporter and despite the fact that the YNF campaign didn't amount to much there seemed good reason for the NF to declare in May 1977, that it was 'clearly capturing the young vote' and that : 'Before very long, the National Front will acquire a virtual monopoly of the

---

Oi
**The name for what might be called the skinhead philosophy of the 1980s;
it involves a neo-Nazi repulsion of perceived outsiders, particularly Asians
and, most importantly, a virulent preservation of ancient white working-
class traditions. The slogan for a style of racist music performed by
skinhead bands.**

---

young vote, especially the 18 year olds casting their first votes. At the same
time, a new generation will be maturing which already feels nothing in common
with the old parties' (*Spearhead*, May, 1977).

By the time the 1979 General Election was over and done with, the appeal
to youth had gained increasing urgency — the life of the party depended on it.
By then it had found a new threat and competitor for youth with the rise of the
British Movement, a direct descendant of the National Socialist Movement
formed by Jordan in 1968. In the mid-1970s, the BM had hit rock bottom:
Jordan had resigned after being found guilty of shop-lifting from a departmental
store, active membership was hovering around the fifty mark and it had little
money to produce leaflets or pamphlets. Jordan was replaced by Michael
McLaughlin in 1975 and, under his leadership, the party was invigorated:
membership rose to about 3,000 by 1981 as the party 'sought to exploit the
(reborn) skinhead youth culture by emphasising the sympathetic components of
its own ideology, like racism and territorial exclusivity' (Taylor, 1981b, p. 539).

Although some writers, like Dick Hebdige, reckon that the political links
between the skinhead and the BM/NF have been exaggerated, these movements
did unquestionably prosper from the strong anti-Asian feelings prevalent
amongst some sectors of working-class youth in the early 1980s (1981, p. 40).
Simon Frith believed this so because the BM/NF ' "politics" involve little more
than a legitimating gloss on the skins' existing activities — defending territory,
dressing in uniform, hitting strangers and women' (1981, p. 5). The skinhead
philosophy and its resonances with the BM/NF stance are neatly captured by
Trevor Griffiths in his play, *Oi! For England*, the title of which derives from the
skinhead's own brand of music called 'Oi!'. One of the skinheads in the play
justifies his attack on an Asian:

> I'm WHITE. I'm proud of it. I think it's the best thing ter be . . . I
> ain't tekin' second place to no niggers 'n' Yids in me own country'
> (1982, p. 29).

The so-called paki-bashing episodes took on new dimensions in 1982 when
unprovoked skinhead attacks resulted in two Asian deaths through stabbings,
both incidents happening in the trouble-torn Midlands city of Coventry.

Although the skinheads have been castigated as social menaces, writers of quite different political persuasions see them as little more than caricatures of older working-class generations. For example, the NF publication *Nationalism Today* theorized:'Skinheads share many of the attitudes of their parents, but with the difference that they do not have the old political loyalties of their parents, and they are also willing to act' (April, 1982, p. 1). Hebdige sees them in the same light, standing for:

> A way of life, a set of values and attitudes which, according to some social historians, did not emerge until the late 19th century when the British Empire was at its most powerful when imperialism, nationalism and Toryism were beginning to figure prominently in the language of the pubs and the music halls (1981, p. 40).

We might even see the skinhead revival as white ethnicity in an atmosphere of rising unemployment, which, as we have seen, can generate feelings of hostility and anger towards perceived outsiders and result in the process of scapegoating discussed in chapter 2.

These, then, are the main tendencies of fascism in modern times. They have taken on different forms, but retained the basic racist-elitist impulse. The various groups' members have sought to further this impulse with obvious and visible displays of hostility towards their perceived enemies. Yet there are other, far less visible, we might say subterranean, movements equally fascist in their aims and philosophies, yet preferring to operate at more covert levels. By far the most important of these grew out of the turbulence of post-bellum America; its effects were still being felt in the States and the UK over 100 years after its birth. We now look at its development.

KKK: the invisible empire

Freed slaves of the southern states of America were reputedly superstitious people. So when they encountered white-robed hooded horsemen in the middle of the night, they took them to be the ghosts of confederate soldiers killed in the American War of Independence. In fact, the night riders were members of an underground resistance movement who were alarmed at the effects of Emancipation and wanted to frighten the ex-slaves back into working the plantations. According to William Randel, the riders would arouse terrified blacks in the night and bid them to shake hands, extending a skeleton's arm from beneath their robe (1965, p. 9). The resistance took on more sinister dimensions when the night riders burned down blacks' homes and engaged in ritualistic lynchings.

The end of the American Civil War in 1865 meant that four million blacks were suddenly granted the legal and social rights southern whites had felt to be exclusively their own. Slave labour was at an end. In the same year, six men formed an organization, taking its name from the Greek word for band or circle, *kuklos*, and adapting the Scottish concept of clan to make the Ku Klux Klan. At various stages in its development thereafter, the KKK opposed blacks, Jews, Catholics and Mormons whilst retaining one constant; as Randel points out: 'the one continuing underlying principle of the Klan is the preservation of white supremacy' (1965, p. xiii). The Klan stood for the purity of the white Anglo-Saxon Protestant, the WASP.

As with other fascist movements, the KKK was fuelled by a vision in which a white race reigned supreme. For two hundred years of its history, America had a majority of Protestants of English descent, Anglo-Saxons. That God looked over them, protected them and designated them as the number one people was obvious, according to the KKK. It was demonstrated by their material well-being compared to the other two main groups. American Indians were subhuman savages fit only for mass extermination. Blacks were also less than human, a form of property used to relieve white men of the harder forms of labour. The myth of Anglo-Saxon superiority gained purchase over these centuries.

The movement's basic philosophy was that there was a divine plan in which the WASP was to lead. The plan had been violated by the freeing of slaves and the growing presence of Catholics. Randel quotes from a KKK manifesto:

> Our main and fundamental objective is the MAINTENANCE OF THE SUPREMACY OF THE WHITE RACE in this republic. History and Physiology teach us that we belong to a race which nature has endowed with an evident superiority over all other races, and that the Maker, in thus elevating us above the common standard of human creation, has intended to give us over inferior races a dominion from which new laws can permanently derogate. (1965, p. 15).

The methods chosen by the Klan to fulfil its aims were diverse: at the most respectable extreme it essayed in national politics (independently and through the Democratic Party) and at the other extreme, it simply annihilated people. The burning cross was the symbol of its presence, though burning of 'KKK' with acid onto the foreheads of blacks was another way of establising terror.

From the 1920s, the movement acquired an organizational structure mainly through the influence of William Simmons. Ostensibly, it took on the form of a secret society, much like the Freemasons with their lodges. The Klan developed a network of communication throughout the USA and a hierarchy, the head of which was the Imperial Wizard. Among those under his command were Grand

Dragons, Grand Titans and Lictors (the Roman title for executioners, later adopted by Mussolini). Collectively, the membership became known as the Invisible Empire.

The new organization gained impetus in the 1920s and Randel somehow estimates that, at this time, 5 million people were affiliated (1965, p. xiii). It may sound an exaggerated total, but this was a time when racism was rife and hostility to the new immigrants from Europe was on the increase. The Klan broadened the scope of its hostilities to encompass Jews, Catholics and, basically, anyone who didn't conform to the WASP. Charles Alexander writes of the southern branches in the period: 'The Klan was only doing what the regional majority wanted — preserving the American way of life as White Southerners defined it' (1965, p. xiii).

In fact, it was widely regarded as a positive moral force and this image was fostered with philanthropic activities and church-like rituals. Support was gained through charity appeals, aiding widows and so on. By the end of the 1920s, Alexander reasons, it was far too complex and far-reaching 'to be dismissed as representing the antics of a few on the lunatic fringe' (1965, p. 106).

The persistence and virulence of the Klan in the States is evidenced by the Greensboro massacre we described at the start of this chapter; though perhaps its most famous atrocity was in 1963 when it was responsible for a bomb attack on a church in Birmingham, Alabama, in which four black girls were killed; its American membership today is difficult to establish simply because it maintains its status as a secret organization. International link-ups with other extremist movements are beyond doubt, as John Tomlinson, amongst others, has shown (1981, pp. 227–35).

In 1965 evidence of the Klan's presence in the UK arrived in the form of burning crosses either nailed to or laid at the doors of selected persons. *The Sunday Times* reported that a meeting in Birmingham established a British KKK with a membership of 200 (13 June 1965). Robert Shelton, the then Imperial Wizard, announced his intention to visit the UK, though he was warned off by the Home Secretary who threatened to refuse him entry. The Klan actually had representatives working underground in British cities for at least nine years before the burning cross incidents. A *Weiner Bulletin* report documented its operations thoughout the late 1950s (Autumn 1965). Mosley's followers disclaimed any connection with the Klan and other movements of the kind discussed in previous sections also denied any links. Jordan's British National Party threatened its members with expulsion if they had anything to do with what it called 'this childish organization'. But there was nothing childish about the Klan's methods and in the mid-1960s it terrorized immigrants and their families in many British cities.

The next 'hard' evidence of the Klan in Britain came via a *News of the World* exposé. 'Britain is ready for us', announced Bill Wilkinson, the Imperial Wizard from Louisiana in 1978 (1 January). 'I reckon your political climate is about right'. A series of reports detailed how the KKK was gearing operations in Britain to a series of assassinations of selected politicians and community leaders. Stories of 'a secret army . . . as skilled, disciplined and trained as the crack SAS British army group' came through. Wilkinson himself illegally entered Britain in March 1978, though it seems his efforts were not particularly successful as the Klan made no impact in the 1970s comparable with its mid-1960s campaign.

However, the KKK has for long been the most infamous of secret fascist organizations in the UK. Others include the paramilitary Column 88 formed in 1970 (the two 8s signifying the eighth letter of the alphabet 'H' for 'Heil Hitler') which maintains active links with other guerrilla outfits in Europe and elsewhere. Another is the League of St. George which was started in 1974 by disaffected members of Mosley's Union Movement, who thought their former leader's brand of anti-Semitism too moderate.

Media reports, such as the *News of the World*'s KKK investigation, in their way help create new elements of race relations situations. So complex and sensitive are some areas and issues that the media's handling of particular, perhaps isolated and, at first, insignificant events, can have decisive impacts on the future shape of race relations. We will expand this argument in the next chapter.

Further Reading

The Fiery Cross by W. Craig (1987) is an analysis of the Ku Klux Klan in modern USA. Far from viewing the Klan as an aberrant organization deviating from central values and norms, the author sees it as what he calls 'an American institution'.

Immigration and Politics is the theme of a special issue of the *European Journal of Political Research* (Vol. 16, No. 6, 1988). Edited by Zig Layton-Henry it includes a paper by Christoper Husbands on the dynamics of racial exclusion and expulsion which centralizes the concept of political racism. Support for political racism according to Husbands, ebbs and flows not only in relation to attitudinal racism of the electorate but also in response to sensitivities to particular issues. His theoretical exploration of political racism is complemented by case studies of its contemporary expression in four Western European societies: France, the Federal Republic of Germany, the Netherlands and Switzerland. The journal also includes papers on the political significance of immigration in Western Europe with particular attention given to France, the Netherlands, Sweden, Austria and Switzerland.

Under Siege by Keith Thompson (1988) builds on the idea that racism as it is articulated at the highest political levels matters much more than street-level responses. 'The indigenous white working class is neither the originator nor the chief bearer of responsibility for racism', the author insists. 'At a time of heightened social tension and strengthened patriotic sentiments the "man in the street" [sic] was more anti-racist than racist. Racial ill-feeling was much more the property of politicians than of the mass of populations'. This is a rather crude polemic, but lively nonetheless.

Anatomy of Adolescence by Adrian Furnham and Barrie Gunter (1989) is based on an interpretation of their survey data about adolescents' views, leisure interests, expectations and aspirations. The authors' view that young white people are more accepting of the multicultural society and less prejudiced towards blacks than their parents were is discrepant with evidence of the accelerated growth of racist harassment in and beyond the school gates. The CRE's **Learning in Terror** (1988), for instance, gives a less sanguine perspective on contemporary 'race relations' amongst young people.

Traditions of Intolerance edited by Tony Kushner and Kenneth Lunn (1989) is subtitled 'Perspectives on fascism and race discourse in Britain'. The volume represents a selection of papers delivered at a conference in September 1987 and covers a broad range of salient topics and themes, both historical and contemporary. Roger Eatwell's 'Fascism and political racism in post-war Britain' and Christopher Husbands' chapter on racial attacks in the UK are of particular significance.

9
Media — racism — reality

- Do the media reflect or shape attitudes?
- How are colonial images portrayed in the media?
- What is the self-fulfilling prophecy?
- Did the media help or injure the NF?
- Were the media responsible for the 1981 riots?

The sambo type

Suppose one moring we have breakfast, as usual, to the accompaniment of the radio. 'We interrupt this programme to bring you a newsflash,' an announcer's voice breaks into the music. We stop eating and listen attentively. 'Groups of blacks have mounted a series of attacks on police headquarters in twelve major UK cities. This is the largest organized black offensive known in the UK: urban guerrilla tactics are being used in a spate of sustained violent assaults. Automatic guns, crude bombs and various explosive devices have been used...'.

We live in a city housing a large black population. In fact, we live adjacent to a principally black district. Suddenly, there is noise in the streets: the neighbours seem to be panicking as they rush about brandishing makeshift weapons and shouting warning to others to arm themselves. We go outside and sense a crazed atmosphere: frenzy sweeps the streets as loosely assembled gangs of whites converge on the nearby black ghetto. We are carried along with them and witness the first hostilities as blacks, expecting the confrontation, lock themselves in combat to produce mass violence.

Back home, the radio is still on, but no one is listening as the announcer apologizes for an inaccuracy in the news item: the violence broke out not in twelve but in two cities and they were not in Britain but in the little-known African state of Youké. Meanwhile, the violence continues as police riot squads arrive.

'WAR OF THE WORLDS'
A fictitious news broadcast based on the H. G. Wells novel which told of an invasion of Martians on earth. Orson Welles, the propagator of the hoax, reported the invasion over the radio network of the USA and, almost immediately, the streets filled with panic-stricken crowds; the episode points up the fact that even joke news items can have serious effects and prompt mass action.

Ridiculous? Maybe, but, when Orson Welles presented his 'War of the Worlds' broadcast to a receptive American public and announced that Martians had landed on earth, no one suspected that he was spoofing as they plunged into what amounted to mass hysteria. It's an exaggerated example to make the point that the mass media, though conventionally thought of as conveyors of news, can not only shape our perception of the world, but also affect how we behave and, therefore, in a self-fulfilling way, create realities. Riots in the streets of Britain may exist solely in the imagination of an incompetent newsreader — at first. Extreme as the example is, it's not so far removed from the actual incidents of summer 1981, when several sources blamed overzealous mediamen for amplifying the initial events in Brixton and Toxteth and starting an imitative reaction in which youths in virtually every city styled their behaviour on the media's images of burnin' and lootin' and engaged in what were called the copycat riots.

Similarly, if a respected politician who makes alarming, prophetic warnings about the future of race relations is afforded massive, sensationalist coverage by the news media he might consider the self-fulfilling factor as recommended by Quintin Hogg, who referred to Enoch Powell when he remarked: 'If one is going to say . . . that the streets of our country might one day run with blood . . . one ought to consider whether in the more immediate future, one's words were more likely to make that happen (quoted in Seymour-Ure, 1974, p. 119).

The mass media today possess an enormous capacity to change our conceptions and, ultimately, our actions and, without suggesting that hearing politicians predicting rivers of blood or slipshod newscasters announcing riots will automatically prompt us to make these happen, we can, with confidence, attribute the media with a good deal of influence on all our lives. Very few of us escape the media's effects; they transmit a large volume of information quickly, frequently and to large audiences. It's difficult to think of anyone besides a hermit insulating themselves from media of some sort; whether television, radio, newspaper or film. We are subjected to a steady but intense bombardment of

---

MASS MEDIA
In contemporary society, this term has come to refer to the vast world-wide network of visual and audial channels of communication; it includes the main media of television and radio, plus newspapers, cinema and theatre.

---

processed information that supplied the material on which we base our view of the world.

Here we aren't over-concerned with the precise degree to which the media affect us: this has been explored by others (Halloran, 1970; McQuail, 1977, for example). Suffice it to say that the media do have an impact of some sort and, while we don't assume that people are empty-headed enough to accept uncritically every scrap of information offered in print or over the airwaves, we do suggest that changes in the beliefs people have of one another and, thus, in the relationships between them are affected by the amount and quality of information they have of each other. Attitudes may be modified or confirmed, behaviour might be changed as a result of media-processed information. The media make it possible for us to scan the world, become familiar with people who are otherwise anonymous to us, participate vicariously in events with which we never have direct contact. Perhaps more significantly, the media can change the way we think and act towards people and events we have direct contact with. Consider how the Powell speeches of 1968 influenced the way many people thought about their next-door neighbours.

In the opening examples, we have deliberately mixed falsehood and fact to establish the argument that the media can actually *create* realities rather than merely reflect them. Reporting the possibility of rivers of blood can act as a catalyst in making those rivers flow. And this has a particular relevance to race relations, especially modern race relations which are lent shape and texture by the information provided by the media. Race relations situations, as we've stressed, are structured by the consciousness we have of other groups (and they of us) and the media's impact on this can be severe, as Paul Hartmann and Charles Husband found: 'it is clear that the press (and the newsmedia in general) have not merely reflected public consciousness on matters of race and colour but have played a significant part in shaping this consciousness' (1974, p. 146).

The study on which this statement is based contained both an analysis of the contents of various media and a survey of how peoples' attitudes were affected. On the first count, the investigators concluded that: 'the press has continued to project an image of Britain as a *white* society in which the coloured population is seen as some kind of aberration, a problem, or just an oddity' (1974, p. 145).

On the second, they found that, although 'the heavy consumption of the mass media does not in itself lead to greater or less hostility towards coloured people,' it does reinforce attitudes: 'peoples' attitudes, which are to a large extent a function of whether they live in an "immigrant area" or not, affect the way they *interpret* media material' (1974, p. 94). So that, if a person in a high immigrant area has a negative attitude towards blacks, they have available in the media material that will strengthen their attitudes rather than completely shape them. Alternatively, people who lives in areas which have not experienced the infusion of migrants — areas, for example, such as Devon, East Anglia or Cumbria — are even more likely to rely on the media for information about the size and nature of the migrant communities and their children and for interpretations of the relationship between these communities and the white population.

This dependence on the media was put into perspective by Otto Kerner and his colleagues during their attempts to tease out the effect of the media on the 1967 riots in the USA. They found 'a significant imbalance between what actually happened in our cities and what the newspaper, radio and television coverage of the riots told us what happened' (1968, p. 363). This discrepancy between what had taken place and the media's version of reality led the commissioners to say:

> Lacking other sources of information, we formed our original impressions and beliefs from what we saw on television, heard on radio, and read in newspapers and magazines. We are deeply concerned that millions of other Americans, who must rely on the mass media, likewise formed incorrect impressions and judgements about what went on in many American cities last summer (1968, p. 363).

The influence of the media, therefore, cannot be dismissed lightly: as Stuart Hall and his colleagues point out, radio, TV and the press have an important mediating role 'in the formation of public opinion, and in orchestrating that opinion together with the actions and views of the powerful' (1978, pp. 63–4).

The upshot of the Hartmann-Husband study of the early 1970s was that the media generally present images of blacks and Asians as oddities and that media-derived ideas about minority groups in the UK were 'more conducive to the development of hostility towards them that acceptance' (1974, p. 208). In the course of this chapter, we will assess to what extent this still holds in the 1980s, but, for perspective, let's consider why in the years immediately following the 1968 Race Relations Act, the media were operating a sort of disguised discrimination against blacks.

UNCLE TOM
Named after the central character in Harriet Beecher Stowe's book *Uncle Tom's Cabin*, this nowadays is a disparaging term applied to any black person who appears to accept inferiority or subservience (in the same way as the original Uncle Tom did).

In previous chapters, we have proposed that the colonial mentality has persisted, albeit in changing forms, for four centuries. The vestige of empire, colonialism and slavery has endured in the popular imagination and this has shone through the media — specifically through their reportage of events pertaining to migrants and their offspring. The racist beliefs we went over earlier are interesting relics of a bygone age when Britain ruled the waves and it was the 'white man's burden' to civilize the 'new-caught sullen peoples' to use Kipling's phrase. But the lasting legacy of empire and slavery is evidenced occasionally by the press allusions such as 'Police find forty Indians in "black hole"' to describe the discovery of illegal immigrants in a cellar. The choice of the *Daily Express* (2 July 1970) to mix the imagery of Calcutta with modern day Bradford tended — perhaps unintentionally — to point up the connections between the present situation and the colonial history. The example is extreme, though Hartmann and Husband found many reiterations of the colonial image in relation to modern events, often but not always, in jokes and cartoons. 'The image is used because it exists and is known to have wide currency and therefore enables easier communication' they explained (1974, p. 31).

The researchers argued that the imagery blends nicely with 'a view of the world in which the entitlement of whites is seen as essentially different from that of non-whites' (1974, p. 33). This view can be seen to manifest in many shapes and in many media: as Stuart Hall has remarked, popular literature, in the period of slavery and imperialism, 'is saturated with these fixed, negative attributes of the colonized races. We find them in the diaries, observations and accounts, the notebooks, ethnographic records and commentaries, of visitors, explorers, missionaries and administrators in Africa, India, the Far East and the Americas' (1981, p. 38). Harriet Beecher Stowe's *Uncle Tom's Cabin* clearly demonstrates Hall's argument: Stowe's passive 'good nigger' prototype served many writers well over the centuries and has only recently undergone the metamorphosis characterized in T. Leab as *From Sambo to Superspade* (1975). Other examples are to be found in school textbooks and atlases. Still around in the late 1970s was *A School Economic Atlas* published in 1921 (fifth edition), and written by J. G. Bartholomew — Victoria Gold Medallist of the Royal Geographical Society — so the cover blurb informed us. On page 13 Bartholomew had produced a map of the world showing where 'The Races of Mankind' were purported to have lived. His designation of 'white', 'yellow' and 'black' types followed exactly Gobineau's earlier analysis (see chapter 2). Bartholomew's accompanying commentary read:

> The economic importance of race, as of religion, is very great. For instance, in the case of the Negro, climactic influences — acting direct and through the typical food — lead to the early closing of the 'seams' between the bones of the skull; and thus the development of the brain is arrested, and the adult is essentially unintellectual. On the other hand, he is naturally 'acclimatized' against numerous diseases and other conditions of life and work which are very adverse to the white man. He is, therefore, of great use as a manual labourer in a 'steamy' climate, e.g. on a cane-sugar planation (1921, pp. v–vi).

Now this and other unsavoury taints of colonist racism have generally been expurgated, such as the removal of Helen Bannerman's *The Story of Little Black Sambo* (1975; first published 1899) from school libraries, along with certain volumes of W. E. Johns's *Biggles*, the archetypal boy's adventurer, and Enid Blyton's innocuous *Noddy* whose peace was occasionally threatened by dark-countenanced gollywogs.

The justification for getting rid of these colonial images was that they were racist and, therefore, in breach of race relations laws, and that they were offensive to ethnic groups in portraying people of a darker hue in a negative way. Sambos and gollywogs form part of a collective media image of the black people as inferior the white (can you imagine Mr Plod being renamed Mr Pig?). These pejorative typifications are constant reminders of the negative connotations attached to colonized groups in imperialist days — which have stuck.

As well as being insulting, the sambo and gollywog types are rather poor illustrations with which to educate children, especially about themselves. This, of course, is one of the arguments for the MRE education programmes considered in chapter 6: that material containing negative images of blacks and other minority groups maintains the 'white bias' in education so that ethnic children learn to accept white superiority and have a somewhat devalued self-image.

We have argued before that the colonial mentality's longevity is reinforced from below in the sense that minority groups accept their alleged inferiority in some measure and so contribute to their own subordination. Being presented with negative images in literature, film, the press and other media is one way through which that acceptance is ensured. Ideologies, beliefs and imagery about white superiority are fairly common currency and are conveyed in often disguised ways through the media; this is what Hall refers to as 'inferential' as distinct from 'overt' racism in the media (1981, p. 37). The images help seal the widespread belief about the inevitability of inequality and so strengthen the very structure of that inequality, which in turn is reflected in the media.

Bearing in mind that, at least up to the mid-1960s the media made abundant use of colonial images and that migrants were working mainly in cellar level jobs, living in undesirable areas, their children struggling at school, we can appreciate the context in which Enoch Powell's predictions were made. More significantly for present purposes we can begin to see how the media gave his claims credibility and so influence public awareness.

Those whom the gods wish to destroy

Few people nowadays would accept the naive view that the media somehow reflect an objective picture of the world. There is plenty of evidence to suggest that they are biased in their content, style and analysis. The Glasgow University Media Group, in particular, has done much to dispel any view to the contrary (1976; 1979; 1982).

On the subject of race relations, Husband argues that the media 'have reflected racist assumptions and reported without adequate analysis racist behaviour and racist policy' (1975, p. 27). In contrast to this, however, Peter Braham contends that, in this period when — according to the Rose Survey (1969) — immigrants were perceived by at least 60 per cent of the population as a threat: 'the media gave little or no airing to opinions which . . . were very widely shared among the general public' (1982, p. 280). Braham documents an attempt by the media to play down conflict and prejudice and to have as little coverage of race related issues as possible, the plausible idea being that 'to focus on racial problems at all would merely serve to stir them up' (1982, p. 279). That is, before Powell.

'Those whom the gods wish to destroy, they first make mad,' warned Powell in 1968. 'We must be mad, literally mad, as a nation to be permitting the annual inflow of some 50,000 dependants, who are for the most part the material of the future growth of the immigrant-descended population' (quoted in Seymour-Ure, 1974, p. 104).

It could be argued that Powell was the first to articulate and, because of his political standing, give credibility to, the feelings of 'immigrant-as-threat' of the UK's majority. But, equally, given the preceding remarks about the power of the media, it could be argued that, together, Powell and the media actually created a situation that wasn't there. His speeches on race relations and immigration had the effect of lifting the censorship on race and the media soon

---

CONSENSUS
An agreement of opinion or view, not necessarily unanimous, but by a
sizeable majority of a chosen population; the opposite of CONFLICT of
opinion.

---

catapulted Powell and his inflammatory opinons into public prominence; so
much so that in the days following his first speech, a Gallup poll revealed that as
much as 96 per cent of the UK's adult population were aware of the nature of
Powell's view (Seymour-Ure, 1974, p. 99).

Powell's thrust was to challenge what he considered a false impression of
consensus as conveyed by politicians and the media. He enumerated the residual
immigration of dependants despite immigration control, claimed that the
political acceptance of this was tantamount of self-immolation and spelled out
the wretched implications of this — 'the River Tiber flowing with much
blood'. Seymour-Ure estimates that Powell received correspondence from
180,000 people in the weeks that followed: 'barely 2,000 expressed disapproval
of the speech' (1974, p. 105).

The speech had a mixed reception from newspapers, some decrying the
sentiments, others applauding them. Whatever the tenor of the response, there
was saturated coverge: front-page headlines on all national daily and Sunday
newspapers, many containing emotive language such as: 'Race Blockbuster'
(*Sunday Express*, 21 April), 'Explosive Race Speech' (*Sunday Times*, 21 April),
'Race Row' (*Daily Mirror*, 22 April). For a solid 10 days, there was blanket
coverage of Powell's speech, and its repercussions, two immediate ones of which
were his dismissal from the shadow cabinet and, following this, a one day 'we
back Powell' strike augmented by a protest march by dockers. A Conservative
party politician receiving the backing of traditional Labour voters is a rare
occurence indeed.

Powell's denial of racism belied some of the sinister implications of his
views and, in any case, those views were seized upon and put to racist uses. John
Thackara believed this was assisted: 'the media reinforce Powell's racism by their
failure either to recognise that he uses them as a stage or to ensure that his
contentious ''proposals'' are put in critical context' (1979, p. 111). Simply
reported, what he said and how he was reacted to, served only to bolster racism;
though it should be stated that much of the media's response to Powell took the
form of quite critical evaluation and questioning of his assumptions. But
criticism was negated, as Braham notes:

> Although many of the newspapers condemned what Powell had said in
> their editorials, and most condemned the way in which he said it, this

was outweighed by the sheer intensity and duration of coverge, an intensity which signified that what could now be taken for granted in public debate over race and immigration had changed (1982, p. 281).

In other words, Powell helped to set the agenda for future discussion about race relations; from 1968, the media, politicians and public debate colluded with Powell's interpretation of the situation: a question of numbers became the name of the game. This provides a clear example of the way the media constructs an inferential racist structure, to use Hall's term again (see also Troyna, 1982b).

If we choose to accept the available evidence, we can state that, at the time of the Powell-media link up, the majority of the population saw in immigrants a threat. We argue that the colonial mentality was validated by the subordinate positions of New Commonwealth migrants. Powell may have given air to the feelings of many, but he also, possibly inadvertently, gave fresh force to those feelings.

Powell's motives and intentions, which have been carefully scrutinized by Paul Foot (1969) are largely irrelevant in the context of this chapter, as indeed are those of the mediamen who amplified him. But the effects were relevant in establishing what amounted to racist ideas as political programmes. 'Blacks are below us and are suited to work in dirty jobs and live in inferior homes. Still, there are more and more of them breeding and coming into our country and preety soon they'll be taking over,' was the type of reasoning given political intelligibility, particularly by Powell's incitement, 'in this country in fifteen or twenty years' time the black man will have the whip hand over the white man' (quoted in Seymour-Ure, 1974, p. 103).

It's impossible to estimate the overall impact of the media's 'earthquake', as Powell later described the after-effects of his speeches. As we saw in the last chapter, prior to 1968 racist and anti-immigrant views were given a political voice often by discredited figures such as Mosley and Jordan, whose extremism alienated grassroots support. Powell, as a Conservative shadow cabinet member, was a totally different proposition and, although his subsequent dismissal and removal from the party tended to relegate him to the political margins in later years, his popularity, as documented by several surveys in the mid-1960s, indicates that he and the media provided some form and clarity to a coherent racism and, significantly, lent it legitimacy. This was possible only because the media afforded Powell massive coverage and so focused sharply on the apparent exposé. Hence the self-fulfilling element, as Braham points out: 'the moment a politician of Enoch Powell's prominence draws attention to it, it's amplified and so a problem of a different magnitude is created' (1982, p. 282). If there was a sense of threat and discontent before Powell, it was certainly intensified as a result of the media's seismic treatment of his claims.

SELF-FULFILLING PROPHECY
'Tell a child he's stupid for long enough and, eventually, he'll become stupid' is the type of reasoning behind the SFP: an initial definition of someone or something may be false, but, if exposed to it long enough (by, for example, teachers), the person may believe it himself and so behave in a manner that suggests the original definition was correct. Similarly, if we say conflict is bound to occur, actually saying this might promote the probability of conflict taking place.

The media's handling of the Powell speeches exemplifies what Hartmann and Husband criticize them for: not addressing the questions of housing, education and employment that underlie race relations; concentration on the immigrant-as-threat issue, instead. Yet, some ten years after the Powell speech when the man's notoriety had completely subsided, the basic criticism still seemed to hold good. The immigrant-as-threat still constituted an important theme for the media in a way it hadn't before the advent of Powell.

We don't want to inflate the importance of the media in shaping peoples' awareness of the race-related issues. Even so, we find totally unacceptable the view of Harold Evans, former editor of the *Sunday Times*, that the media simply passed on Powell's message to the public (1971). The press, TV and radio are not passive conduits of information from Westminster or anywhere else for that matter; nor does the news constitute 'random reactions to random events' as the journalist, John Whale, once claimed (1970, p. 510). On the contrary, what appears in newspapers or on TV and radio news bulletins has been carefully selected from a vast pool of potentially newsworthy items and the process of news-gathering is directed by a set of unwritten, though widely shared criteria, or 'news values'. How could it be otherwise when, as C. MacDougall points out, 'At any given moment billions of simultaneous events occur throughout the world' (1968, p. 12).

The old maxim that 'man bites dog' is news but 'dog bites man' isn't, provides a clue to at least one of the criteria used by journalists to define the worthiness of an event: its extraordinary or unusual features. Other news values invoked by journalists include the immediacy and drama of an event, the presence of an established personality, and negative elements which are part of, or a consequence of an event. The greater the number of these elements present in an item, the more likely it is to appear as a news story. It's in the context of the overriding importance of such news values in determining what is and what isn't reported, that we can understand why Powell's speech received such prominent and generous coverage in the media. Seymour-Ure has shown precisely how Powell ensured that this speech (which was not so different in content from an earlier speech which he had given in Walsall and which had been sparsely reported) received wide coverage in the press and on radio and TV (1974, pp. 111–12). Harold Evans is on stronger ground, however, when he claims that 'the way race is reported can uniquely affect the subject itself' (1971, p. 42). We have already indicated how Powell's speech had the effect of reinstating the issues of race and immigration as salient issues in political and public debate; and there are other examples. The artificially high levels of electoral support for the NF in the 1976 local elections may, for instance, be largely explained by the media's coverage of the inflow of Goan Asians from Malawi and, in particular, reports of two homeless families newly arrived from Malawi, who were provided with four-star hotel accommodation by West Sussex County Council at a cost of £600 a week. Headlines such as 'Scandal of £600-a-week Asians' (*The Sun*, 4 May) and 'We want more money, say the £600-a-week Asians' (*Daily Mail*, 5 May) gave the impression that the immigrants had come to the UK primarily to 'sponge' off the welfare state. As Peter Evans has pointed out, this sensationalist, often irresponsible reporting enhanced peoples' anxieties about the level of immigration into this country from the New Commonwealth and East Africa (1976). It's therefore more than coincidence that the NF attacted most support in those areas where it was anticipated that the Malawi immigrants would settle: Leicestershire, the West Midlands and parts of Yorkshire.

Powell's speech and the Malawi Asian episodes highlight the dilemma facing journalists, especially those involved in reporting sensitive issues such as race relations, in their search for 'good' news. On the one hand, their routine journalistic values and assumptions about what constitutes newsworthy issues impels them towards such events; on the other, many journalists are conscious of the fact that coverage of such issues may have a deleterious impact on relations between black and white communities. The National Union of Journalists (NUJ) has recognized this dilemma and, in 1975, issued a series of guidelines on 'race reporting' to its members. These were intended to put some flesh on clause 10 of the NUJ's code of conduct: 'A journalist shall not originate material which encourages discrimination on grounds of race, colour, creed, gender or sexual orientation.' But the guidelines are not enforceable; in fact even if they were put into practice they would effect little more than superficial changes to the way such issues are reported; as James Halloran points out, the way in which race relations are covered will not be substantially altered because basic news values will remain the same (1981, p. 8).

The pertinence of Halloran's observation can be demonstrated by the stubborn position taken by *The Sun* newspaper in response to Peter Evans's pamphlet, *Publish and Be Damned?* (1976). Evans had specifically criticized *The*

Sun for its sensationalist coverage of the Malawi Asian affair. *The Sun*'s editorial reply: 'In the reporting of racial matters there is one safe guideline, the good old fashioned one of news value. We stand by that.' (5 January 1977). If the reporting of race relations, generally, exemplifies the tension between journalists' habitual professional practices and their social and political implications then the growth in the late 1960s and '70s of organizations such as the NF pinpointed another seemingly irreconcilable issue: how do you report an avowedly racist organization which, at the same time, ostensibly shares with the other mainstream political parties a commitment to parliamentary democracy?

Beyond the pale?

Whichever newspaper you read, there is one important strand which is common to all in their coverage of political news; they share an unswerving belief in parliamentary democracy as the only legitimate channel for effecting social and political change in the UK. It is a commitment which transcends their different political orientations and is also shared by both BBC and IBA networks. This is not to say that all other expressions of dissent are routinely ruled out of court, however. The ideology of the media is sufficiently liberal to recognize that many views and opinions exist over many issues and that these may be legitimately expressed outside parliament through, for example, peaceful campaigns. In other words, while certain newspapers may not agree with the views of CND or civil rights demonstrators they respect the rights of those marchers as long as they, themselves, respect the sovereignity of the rule of law and the democratic processes which it underwrites. Once dissent takes on a violent face, however, and the demonstrators begin to take direct political action then, quite regardless of the legitimacy of the grievance, those people and their organizations are declared as being 'beyond the pale'. Terry Ann Knopf makes a similar point:

> Both the general public and the media share the same dislike of protestors: both are unable to understand violence as an expression of protest against oppressive conditions: both prefer the myth of orderly, peaceful change, extolling the virtues of private property and peaceful decorum. People are expected to behave in a certain way; they just don't go around yelling or cursing or throwing rocks (1970, p. 858).

The most vivid and dramatic example of this process is provided by the media's coverage of the IRA: having taken the law into its own hands and embarked on a strategy of 'indiscriminate' bombing, the organization is unanimously condemned in the media; discussion of the legitimacy, or otherwise, of the IRA's grievances is firmly subordinated to a consideration of how the organization can be repressed. This is well illustrated in the editorial coverage which followed the IRA's bombing of the Household Cavalry and a bandstand in Regent's Park, London in July 1982. The *Daily Mirror* comment, under the heading, 'Evil, Pitiless', summed up Fleet Street's general reaction when it described the IRA as 'the most consistently wicked gang of killers in the Western world'. It continued: 'They claim to fight for a cause. But no cause could justify such evil' (21 July 1982). Defining the IRA in such terms precludes any efforts to discuss their cause dispassionately or objectively. Instead, the IRA is 'routinely signified as illegitimate by the media and placed in the "twilight zone" of thugs, anarchists and subverters of the established social order' (Troyna, 1982b, p. 260).

When the media turned their attention to the NF, the ascription of legitimate or illegitimate status to the party is not so easily resolved, however. On the one hand, as we saw in the last chapter, the political programme of the NF was openly racist and fascist. It therefore represented an ideology which fell outside the limits of political beliefs which are conventionally accepted as legitimate by the media. At the same time, however, the NF made a substantial effort to win support and gain power through conventional parliamentary channels and procedures during the 1970s. In this sense it differed from the subterranean fascist groups we considered in the last chapter.

The NF, like the mainstream political parties, ostensibly adhered to the rules of parliamentary democracy by contesting elections and invoking the principles of free speech, freedom of assembly and so on. The essence of the NF's ambivalent relationship with media ideology should now be clear. If the party's fascist beliefs were seen as its preeminent feature, then there was a strong case for the media to treat it differently from other political parties, such as the Labour party. If, however, the way in which the NF operated was taken as crucial criterion of how to cover it then it was difficult for reporters not to ascribe it equivalent status to other parties. Of course, it would be naive to assume that NF leaders themselves had no part to play in generating this dilemma. From the party's formation in 1967, leading members such as Chesterton, Tyndall and Webster stressed how important a role the media could play in facilitating the increase in membership and electoral growth of the party; they therefore implored members to refrain as far as possible from becoming involved in activities which would undermine the conception of the NF as a democratic party (Troyna, 1982b, pp. 268–70; see also Fielding, 1981).

Concern about the media's relationship with the NF reached a peak in the late 1970s, particularly during the build-up to the 1979 General Election. As we saw in the last chapter, the party had managed to field 303 candidates, the 'largest scale challenge of any "insurgent" party since the Labour party in 1918,' according to Stan Taylor (1982, p. xi). As part of a broadly based campaign against the NF, the Anti-Nazi League, Campaign Against Racism in the Media and some members of the NUJ argued that journalists should report NF-related news critically and should inform readers, viewers and listeners that the NF and its leading members endorsed and promoted many fascist ideas. In fact, they went further by instigating the 'pull the plugs' campaign in which they argued that the NF should not be given the opportunity to hold party political broadcasts. David Edgar spelled out the reasons for this campaign in the *Sunday Times* (1 October 1978). According to Edgar, 'the factor that could, and I believe should, exclude [the NF] from uncritical TV coverage is a form of racial-ideology that threatens the freedom of biologically defined groups, not only to speak, but also to be.' He continued:

> Of course, there are parties in Britain (on the left and right) which are abusive and even intimidating towards groups of people on the grounds of their income or their method of earning it; the NF is unique in attacking a group of British citizens not for what they *do* (and could therefore, *in extremis*, stop doing) but for what they *are*, for something they couldn't change even if they wanted to . . . Freedom for the NF to abuse the air waves does mean, in the here-and-now and much more in the future, the *reduction* of the freedom of their racially-defined victims (*Sunday Times*, 1 October 1978, p. 15).

Despite Edgar's well-argued case, the 'pull the plugs' campaign was generally vilified by journalists and failed to carry any weight with the director generals of either the BBC or IBA. 'At the end of the day,' wrote Ian Trethowan, director general of the BBC, in response to the demands to ban NF party political broadcasts, 'we must give fair treatment to all legally constituted political parties seeking the votes of the electorate in a legal way' (quoted in Tracey and Troyna, 1979, p. 13). The politics of a party, according to this view, then, and, in the particular circumstances of a General Election campaign, were of minimal importance to those in the higher echelons of the broadcasting media. What is of greatest importance is how a party sets about promoting those views and attracting public support.

Broadly speaking, Trethowan's response was indicative of the views of many journalists and broadcasters in their handling of NF-related news. Parliamentary democracy is, according to media ideology, sacrosanct and any political group which adheres to the rules and procedures of that system must be protected and allowed to function, however distasteful or offensive its political beliefs might be. Yet, as Edgar suggested, the freedom of speech accorded the NF by the media had the potential to restrict, if not completely remove, various freedoms of the nonwhite population in the UK — including, of course, freedom to exist. This says much about how the media reflect the presence of this population. In the early 1970s, Hartmann and Husband had argued that 'coloured people have not on the whole been portrayed as an integral part of British society' (1974, p. 145). The way in which the media resolved its crisis over the management of NF-related news in the late 1970s indicated that the position had, to all intents and purposes, remained the same. At that time, the media represented the UK's black population in a generally negative light. The media's coverage of the 1981 urban riots in the UK did much to confirm this impression as we will now see.

The copycat effect

Writing in the *Daily Mail* on 14 July 1981 — the second major week of rioting in the UK's major cities — Mary Whitehouse of the National Viewers and Listeners Association (NVALA), informed readers of a telegram she had recently sent to both the BBC and ITN asking them to consider 'whether the televising of acts and vandalism and violence did not contribute to the spread of riots by creating excitement, encouragement, imitation and actually teaching the techniques of violence.' The effect of Whitehouse's telegram and article was to rekindle interest in the part played by the media in the escalation of violence both specifically in relation to the events of 3–16 July, and more generally in contemporary society. Until then, the copycat influence of the media, especially TV, in relation to the riots, had not been a major topic of concern. For the remaining period of the riots, however, and long after the violence had receded, the copycat effect became a prominent theme in leader articles in the press and also became a focus for more general political and public debate. For instance, Milton Shulman, writing in *The New Standard* (16 July 1981) asserted: 'If Lord Scarman is seriously concerned with long-term solutions to the nation's plight, he should study the case against television.' Not that the copycat phenomenon was a new issue; as we indicated earlier, the Kerner Commission on the US riots had also investigated whether or not there was a link between the media's presentation of the disorders and the growth of violence in various US cities between 1966–7.

Claims that the media have played a direct role in the degeneration of contemporary Western countries into violent societies have gained increasing pace and credibility. Social psychologists such as William Belson (1978), for instance, claim to have provided empirical support for the proposition that there is a causal relationship between exposure to deviant images on TV and adolescent involvement in delinquent behaviour. Similar claims have been proposed by Hans Eysenck and David Nias in their book, *Sex, Violence and the Media* (1978). Such views have largely been translated into conventional wisdom; as Shulman wrote: 'the connection between TV violence and the current malaise among the young has been proved beyond reasonable doubt.' But this neglects the important evidence adduced by many media researchers which largely refute the arguments of Belson, Eysenck and others (see Halloran, 1978; Howitt and Cumberbatch, 1975; Murdock and McCron, 1979). In fact, Halloran has commented that, 'No case has been made where television (or the other media) could be legitimately regarded as a major contributory factor to any form of violent behaviours. At most they play a minor role' (1978, p. 827). Whatever the view taken, it seems justifiable to conclude that the mass media do provide the most persuasive source of representations of violence, crime and socially disapproved behaviour and, as Denis McQuail puts it, 'provide the materials for shaping personal and collective impressions' (1977, p. 83). This is an important point because whatever one thinks is the precise role of the media in the cause of a growth in violent and delinquent behaviour, it's clear that through their frequent protrayal of such activities they have enormous potential to extend the tolerance of aggression beyond current social limits.

But how tenable is the proposition that the media produced a copycat effect either in the riots which throught swept the US or the UK? Well, in both cases the evidence adduced tends to be more circumstantial than empirical. In other words, emphasis is placed on the importance of the media as conveyors of news and on their potential to encourage particular forms of activities, rather than on explicating the specific role which they've played in inciting riotous behaviour. Were young people on the streets because of what they'd seen happening in other cities on the television? This is a question which has been left unresolved. The reasons why are not difficult to identify however; as Howard Tumber admits in his pamphlet, *Television and the Riots*: 'Finding a "rioter" is not easy' (1982, p. 11). Trying to establish the influence of the media on a person's decision to take to the streets is even more difficult. Nevertheless, Tumber reports that the youths he interviewed in Toxteth, Liverpool, were resentful of the suggestion that they had simply imitated the postures of youths in other cities where violence had flared up. 'We're fighting for our rights — against the police — it's not copycat' was typical of the comments Tumber received (1982, p. 12). This suggests a greater degree of volition than is often accorded to the participants and is generally sustained by Peter Southgate's interviews with young residents in Handsworth, where rioting also took place. Of the 532 people he spoke to, only one-quarter believed that 'copying other areas' had been one of the principal causes of the local disturbances (1982, p. 49). At the same time, however, he points to the role of rumour that 'something was about to happen' as an important source of information. But it was mainly amongst the older members of his sample, those aged between 30–34 (and who did not take as active a part in the riots as those aged under 20), who said that they first heard of something happening via TV reports (1982, p. 53). This both corresponds with and substantiates Tumber's conclusions that:

> The most obvious point of agreement between the police, the broadcasters and the young people on the streets was that wherever the rioters got their information from it was not television. This is not surprising since the BBC daily survey of listening and viewing taken during the riots showed the proportion of 12 to 19 year olds viewing even the most popular news bulletin did not reach 10% (1982, pp. 45–6).

Does this truly absolve the media from responsibility for generating a copycat effect? Well, despite the above observations and the important point that there was a three-month gap between the Brixton riots (10–12 April 1981) and those in Toxteth, Handsworth, Moss Side, Highfields and elsewhere, Lord Scarman, for one, wasn't convinced. 'The media, particularly the broadcasting media,' he wrote in his official inquiry, 'do in my view bear a responsibility . . . for the imitative element in the later disorders elsewhere' (1981, p. 111). His assertion, which is totally unsubstantiated by the evidence he received, contrasts sharply with the more circumspect conclusion offered in 1968 by Kerner and his colleagues. They were heavily critical of the distorted portrayal which the news media presented of the US disorders and claimed that the media's presentation of a black-white confrontation was inaccurate and potentially harmful. Even so, they maintained: 'Our criticisms, important as they are, do not lead us to conclude that the media are a cause of riots, any more than they are the cause of any other phenomena which they report' (1968, p. 366). It is worth quoting their subsequent comments if only because they reveal a critical awareness and form of argument which is lacking in Lord Scarman's discussion:

> It is true that newspaper and television reporting helped shape peoples' attitudes towards riots. In some cities people who watched television reports and read newspaper accounts of riots in other cities later rioted themselves. But the causal chain weakens when we recall that in other cities, people in very much the same circumstances watched the same programs and read the same newspaper stories but did not riot themselves. (Kerner, 1968, pp. 336–7).

These remarks tie in with what we said earlier: the media are more likely to support than change attitudes. If, as Eric Moonman has suggested, TV's portrayal of Northern Ireland in which the 'violent defiance of authority, street fighting and neighbourhood strife' is routine, largely 'dictated the form of action' taken in Toxteth and elsewhere (1981, p. 1); if young people in Moss Side, Handsworth and Highfields imitated the activities of their counterparts in

---

CAUSAL CHAIN
Said to exist when one event actually causes another event to happen and
the second event could not possibly have occurred without the original
presence of the first. So for example, one event (A) might be the media's
sensationalistic coverage of the violence; if this is followed by another
event (B) like riots in the street and (B) could not happen without the prior
event (A), then a causal chain or relationship might be said to exist. There
is a popular attribution of causal power to the media: they are thought to
cause violence (by showing violent programmes — like 'Tom and Jerry'),
increases in sexual attacks (by screening and reporting sexual offences)
and delinquency (by reporting youths' activities), amongst other things.
The evidence on whether they play a causal role in the relationship is,
however, very scarce and it seems impossible to establish whether the
media are actual causes or mere influences.

Brixton then it was because they were already predisposed to those activities.
Seeing the media as the chief culprit diminishes the political motives of the
'rioters' and necessarily deflects our attention away from the underlying
conditions of unemployment, bad housing, intimidating police practices and
racism. As Field indicates: 'If television reports on the events of Southall and
Toxteth were sufficient to break the social controls on young people in other
cities then those controls must have already been stretched to the point of
breaking' (1982, p. 26). In other words, the social disorders were amplified and
perhaps exaggerated by the media which most certainly transformed the eventual
cycle of riots, but the original disturbances had their roots independent of the
media — in the oppression of black people.

News value

The essentially limited and ethnocentric picture of the world which the mass
media continue to project derives from a complex set of factors which, at the risk
of over-simplification, may be reduced to the combination of, on the one hand,
racist values which suffuse the society and therefore affect the way journalists
report race-related phenomena, and, on the other, the nature of news values
which orient the journalist towards the sensational, the extraordinary, the
negative. Let's briefly develop this point.

Despite the recent growth of newspapers, magazines, TV and radio
programmes aimed principally at the UK's ethnic minority communities, the

ownership, control and staffing of the news media in this country continue to be dominated by white interests to the extent that in 1975 Lionel Morrison estimated that: 'Of the 28,000 journalists working on British newspapers and magazines, less than 2 dozen (or 0.1%) are black' (1975, p. 167). Futhermore, journalists tend to be drawn from either lower middle-class or middle-class backgrounds. As John Clare, BBC Community Relations correspondent admitted in 1980: 'We're like clones, all with very similar backgrounds, the majority Oxbridge graduates' (quoted in Golding and Middleton, 1982). Not surprisingly, therefore, news about race-related events and issues tends to reflect a particular white middle-class interpretation; simply, it will lack the benefits of insight. However, although this point about the domination of white interests in the news media is important it's not sufficient in itself to explain why certain race-related issues come to be 'news' or why particular news angles are emphasized in a story. Here we come back to the 'good old-fashioned guideline of news value.' As we've already said, despite the attempts by the NUJ and others to alert their colleagues to the potentially damaging impact which a sensationalist, inaccurate report on race relations may have, guidelines on race reporting can, at best, lead only to cosmetic improvements in the treatment of the subject; they will not affect the news 'process' itself. It's for this reason that one recent study into race reporting found that black people tended to get into the news for negative reasons, a finding which may have been predicted from the seemingly immutable nature of 'news values' which remain an important guideline for the selection and presentation of all kinds of news (Troyna, 1981).

As chairman of the Press Council between 1964–69, Lord Devlin had made the point that in the reporting of race, 'News value ceases to be the only criterion,' the normal test becomes whether publication will or will not sufficiently raise the temperature' (1971, p. 10). The evidence, however, suggests that this injunction continues to fall on deaf ears.

Our conclusions to this chapter, then, are no more positive than they are in previous chapters. The media have done little more than generate the material on which the colonial mentality is sustained and the signs are that they will effect no radical change in the near future. But what of this future? If the media perpetuate inaccuracies, racist organizations continue to proliferate, ethnicity transforms adherents into militants, education, housing and work remain generators of inequality, laws disadvantage New Commonwealth citizens, what's the probably course of development for race relations? We will speculate on this in the final chapter.

Further reading

News Analysis by Teun A. van Dijk (1987) contains a section on 'Racism and the press' which is based on case studies, the main one being of the Dutch press' treatment of ethnic minorities. The author notes the influential role of the mass media in 'the reproduction of racism'.

Black People and the Media is edited by Joe Harte (1988) and derives from a seminar on 'Employment prospects for black people in the media' held in Lewisham, London in May 1988. It covers a wide array of pertinent themes crystallizing around issues of equal access to and representation in the media. It includes contributions from practitioners, academics, management and trades union activists. Although the focus is on the UK, parallels are drawn with the situation in the USA where, according to John Downing: 'Superficially, there certainly seems to be much greater progress and self-confidence among ethnic minorities . . . ' which is reflected in their relationship with the media industry.

The Black and White Media Show Book is edited by John Twitchin (1988). It contains a number of articles identifying the racist orientation of media representations of blacks. Salman Rushdie, Bhikhu Parekh and Gajendra Verma are amongst its contributors. In addition, its includes strategies and resources for teaching media literacy in schools. Amongst these, the checklist for identifying racist imagery in books and the media is of especial value.

'Media and racism' by Guy Cumberbatch (in **Dictionary of Race and Ethnic Relations**, 1988) has a short summary of the major research findings in this area and a contentious argument: 'The media may not have a powerful effect on prejudice as conventionally defined in the literature on race relations, but they may well have an important impact on self perceptions'. In other words, the most insidious effects of the media are on ethnic minorities themselves.

Daily Racism: The Press and Black People in Britain is by Paul Gordon and David Rosenberg (1989). It pays attention to the way in which antiracist policies have been criticized in the press, especially tabloid newspapers. It also reinforces earlier studies of race and the media by illustrating how black people continue to be typified as a problem in media discourse. This work may profitably be read in conjunction with **Race relations as news**, a US study by Herman Gray (in *American Behavioural Scientist*, Vol. 30, No. 4, 1987). Gray argues that black protest has been defined as 'illegitimate and threatening'. In a later passage, the author warns that: 'The immediacy and potency of the television (news) image . . . contributes to the relaxation of critical insight by the viewer'.

The Punjabi Press by Darshan Singh Tatla and Gurharpal Singh in *New Community* (Vol. 15, No. 2, 1989) is one of the few studies available that looks into the ethnic press. It considers the fortunes of this venture in the UK since the mid-1960s. The authors look at the motives behind the setting up of such publications, the problems experienced and factors likely to influence its future. They maintain that the Punjabi press 'will remain as a medium which both provides a self-image for the Sikh community and reflects its changes'.

10
Conclusion

- **What of the future?**
- **How are blacks improving their positions in the US?**
- **Is there a crisis in race relations?**
- **Will there be class conflict or ethnic conflict?**
- **How can the vicious circle be broken?**

The next stage

One of the recent, preoccupying questions in race relations is: what were the causes of the British riots? The same question could be asked of Miami in 1980, Soweto in 1976, Detroit in 1967 or any other place where nonwhites have issued notices of their discontent with social conditions. This book has, in a way, inverted that question and attempted to answer why, for long periods in history, those groups have conceded? Why haven't they rioted more frequently?

Each of the chapters in this book has dealt with a different dimension of the race issue; collectively they form an argument that race relations situations are very much alive in contemporary society. And where race relations situations exist, so does inequality. And where inequality exists for longish periods one expects conflict.

There is conflict and that is certain, but only sporadically does it manifest itself. What we have tried to do is show how class and power interlock with consciousness to inhibit manifestations of conflict. We have done this by tracing modern race relations back to the early days of colonialism and European empire-building, by taking note of the class divisions that have produced racial divisions and split working-class commitments and by emphasizing the all-pervasive consciousness we described as the colonial mentality. The images carved out of colonialism have a longevity that is sustained and supported by class relations.

Some liberal critics of certain aspects of capitalism might argue that those colonial images and the racism they foster are outmoded relics of a by-gone age. They have persisted as an anachronism, but will surely be swept away as industrial society advances and enlightenment brings fresh perspectives. This was the type of view popularized by social scientists in the early 1960s. 'It's just a matter of getting used to the newcomers' was the gist of the argument: racism was seen more or less as a form of ethnocentrism (or even xenophobia) and so gradual expansions of consciousness would lead to harmony amongst different groups from different backgrounds. In sum, the sanguine prediction was that racism was based on pure ignorance and that greater, sustained contact would systematically reduce that ignorance, thus paving the way for an enlightened society.

This was a rather naive and, in many respects, superficial view which failed to x-ray the social structures lying behind the race relations situation — structures that effectively supported racism. Our argument has been that race relations cannot be fully understood by concentrating on the present or indeed the social structure of the UK since the war (the starting point for many studies), but only by probing into history and trying to uncover the manifold functions racism has performed over the decades and centuries.

Why racism exists has not been our guiding concern; in our analysis, it seems for the working class an almost rational response to changing social circumstances. We could say that the problematic of this book is: why isn't there more racism about? It seems perfectly feasible in our frame of reference to suppose that racism and the conflict it generates could be more intense than they actually are. Our task has been to explain why and show how, in the future, things will not escalate as some of our more pessimistic contemporaries might expect, at the same time not falling into the trap of giving too much false hope for the future.

Things are changing, of course and efforts are being made in both the UK and USA to equalize opportunities in all possible spheres. But the changes are suprisingly recent and, in many instances, motivated by the dread of consequences rather than guided by a vision of equality. Take the infamous English 'Sus Law' for example. Throughout the 1960s and 1970s, an increasing number of black youths were prosecuted under the ancient Vagrancy Act, 1874.

In 1977, of all the youths charged under the act, 42 per cent were black; considering they constituted about 1.78 per cent of the UK's total population, the statistic was revealing (see Roberts, 1982, for a total analysis of the act). Basically, evidence for prosecution under 'Sus' (for suspicion) rested on the often uncorroborated testimonies of police officers; to grant an acquittal, the magistrate more or less had to repudiate police evidence. The over-representation of young blacks, therefore, suggested a pronounced racialist bias in the whole operation of the law. At a time when the NF were gaining in ascendancy, the issue of 'Sus' became paramount. Remi Kapo put it forcefully when arguing: 'Politically, in the wake of the white racial insurgency against blacks, the Vagrancy Act by its obvious misuse is nothing more than an instrument of repression' (1981, p. 51)

It seems no small coincidence that the repeal of the law came at a time when the statistics showed an astonishing imbalance, when hatred against blacks seemed on the upswing and when black youths' rage was reaching critical point.

Change to flatten out inequalities doesn't just evolve: it is pushed along by circumstance. Positive discrimination, as we noted in chapter 4, is quite an old, benevolent strategy for improvement. But witness the dramatic steps taken by the Reverend Jesse Jackson's Chicago-based organization, PUSH, which forced blacks onto boards of directors and into executive positions by threatening boycotts should the company fail to cooperate. Suppose PUSH approaches Coca Cola: 'Let's see some rapid promotions for blacks or else blacks won't buy your product'. If Coke figure out that the black market is worth $300 million per year to them, they think very seriously about the proposal!

This we see as precisely the type of tactic to ensure effective equalization. As we quoted in chapter 1, 200 years of seeing someone as coolie — or, indeed, a slave — does not end in thirty-five years; and if it ends at all it will probably be through the efforts of committed descendents of coolies and slaves struggling to throw off the invisible coolie hats and shackles. Chiselling out breaks in work and eduction can work to undermine exactly those prejudices on which racism rests. In the States, blacks are no longer waiting for the breaks: they are making them. And as William J. Wilson notes: 'Because of increasing opportunities for education and skilled training, subordinate members find themselves in a position to challenge the authority of the dominant group and exhibit degrees of competence and expertise that invalidate racial stereotypes' (1976, p. 59).

A condition of proliferating unemployment is hardly conducive to this, however, and restrictions on opportunities to 'exhibit degrees of competence and expertise' may prevent the invalidation of stereotypes. Nowadays, it seems slightly ridiculous to think of blacks living in the inner cities as a reserve army of labour. The first waves of immigrants in the 1950s and 1960s may once have been brought into the metropolitan centre as productive auxiliaries, but, nowadays, they and their children more closely resemble what Cross calls 'an abandoned army' supported by welfare (1982c, p. 7).

The UK riots of 1981 were seen by many, including ourselves as monumentally important in the development of race relations, yet their total effect on the lives of black people in the modern UK can be over-estimated. Brixton in the London district of Lambeth was the centre of gravity of the riots, yet, in the twelve months after the outbreaks, unemployment amongst black youths in the area rose by 79 per cent and amongst whites 33 per cent: what is more, housing opportunities declined. In 1981–2, the inner cities, where the majority of blacks and Asians dwell, were singled out for much bigger cuts in state aid than other areas. City housing authorities had their resources greatly diminished.

These more than balanced the positive changes made: the appointment of a Minister for Race Relations within the Environment Department with little money or power and only a general brief; an experimental assessment of black recruitment in a civil service department; the monitoring of the Criminal Attemps Act (which replaced the Vagrancy Act). There were no attempts even to implement some of the proposals of Lord Scarman (1981) like the establishment of statutory liaison committees to ensure greater police accountability, or the reform of police complaints procedure. Racialism by police officers remains a vague rather than specific disciplinary offence. The riots made the headlines and made it crystal clear that there was a huge problem of black youth, but the changes that followed in their aftermath were not significant.

Our view is that equalization will be approached via concerted action by black and Asian organizations with firm goals, plans and strategies for implementing them. The PUSH model is an interesting and, in all probability, effective one over the long term; it is clear in its objectives, sensible in its proposals and weighty in its bargaining. It remains to be seen how much big business and industry — capital — needs blacks.

The problem is, however, that such compromises may lead to an exaggerated version of Franklin Frazier's depiction of the US scene in which a few blacks joined an exclusive black bourgeoisie and the majority stayed fixed at the cellar level. Those wary of this possibility would anticipate a gradual incorporation of some blacks and Asians into the system, but no serious calling into question of that system. Improvements in the conditions and chances of some blacks and Asians tend to knock the sharp edges off the challenge and leave the impression: 'Well, we made it good, so the system must work; you haven't because you weren't capable or didn't work hard enough'.

For those fearing this type of scenario, nothing short of a wholesale disruption of the capitalist system from which all evils emanate will suffice. Presumably, mass action by the working class will prompt this, though, as we've seen, the acceptance of blacks and Asians by the working class and its organizations has been ponderously slow. Further complicating this possibility is the fact that, although the majority of blacks and Asians are members of the working class by virtue of their lack of ownership of the means of production, they are, in many senses, dislocated from that class. In work, housing and education, they are out of joint with the rest of the working class and, as we saw in chapter 8, there are pressures from many whites to push them further out of joint.

There are others who take the opposite view and that is that the answer to the question of inequality lies in the establishment of institutions such as the CRE. Yet what limited successes have come the way of blacks and Asians have come with the help of black or Asian minority organizations. At the end of the 1970s, Rex wrote of such organizations: 'I expect these groups to use a violent rhetoric and one which talks of war with British society, but I also expect that in the long run their main effect will be to provide necessary protection for blacks in a hostile world' (1979, p.91).

Whilst agreeing that minority organizations will function protectively, we also foresee the possibility of increased political action and more pay-offs. Successes are more likely to come through direct action than through either working-class integration or liberal paternalism.

William Wilson has reasoned that: 'A sense of futility would seem to work against the development of morale and hope required for a militant vision' (1976, p.48). We indicated in chapter 7 that such a sense may have been found in the 1950s and 1960s, but it is fast dissolving and being replaced with an energy and incentive to force changes in the positions of blacks and Asians. We have seen the violence of Watts, Detroit, and Miami replicated, albeit on a smaller scale, in the UK and this reflects not apathy or despair, but a willingness to challenge assumptions about the conditions of blacks and Asians.

One difference between the American riots and the British outbreaks is that the gap dividing blacks from their white working-class equivalents in the States was large enough to make the riots about blacks; in the UK, social conditions are such that the gap, particularly between black and white working-class youths, has closed to the extent that white youths are actually joining in to make the riots expressions of class discontent as well as black anger. Despite this increase in motivation to overcome present conditions, the attempts will continue to be abortive. We envisage that the less spontaneous, better coordinated efforts will prove the more effective in the implementation of change.

Faith in white working-class organizations has lapsed, and confidence in official white-dominated agencies like the CRE had never been totally there in the first instance. A prolonged period of rising expectations and gradually increasing gratifications (like social mobility, better housing) has been followed in the UK by a short period of sharp reversal. A gap between what was anticipated and what is being experienced has opened and there seems little hope of its being closed. There seems to be a growing belief in the black and Asian communities, especially among younger elements, that desired changes can only be successfully accomplished by accelerating and intensifying protests. Only the more articulate and better coordinated ones will gain reception.

In our previous work, we wrote of *Black Youth in Crisis* and it is a crisis

THE MELTING POT
The title of a play by Israel Zangwill, used to describe early twentieth-century USA. The plot involves a poor Jewish boy who marries a Christian girl; animosities between their families dissolve. This, in brief, is the theme of the play: how cultural and religious differences can melt away in a new environment — particularly the USA, at the time populated by many diverse groups from many countries. The concept's viability is assessed by Nathan Glazer and Daniel Moynihan (1970).

which has not yet passed (1982). Indeed, it is a crisis which may yet have ramifications for all groups perceived by whites as racial minorities. So, the stage is set for more ethnic conflict; we suggest that the collective actions witnessed in western societies over the past twenty years will continue, possibly taking on more obviously political functions. And, on the evidence of previous episodes, we forecast that ethnicity will be a more effective basis than social class when it comes to organizing for action. Does this mean that ethnicity will replace social class as the main unit of conflict in the modern world? Certainly, some writers have reasoned that ethnicity has already displaced class as the major form of social cleavage. Glazer and Moynihan, fathers of the 'melting pot thesis', compare the two forms and conclude that ethnicity is 'a more fundamental source of stratification' (1975, p. 17).

Whilst our general argument in this book compels us to hold severe reservations about totally agreeing with this, we believe that there's material enough to make us recognize that ethnicity and ethnic conflict will be, in the future, at least as significant as class and class conflict. Quite obviously, we do not favour some form of 'ethnic analysis' over 'class analysis' nor any similar artificial division. Race relations, as the discipline we have outlined, must attempt to integrate both these elements of social stratification and conflict.

Blacks and Asians in the UK and, for that matter, in the USA have collectively been described as an underclass, class fraction and sub-proletariat; all of which denote one thing — that they are part of the working class (that is, not owners of the means of production), yet remain a splinter group of that class. In other words, their position is beneath that of the white working class. That position is marked by their alleged race. So, they are stratified by both class and what others take to be their race. What convinces us that this twofold stratification will continue is the apparent unwillingness of the majority of the white working class to incorporate blacks and Asians into the organized labour movement, let along campaign vigorously for the improvement of the general condition of these workers (or non-workers as is increasingly the case). This policy of virtual exclusion is referred to by Frank Parkin as 'exploitation by proxy' since the working class reaps the short-term rewards of keeping blacks and Asians down, but the grand beneficiaries and initiators of the tactic are the more powerful bosses (1979, p. 90).

Exploitation by proxy is witnessed vividly in Canada; for example, in the late nineteenth century when the Working Men's Protective Association campaigned for a shut-out of Chinese labourers and, in 1951, when the Trades and Labor Congress called for a total ban on immigration (Cashmore, 1978). Similarly, the Australian labour movement playing an important part in developing the White Australia policy aimed at keeping Asian labour out of the domestic work scene (Parkin, 1979, p.91). And white South African trade unions fought belligerently for all-white labour policies designed to reinforce apartheid barriers (Simons and Simons, 1969, p. 618-9). Historical examples these may be, but they give little cause for expecting future broad working-class alignments in efforts to improve the lot of blacks and Asians. Yet, this isn't meant as an attack on the working class and its perverse xenophobia: the actions in all cases have been most rational and comprehensible in terms of straightforward defences of interests. Let's put it this way: if you're a railway worker and a seemingly endless stream of migrant workers enter your industry, prepared to do your job at cut-rates, then they appear a threat: so you want to protect yourself by keeping them out. To bring matters up-to-date: if you're a working-class engineer and clinging on to your job when all about you are seeming to lose theirs as unemployment grows month by month, you might make the plausible calculation that: (1) There are three million others out of work and looking for jobs; and (2) That three million might be halved if all the blacks and Asians weren't around — thus making the job a bit safer. It's just a matter of limiting competition and, with unemployment in the western world spiralling, the 'abandoned army' can expect little help from a white working-class preoccupied with its own survival.

So, when we predict how blacks and Asians may organize themselves on ethnic lines and push for changes to improve their lives, we can simultaneously forecast resistance from the white working class to such measures. We foresee a degree of willingness on the behalf of big business and the State to accede to the demands of ethnic organizations, if only because it represents no effective disturbance of their positions and it serves to assuage sometimes troublesome conditions, like black boycotts, for instance. And it presents the image of benign liberalism, even though a more sinister interpreter might see the moves as motivated by the wish to create more tensions amongst the working class. If this were the case, then it might well be completely effective: opening up gaps in the occupational hierarchy especially (and exclusively) for blacks and Asians could be a heaven-sent strategy to stimulate antagonisms amongst workers. And who gains most? A few blacks and Asians and a lot of people with vested interests in business and industry.

Whichever way you cut it, our conclusions aren't very encouraging — not unless you're amongst the privileged minority, that is. We do see improvements for blacks and Asians: there will be better housing available, educational standards will go up — but not dramatically — and there will be more seats on boards of directors, executive posts, political positions, etc. for blacks and Asians. But these opportunities will be rather limited and they will be fought for, not simply granted. They will also meet with anger and possible opposition from the white working class and will so undermine any possible 'uniting of common interests'.

Vicious circle

Our argument ends, then, with the race issue as virulent as ever; it persists as a great divider of human populations. To summarize, we contend that the concept of race itself and the philosophy of racism it feeds are not merely creations of capitalism: we have shown that the category of race as a way of comprehending the bewildering diversity of human populations existed way before the colonial expansion of the seventeenth and eighteenth centuries.

However, this crucial period did see the process of what Banton calls the racializing of the west and the race concept most certainly took on a different significance as a unit of ordering populations hierarchically in this phase. The type of racism that grew in this time quite obviously both facilitated the gross and, often savage, exploitation of others deemed naturally inferior and offered some form of justification — or even explanation — of that exploitation.

Without doubt, racism has, over the years, been a great servant of capitalism in splitting working-class loyalties and introducing antagonisms between workers. Yet, we do not view this as in any way a pure product of some conspiracy of the heads of capitalism. Instead, we see a complementarity in which racism has bolstered capitalism. And, as we indicated earlier, we see racism continuing to support capitalism, albeit in a slightly different way in the future (through for example, the gradual incorporation of blacks and Asians into executive positions).

That very racism is itself a legacy of capitalism: it gained credibility in centuries gone by and has endured as a set of beliefs ever since. Its form has changed and taken on new dimensions with the post-war migration to the UK, but the premise of a fundamental, natural inequality of people remains. That belief in inequality has dictated that whites — the original colonialists — have kept their positions at the top (in their eyes, at least) and this belief is built into the colonial mentality.

The conditions in which black and Asian migrants found themselves in the UK in the years after World War II simply gave greater credence to the central principle of the colonial mentality — racial inequality. The conditions and activities of migrants and their children in work, housing and education have since reinforced colonial stereotypes and so lent fresh force to old mentalities. Thus, the black or Asian has been compelled by material circumstances to live up to the stereotype and has become caught, as we mentioned before, in the most vicious of vicious circles.

We have, in this concluding chapter, outlined at least some of the ways in which the circle might be broken. Yet, if there is, as many suggest, a 'logic' of capitalism, it will work to keep that circle secured, for racism may be a relic of colonialism, but it has profound relevance for modern day capitalism. It comes from the past, but lives in the present. This is why racism can in no sense be analysed as an independent factor and always has to be seen in the social context in which it prospers. The present housing conditions, the chronic problems in education and the conflicts at work are not causes of racism, but are exacerbating factors in its continuance; and this makes the vicious circle tighter and tighter. The pressures to keep that circle intact will be unremitting for some time to come.

Further Reading

Strategies for Improving Race Relations edited by John Shaw, Peter Nordlie and Richard Shapiro (1987) examines the 'nuts-and-bolts' of race and ethnicity training and its pragmatic approach can be contrasted with the more critical appraisal of **Racism and Equal Opportunity Policies in the 1980s** edited by Richard Jenkins and John Solomos (1987).

Eliminating Racism edited by P. Katz and D. Taylor (1988) is a US volume with a wide-ranging remit. It covers and evaluates virtually every aspect of policies and programmes designed to confront racism.

Social Policy: A critical introduction by Fiona Williams (1989) has many sections devoted to the efforts of the welfare state in dealing with the eradication of racism. Often the policies can backfire, as the author points out: 'The concept of "*special needs*" or "special treatment" when imbued with connotations of "culture" reinforces racism and lack of opportunities'.

References

ABEL-SMITH, B. and TOWNSEND, P. (1965), *The Poor and the Poorest*, London, Bell.

ADORNO, T. S., FRENKEL-BRUNSWIK, E., LEVINSON, D. J. and SANFORO, R. N. (1950), *The Authoritarian Personality*, New York, Harper & Row.

AFRO-CARIBBEAN EDUCATIONAL RESOURCES PROJECT (1977), *First Annual Report*, London, ACER.

ALDRICH, H. E., CATER, J. C., JONES, T. P. and McEVOY, D. (1981), 'Business development and self-segregation: Asian enterprise in three British cities' in C. Peach, V. Robinson and S. Smith (eds), *Ethnic Segregation in Cities*, London, Croom Helm, pp. 170–92.

ALEXANDER, C. C. (1965), *The Ku Klux Klan in the Southwest*, University of Kentucky Press.

ALIBHAI, Y. (1988), 'Tribal dance', *New Statesman and Society*, 22 July, pp. 18–19.

ALLEN, S. (1971), *New Minorities, Old Conflicts*, London, Random House.

ALLEN, S. (1982), 'Confusing categories and neglecting contradictions', in E. Cashmore and B. Troyna (eds), *Black Youth in Crisis*, London, Allen & Unwin, pp. 143–58.

ALLEN, S. and SMITH, C. R. (1975), 'Minority group experience of the transition from education to work', in P. Brannen (ed.), *Entering the World of Work: Some Sociological Perspectives*, London, HMSO, pp. 71–90.

ALLEN, S., BENTLEY, S. and BORNAT, J. (1977), *Work, Race and Immigration*, University of Bradford School of Studies in Social Science.

ANWAR, M. (1970), *The Myth of Return: Pakistanis in Britain*, London, Heinemann Educational Books.

ARDREY, R. (1966), *The Territorial Imperative*, New York, Atheneum Press.

ARIS, S. (1970), *The Jews in Business*, London, Jonathan Cape.

ARONSON, E. (1980), *The Social Animal*, San Francisco, W. H. Freeman.

BAGLEY, C. (1979), 'A comparative perspective on the education of black children in Britain', *Comparative Education*, vol. 15, no. 1, pp. 63–81.

BAKER, A. (1981/2), 'Ethnic enterprise and modern capitalism: Asian small businesses', *New Community*, vol. 9, no. 3, pp. 478–86.

BAKER, John R. (1974), *Race*, London, Oxford University Press.

BALLARD, C. (1979), 'Conflict, continuity and change', in V. S. Khan (ed.) *Minority Families in Britain*, London, Macmillan, pp. 109–30.

BALLARD, R. and BALLARD, C. (1977), 'The Sikhs', in J. L. Watson (ed.) *Between Two Cultures*, Oxford, Basil Blackwell, pp. 21–36.

BANKS, J. A. (1981), *Multiethnic Education: Theory and Practice*, London, Allyn & Bacon.

BANKS, O. (1955), *Parity and Prestige in English Secondary Education*, London, Routledge & Kegan Paul.

BANKS, O. (1968), *The Sociology of Education*, London, Batsford.

BANNERMAN, H. (1975), *The Story of Little Black Sambo*, London, Chatto & Windus.

BANTON, M. (1977), *The Idea of Race*, London, Tavistock.

BANTON, M. (1979), 'Analytical and folk concepts of race and ethnicity', *Ethnic and Racial Studies*, vol. 2, no. 2, pp. 127–38.

BANTON, M. (1988), *Racial Consciousness*, Harlow, Longman.

BARBER, L. (1982), 'We're Black — And We Mean Business', *The Sunday Times*, 28 March, p. 55.

BARKER, M. (1981), *The New Racism*, London, Junction Books.

BARNETT, A. (1982), *Iron Britannia*, London, Allison and Busby.

BARON, S., FINN, D., GRANT, N., GREEN, M. and JOHNSON, R. (1981), *Unpopular Education*, London, Hutchinson.

BARTHOLOMEW, J. G. (1921), *A School Economic Atlas* (5th ed.), Oxford University Press.

BARZUN, J. (1937), *Race: A Study in Superstitution*, New York, Harcourt, Brace & Co.

BAXTER, P. and SANSOM, B. (eds) (1972), *Race and Social Difference*, Harmondsworth, Penguin.

BEETHAM, D. (1970), *Transport and Turbans*, Institute of Race Relations, Oxford University Press.

BELL, C. (1977), 'On housing classes', *Australian and New Zealand Journal of Sociology*, vol. 13, no. 1, February, pp. 36–40.

BELSON, W. (1978), *Television Violence and the Adolescent Boy*, Farnborough, Saxon House.

BENEWICK, R. (1972), *The Fascist Movement in Britain*, London, Allen Lane.

BEN-TOVIM, G. and GABRIEL, J. (1979), 'The politics of race in Britain 1962–79', *Sage Race Relations Abstracts*, vol. 4, no. 4, pp. 1–56.

BERGER, J. and MOHR, J. (1975), *A Seventh Man*, Harmondsworth, Penguin.

BERGER, P. L. and LUCKMANN, T. (1972), *The Social Construction of Reality*, Harmondsworth, Penguin.

BERNSTEIN, B. (1970), 'Education cannot compensate for society', *New Society*, 26 February.

BETHNAL GREEN and STEPNEY TRADES COUNCIL (1978), *Blood on the Streets*, London, Bethnal Green and Stepney Trades Council.

BIDDISS, M. (ed.) (1979), *Images of Race*, Leicester University Press.

BILLIG, M. (1978), *Fascists: A Social Psychological View of the National Front*, London, Academic Press.

BILLIG, M. and BELL, A. (1980), 'Fascist parties in post-war Britain', *Sage Race Relations Abstracts*, vol. 5, no. 1, pp. 1–30.

BILLIG, M., CONDOR, S., EDWARDS, D., GANE, M., MIDDLETON, D., and RADLEY, A. (1987), *Ideological Dilemmas*, London, Sage.

BIRRELL, T. (1978), 'Migration and the dilemmas of multiculturalism', in R. Birrell and C. Hay (eds), *The Immigration Issue in Australia*, Melbourne, Department of Sociology La Trobe University.

BLACK PEOPLES PROGRESSIVE ASSOCIATION (1979), *Cause for Concern: West Indian Pupils in Redbridge*, London, Redbridge Community Relations Council.

BLAUNER, R. (1972), *Racial Oppression in America*, New York, Harper & Row.

BOCHNER, S. (1982), 'The social psychology of cross-cultural relations' in S. Bochner (ed.), *Cultures in Contact: Studies in Cross-Cultural Interaction*, London, Pergamon Press, pp. 5–44.

BOWLES, S. and GINTIS, H. (1976), *Schooling in Capitalist America: Educational Reform and the Contradictions of Economic Life*, London, Routledge & Kegan Paul.

BRAHAM, P. (1982), 'How the media report race', in M. Gurevitch *et al.*, (eds), *Culture, Society and the Media*, London, Methuen, pp. 267–86.

BRAHAM, P., RHODES, E. and PEARN, M. (eds) (1980), *Discrimination and Disadvantage*, London, Harper & Row.

BRANNEN, P. (ed.) *Entering the World of Work: Some Sociological Perspectives*, London, HMSO.

BROOKS, D. (1975), *Race and Labour in London Transport*, IRR/Oxford University Press.

BRYAN, B., DADZIE, S., and SCAFE, S. (1987), 'Learning to resist: black women and education' in G. Weiner and M. Arnot (eds), *Gender Under Scrutiny*, London, Hutchinson, pp. 90–100.

BULLIVANT, B. (1981), *The Pluralist Dilemma in Education*, Sydney, Allen & Unwin.

BULLIVANT, B. (1987), *The Ethnic Encounter in the Secondary School*, Lewes, Falmer Press.

BURNEY, E. (1967), *Housing on Trial*, Institute of Race Relations, Oxford University Press.

BURT, C. (1966), 'The genetic determination of differences in intelligence' *British Journal of Psychology*, vol. 57, pp. 137–53.

CALLEY, M. J. C. (1965), *God's People*, London, Oxford University Press.

CAMPAIGN AGAINST RACISM and FASCISM/SOUTHALL RIGHTS (1981), *Southall: The Birth of a Black Community*, London, Institute of Race Relations and Southall Rights.

CAMPBELL, M. and JONES, D. (1982), *Asian Youths in the Labour Market: A Study in Bradford (EEC/DES Transition to Work Project)*, Bradford College.

CARBY, H. (1982) 'White women listen! Black feminism and the boundaries of sisterhood' in CCCS, *The Empire Strikes Back*, London, Hutchinson, pp. 212–235.

CARBY, K. and THAKUR, M. (1977), *No Problems Here?*, London, Institute of Personnel Management.

CARTER, B. and WILLIAMS, J. (1987), 'Attacking racism in education' in B. Troyna (ed.) *Racial Inequality in Education*, London, Tavistock, pp. 170–183.

CARTER, T. (1986), *Shattering Illusions: West Indians in British Politics*, London, Lawrence and Wishart.

CASEY, J. (1982), 'One nation: the politics of race' *The Salisbury Review*, Autumn, pp. 23–28.

CASHMORE, E. (1978), 'The social organization of Canadian immigration law', *Canadian Journal of Sociology*, vol. 3, no. 4, pp. 409–29.

CASHMORE, E. (1979), *Rastaman*, London, Allen & Unwin; paperback edition (1983), London, Unwin Paperbacks.

CASHMORE, E and TROYNA, B. (eds) (1982), *Black Youth in Crisis*, London, Allen & Unwin.

CASHMORE, E. (1987), *The Logic of Racism*, London, Allen & Unwin.

CASHMORE, E. (ed.) (1988), *Dictionary of Race and Ethnic Relations*, 2nd edition, London, Routledge.

CASTELLS, M. (1977), *The Urban Question*, London, Edward Arnold.

CASTELLS, M. (1980), *The Economic Crisis and American Society*, Oxford, Basil Blackwell.

CASTLES, S. and KOSACK, G. (1973), *Immigrant Workers and the Class Structure in Western Europe*, IRR/Oxford University Press.

CASTLES, S. and WALLACE, T. with H. BOOTH (1984), *Here for Good: Western Europe's New Ethnic Minorities*, London, Pluto.

CATER, J. (1978), 'Letter', *New Society*, 9 March, p. 565.

CATER, J. and JONES, T. (1978), 'Asians in Bradford, *New Society*, 13 April, pp. 81–2.

CENTRAL ADVISORY COUNCIL FOR EDUCATION (1967), *Children and their Primary Schools*, 2 vols, London, HMSO.

CENTRAL HOUSING ADVISORY COMMITTEE (1969), *Report of the Housing Manangement Sub-Committee, Council Housing: Purposes, Procedures, Priorities* (the Cullingworth Report), London, HMSO.

CENTRE FOR CONTEMPORARY CULTURAL STUDIES (1982), *The Empire Strikes Back: Race and Racism in 70s in Britain*, London, Hutchinson.

CHIVERS, T. (ed.) (1986), *Race and Culture in Education*, Windsor, Berks., NFER-Nelson.

CLUTTERBUCK, R. (1980), *Britain in Agony; The Growth of Political Violence*, Harmondsworth, Penguin.

COARD, B. (1971), *How the West Indian Child is Made Educationally Subnormal in the British School System*, London, New Beacon Books.

COCKERELL, M. (1972), 'Inside the National Front', *The Listener*, 28 December, pp. 982–90.

COHEN, J. (1966), *Burn, Baby, Burn*, London, Gollancz.

COHEN, P. and BAINS, H. (eds) (1988), *Multi-Racist Britain*, London, Macmillan.

COHN, N. (1967), *Warrant for Genocide: The Myth of the Jewish World Conspiracy and the Protocols of the Learned Elders of Zion*, London, Eyre & Spottiswoode.

COLEMAN, J., CAMPBELL, Q., HOBSON, C. (1966), *Equality of Educational Opportunity* in 2 vols, Washington, DC, Government Printing office.

COLLS, R. and DODD, P. (eds) (1987), *Englishness: Politics and Culture, 1880 1920*, Beckenham, Croom Helm.

COMMISSION FOR RACIAL EQUALITY (1979), *Looking for Work: Black and White School-leavers in Lewisham*, London, CRE.

COMMISSION FOR RACIAL EQUALITY (1979), *Brick Lane and Beyond: An Inquiry into Racial Strife and Violence in Tower Hamlets*, London, CRE.

COMMISSION FOR RACIAL EQUALITY (1980), *Equal Opportunity in Employment: Why Positive Action?*, London, CRE.

COMMISSION FOR RACIAL EQUALITY (1980), *Ethnic Minority Youth Unemployment: A Paper Presented to Government*, London, CRE.

COMMISSION FOR RACIAL EQUALITY (1987), *Living in Terror*, London, CRE.

COMMISSION FOR RACIAL EQUALITY (1988), *Learning in Terror*, London, CRE.

COMMITTEE OF INQUIRY INTO THE EDUCATION OF CHILDREN FROM ETHNIC MINORITY GROUPS (1981), *West Indian Children in our Schools (Interim Report)*, Cmnd, 8273, London, HMSO.

COMMUNITY RELATIONS COMMISSION (1977), *Education of Ethnic Minority Children. From the Perspectives of Parents, Teachers and Education Authorities*, London, CRC.

COMMUNITY RELATIONS COMMISSION (1977), *Housing Choice and Ethnic Concentration*, London, CRC.

COX, O.C. (1948), *Caste, Class and Race: A Study of Social Dynamics*, New York, Doubleday.

COX, O.C. (1976), *Race Relations: Elements and Dynamics*, Detroit, Illinois, Wayne State University Press.

CRAFT, M. and CRAFT, A.Z. (1981), *The Participation of Ethnic Minorities in Further and Higher Education*, (summary and conclusion of a report), Oxford, Nuffield Foundation study.

CRAIG, W. (1987), *The Fiery Cross*, New York, Simon and Schuster.

CROSS, C. (1961), *The Fascists in Britain*, London, Barrie & Rockliff.

CROSS, C. (1965), 'Britain's racialists', *New Society*, 3 June, pp. 9–11.

CROSS, M. (1982a), 'Race and social policy: The case of the CRE', in O. Stevenson and C. Jones (eds), *Yearbook of Social Policy 1981*, London, Routledge & Kegan Paul.

CROSS, M. (1982b), 'Black youth unemployment and urban policy', in J. Rex and M. Cross, *Unemployment and Racial Conflict in the Inner City*, Birmingham, Research Unit on Ethnic Relations, pp. 15–30.

CROSS, M. (1982c), 'Race and class theory', paper presented to the Research Committee on Ethnic, Race and Minority Relations at the *World Congress of Sociology*, Mexico City, August.

CROSS, M. (1988), 'The black economy', *New Society*, 24 July, pp. 16–19.

CROSS, M., EDMONDS, J. and SARGEANT, R. (1982), *Special Problems and Special Measures: Ethnic Minorities and the Experience of YOP*, Birmingham, Research Unit on Ethnic Relations.

CROSSMAN, R. (1975), *Diaries of a Cabinet Minister*, London, Hamish Hamilton/Cape.

CUMBERBATCH, G. (1988), 'Media and racism' in E. Cashmore (ed.) *Dictionary on Race and Ethnic Relations*, 2nd edition, London, Routledge, pp. 184–186.

DAHYA, B. (1974), 'The nature of Pakistani ethnicity in industrial cities in Britain' in A. Cohen (ed.) *Urban Ethnicity*, London, Tavistock (ASA Monograph 12), pp. 77–117.

DANIEL, W.W. (1968), *Racial Discrimination in England*, Harmondsworth, Penguin.

DAVIES, J.G. and TAYLOR, J. (1970), 'Race, community and no conflict', *New Society*, 9 July, pp. 67–9.

DAVISON, R.B. (1962), *West Indian Migrants*, Institute of Race Relations, Oxford University Press.

DEAKIN, N. (1978), 'The vitality of a tradition', in C. Holmes (ed.) *Immigrants and Minorities in British Society*, London, Allen & Unwin, pp. 158–85.

DEAKIN, N. and COHEN, B.G. (1970), 'Dispersal and choice: towards a strategy for ethnic minorities in Britain', *Environment and Planning*, vol. 2, pp. 193–201.

DEPARTMENT OF EDUCATION AND SCIENCE (1965), *The Education of Immigrants (Circular 7/65)*, London, HMSO.

DEPARTMENT OF EDUCATION AND SCIENCE (1985), *Education for All: The Report of the Committee into the Education of Children from Ethnic Minority Groups*, Cmnd. 9543, London, HMSO.

DEPARTMENT OF THE ENVIRONMENT (1975), *Race Relations and Housing*, (Cmnd 6232), London, HMSO.

DEVLIN, LORD (1971), 'Introduction' in *Race and the Press*, London, Runnymede Trust, pp. 7–11.

DHONDY, F., BEESE, B. and HASSAN, L. (1982), *The Black Explosion in British Schools*, London, Race Today Publications.

DHOOGE, Y. (1981), 'Ethnic difference and industrial conflicts,' *Working Paper on Ethnic Relations, No. 13*, Birmingham, Research Unit on Ethnic Relations.

DIXON, B. (1977), *Catching Them Young: Sex, Race and Class in Children's Fiction*, London, Pluto Press.

DOERINGER, P. B. and PIORE, M. J. (1971), *Internal Labor Markets and Manpower Analysis*, Massachusetts, D. C. Heath.

DOHERTY, J. (1969), 'The distribution and concentration of immigrants in London', *Race Today*, vol. 1, no. 8, December, pp. 227–31.

DOLLARD, J. (1938), 'Hostility and fear in social life', *Social Forces*, 17, pp. 15–26.

DORN, A. (1982), *LEA Policies on Multiracial Education*, unpublished document, CRE.

DORN, A. and TROYNA, B. (1982), 'Multiracial education and the politics of decision making', *Oxford Review of Education*, vol. 8, no. 2, pp. 175–85.

DRIVER, G. (1980a), 'How West Indians do better at school (especially the girls)', *New Society*, 17 January, pp. 11–14.

DRIVER, G. (1980b), *Beyond Underachievement: Case Studies of English, West Indian and Asian School-leavers at Sixteen Plus*, London, CRE.

DUMMET, A. (1978), *A New Immigration Policy*, London, Runnymede Trust.

DUMMETT, A. and DUMMETT, M. (1969), 'The role of government in Britain's racial crisis', in L. Donnelly (ed.), *Justice First*, London, Sheed & Ward, pp. 25–78.

DWORETZKY, J. P. (1982), *Psychology*, St Paul, Minn., West Publishing.

DWORKIN, R. (1977), *Taking Rights Seriously*, London, Duckworth.

EDGAR, D. (1977), 'Racism, fascism and the politics of the National Front', *Race and Class*, vol. 19, no. 2, pp. 111–31.

EDGAR, D. (1978), 'Why the Front is beyond the pale', *The Sunday Times*, 1 October, p. 15.

EDWARDS, J. and BATLEY, R. (1978), *The Politics of Positive Discrimination*, London, Tavistock.

EKBERG, D. L. (1979), *Intelligence and Race*, New York, Praeger.

EVANS, P. (1976), *Publish and Be Damned?*, London, Runnymede Trust.

EVANS, B. and WATES, B. (1981), *I. Q. and Mental Testing*, London, Macmillan.

EVANS, H. (1971), 'A positive policy', in *Race and the Press*, London, Runnymede Trust, pp. 42–53.

EVETTS, J. (1973), *The Sociology of Educational Ideas*, London, Routledge & Kegan Paul.

EYSENCK, H. J. (1971), *Race, Intelligence and Education*, London, Temple Smith.

EYSENCK, H. and NIAS, D. K. (1978), *Sex, Violence and the Media*, London, Temple Smith.

EYSENCK, H. and ROSE, S. (1979), 'Race intelligence and education', *New Community*, vol. 7, no. 2, pp. 278–83.

FIELD, S. (1982), 'Urban disorders in Britain and America: a review of research', in S. Field and P. Southgate, *Public Disorder*, London, Home Office Research Study, no. 72, pp. 1–41.

FIELD, S., MAIR, G., REES, T and STEVENS, P. (1981), *Ethnic Minorities in Britain: A Study of Trends in their Position since 1961*, Home Office Research Study, no. 68.

FIELDING, N. (1981), *The National Front*, London, Routledge & Kegan Paul.

FLETT, H. (1977), 'Black council house tenants in Birmingham', *SSRC Working Papers on Ethnic Relations, No. 12*, Birmingham , Research Unit on Ethnic Relations.

FLETT, H. (1979), 'Dispersal policies in council housing: arguments and evidence', *New Community*, vol. 7, No. 2, pp. 184–194.

FLETT, H. (1981), 'The politics of dispersal in Birmingham', *Working Papers on Ethnic Relations, No. 14*, Birmingham, Research Unit on Ethnic Relations.

FLETT, H., HENDERSON, J. and BROWN, B. (1979), 'The practice of racial dispersal in Birmingham, 1969–1975', *Journal of Social Policy*, vol. 8, no. 3, pp. 289–309.

FLYNN, J.R. (1980), *Race, IQ and Jensen*, London, Routledge & Kegan Paul.

FONER, N. (1977), 'The Jamaicans', in J. L. Watson (ed.), *Between Two Cultures*, Oxford, Basil Blackwell, p. 120–50.

FONER, N. (1979), *Jamaica Farewell*, London, Routledge & Kegan Paul.

FOOT, P. (1965), *Immigration and Race in British Politics*, Harmondsworth, Penguin.

FOOT, P. (1969), *The Rise of Enoch Powell*, Harmondsworth, Penguin.

FORESTER, T. (1978), 'Asians in Business', *New Society* 23 February, pp. 420–3.

FRAZIER, E. F. (1957), *Black Bourgeoisie*, New York, Free Press.

FRITH, S. (1981), 'Dancing in the streets', *Time Out*, no. 570 (March 20–26), p. 5.

FRYER, P. (1984), *Staying Power*, London, Pluto Press.

FRYER, P. (1988), *Black People in the British Empire: An Introduction*, London, Pluto Press.

FURNHAM, A. and GUNTER, B. (1989), *Anatomy of Adolescence*, London, Routledge.

GANS, H.J. (1972), *People and Plans*, Harmondsworth, Penguin.

GASMAN, D. (1971), *The Scientific Origins of National Socialism*, London, Macdonald & Co.

GESCHWENDER, J. A. (1977), *Class, Race and Worker Insurgency*, New York, Cambridge University Press.

GIBSON, M. A. (1976), 'Approaches to multicultural education in the United States: some concepts and assumptions', *Anthropology and Education Quarterly*, vol. 7, no. 4, pp. 4–9.

GILBERT, T. (1975), *Only One Died*, London, Kay Beauchamp.

GILES, R. (1977), *The West Indian Experience in British Schools*, London, Heinemann Educational Books.

GILROY, P. (1987a), *There Ain't No Black in the Union Jack*, London, Hutchinson.

GILROY, P. (1987b), 'The myth of black criminality' in P. Scraton (ed.), *Law, Order and the Authoritarian State*, London, Open University Press, pp. 107–120.

GLASGOW, D. (1980), *The Black Underclass*, New York, Jossey Bass.

GLASGOW UNIVERSITY MEDIA GROUP, (1976), *Bad News*, London, Routledge & Kegan Paul.

GLASGOW UNIVERSITY MEDIA GROUP (1979), *More Bad News*, London, Routledge & Kegan Paul.

GLASGOW UNIVERSITY MEDIA GROUP (1982), *Really Bad News*, London, Writers and Readers Publishing Co-operative.

GLASS, R. (1960), *Newcomers: the West Indians in London*, London, Allen & Unwin.

GLAZER, H. (1978), *The Cultural Roots of National Socialism*, London, Croom Helm.

GLAZER, N. (1975), *Affirmative Discrimination*, New York, Basic Books.

GLAZER, N. and MOYNIHAN, D. P. (1970), *Beyond the Melting Pot*, London, MIT Press.

GLAZER, N, and MOYNIHAN, P. (eds), (1975), *Ethnicity*, Cambridge, Mass, Harvard University Press.

GOLDING, P. and MIDDLETON, S. (1982), *Images of Welfare*, Oxord, Martin Robertson.

GOODMAN, W. (1975), 'Integration, yes; busing, no', *The Education Digest*, vol. 41, November, p. 6.

GORDON, P. (1985), 'Police and black people in Britain', *Sage Race Relations Abstracts*, vol. 10, no. 2, pp. 3–33.

GORDON, P. (1989), *Citizenship for Some?* London, The Runnymede Trust.

GORDON, P. and ROSENBERG, D. (1989), *Daily Racism: The Press and Black People in Britain*, London, The Runnymede Trust.

GORMAN, R. M. (1977), 'Racial Antisemitism in England: the legacy of Arnold Leese', *Weiner Library Bulletin*, nos. 43–4, pp. 65–74.

GRAEF, R. (1989), *Talking Blues*, London, Collins Harvill.

GRAY, H. (1987), 'Race relations as news', *American Behavioral Scientist*, vol. 30, no. 4, pp. 381–396.

GREELEY, A. M. (1974), *Ethnicity in the United States*, London, Wiley.

GREEN, P. (1981), *The Pursuit of Inequality*, Oxford, Martin Robertson.

GRIFFITHS, T. (1982), *Oi! for England*, London, Faber & Faber.

HALL, S. (1981), 'The whites of their eyes', in G. Bridges and R. Brunt (eds), *Silver Linings*, London, Lawrence & Wishart, pp. 28–52.

HALL, S. (1980), 'Race, articulation and societies structured in dominance', in *Sociological Trends: Race and Colonialism*, Paris, Unesco, pp. 305–346.

HALL, S., CRITCHER, C., JEFFERSON, T., CLARK, J. and ROBERTS, B. (1978), *Policing The Crisis: Mugging, the State and Law and Order*, London, Macmillan.

HALLORAN, J. D. (1978), 'Mass communication: symptom or cause of violence', *International Social Science Journal*, vol. 30, no. 4, pp. 816–33.

HALLORAN, J. D. (1981), 'Preface' in B. Troyna, *Public Awareness and the Media*, London, CRE, pp. 6–9.

HALLORAN, J. D. (ed.) (1970), *The Effects of Television*, London, Panther.

HALSEY, A. H. (1982), 'Doing good by doing little', *New Society*, July, pp. 91–3.

HALSEY, A. H., FLOUD, J. and ANDERSON, C. A. (eds) (1961), *Education, Economy and Society*, London, Collier Macmillan.

HALSEY, A. H., HEATH, A. F. and RIDGE, J. M. (1980), *Origins and Destinations: Family, Class and Education in Modern Britain*, Oxford, Clarendon Press.

HALSTEAD, M. (1988), *Education, Justice and Cultural Diversity*, Lewes, Falmer Press.

HAMMER, T. (ed.) (1985), *European Immigration Policy: A Comparative Study*, Cambridge, Cambridge University Press.

HARROP, M. and ZIMMERMAN, G. (1977), 'Anatomy of the National Front', *Patterns of Prejudice*, vol. 11, pp. 12–13.

HARROP, M., ENGLAND, J. and HUSBANDS, C. T. (1980), 'The bases of National Front support', *Political Studies*, vol. 27, no. 2, pp. 271–83.

HARTE, J. (ed.) (1988), *Black People and the Media*, Warwick, London Borough of Lewisham/CRE/University of Warwick.

HARTMANN, P. and HUSBAND, C. (1974), *Racism and the Mass Media*, London, Davis Poynter.

HARTNETT, A. (ed.) (1982), *The Social Sciences in Educational Studies*, London, Heinemann Educational Books.

HATCHER, R. (1987), ' "Race" and education: two perspectives for change' in B. Troyna (ed.) *Racial Inequality in Education*, London, Tavistock, pp. 184–201.

HAYES, P. M. (1973), *Fascism*, London, Allen & Unwin.

HEATH, A. (1981), *Social Mobility*, London, Fontana.

HEBDIGE, D. (1981), 'Skinheads and the search for white working-class identity', *New Socialist*, September October, pp. 39–41.

HENRIQUES, J. (1984), 'Social psychology and the politics of racism' in J. Henriques, W. Holloway, C. Urwin, C. Venn and V. Walkerdine, *Changing the Subject*, London, Methuen, pp. 60–90.

HERRNSTEIN, R. J. (1973), *IQ in the Meritocracy*, Boston, Little Brown.

HILL, C. (1970), 'Some aspect of race and religion in Britain', in D. Martin and M. Hill (eds), *A Socilogical Yearbook of Religion*, vol. 3, London, SCM Press, pp. 30–44.

HILL, C. (1971), 'Pentecostal growth — result of racialism?' *Race Today*, vol. 3, pp. 187–9.

HIRO, D. (1973), *Black British, White British*, Harmondsworth, Penguin.

HOLMES, C. (1979), *Anti-Semitism in British Society 1876-1939*, London, Edward Arnold.

HOLMES, C. (1980), 'Anti-semitism and the BUF', in K. Lunn and R. Thurlow (eds), *British Fascism*, London, Croom Helm, pp. 114–34.

HOME OFFICE (1965), *Immigration from the Commonwealth*, (Cmnd, 2739), London, HMSO.

HOME OFFICE (1977), *Policy for the Inner Cities*, (Cmnd. 6845), London, HMSO.

HOME OFFICE (1981), *Racial Attacks*, London, Home Office.

HONEYFORD, R. (1984), 'Education and race — an alternative view', *The Salisbury Review*, winter, pp. 30–32.

HORSMAN, R. (1981), *Race and Manifest Destiny*, Cambridge, Mass., Harvard University Press.

HOUSE OF COMMONS (1981), *First Report from the Home Affairs Committee, Session 1981-2: Commission for Racial Equality*, vol. 1, London, HMSO.

HOVLAND, C. and SEARS, R. (1940), 'Minor studies of aggression', *Journal of Psychology*, 9, pp. 301–10.

HOWITT, D. and CUMBERBATCH, G. (1975), *Mass Media, Violence and Society*, London, Elek Science.

HUBBUCK, J. and CARTER, S. (1980), *Half a Chance: A Report on Job Discrimination Against Young Blacks in Nottingham*, London, CRE.

HUMPHRY, D. and JOHN, G. (1971), *Because They're Black*, Harmondsworth, Penguin.

HUSBAND, C. (ed.) (1975), *White Media and Black Britain*, London, Arrow.

HUSBAND, C. (ed.) (1987), *'Race' in Britain: Continuity and Change*, (2nd Edition), London, Hutchinson.

INSTITUTE OF RACE RELATIONS (1981), *Police Against Black People*, London, Institute of Race Relations.

JACKSON, P. (1989), *Maps of Meaning: An introduction to cultural geography*, London, Unwin Hyman.

JACKSON, P. and SMITH, S. (eds) (1981), *Social Interaction and Ethnic Segregation*, London, Academic Press.

JENCKS, C. (1972), *Inequality*, New York, Basic Books.

JENKINS, J. (1989), 'The return of "sus" ', *New Statesman and Society*, 4 August, p. 16.

JENKINS, R. (1982), 'Managers, recruitment procedures and black workers', *Working Papers on Ethnic Relations, No. 18*, Birmingham, Research Unit on Ethnic Relations.

JENKINS, R. (1986), *Racism and Recruitment*, Cambridge, Cambridge University Press.

JENKINS, R. and TROYNA, B. (1983), 'Educational myths, labour market realities', in B. Troyna and D. Smith (eds), *Racism, School and the Labour Market*, Leicester, National Youth Bureau.

JENKINS, R. and SOLOMOS, J. (eds) (1987), *Racism and Equal Opportunity Policies in the 1980s*, Cambridge, Cambridge University Press.

JENSEN, A. R. (1969), 'How much can we boost IQ and scholastic achievement?' *Harvard Educational Review*, vol. 39, no. 1, Winter, pp. 1–123.

JENSEN, A. R. (1972), *Genetics and Education*, New York, Harper & Row.

JONES, C. (1977), *Immigration and Social Policy in Britain*, London, Tavistock.

JONES, K. (1989), *Right Turn: The conservative revolution in education*, London, Hutchinson.

JONES, P. N. (1978), 'The distribution and diffusion of the coloured population in England and Wales, 1961–1871', *Transactions Institute of British Geographers*, vol. 3, no. 4, pp. 515–32.

JONES, S. (1988), *Black Culture, White Youth: The reggae tradition from JA to UK*, London, Macmillan.

JONES, T. (1981/2), 'Small business development and the Asian community in Britain', *New Community*, vol. 9. no 3, pp. 467–77.

JORDAN, W. (1974), *The White Man's Burden*, New York, Oxford University Press.

JOSEPH, SIR K. (1986), 'Without Prejudice: Education for an ethnically mixed society', *Multicultural Teaching*, vol. 4, No. 3, pp. 6–8.

KAMIN, L. J. (1977), *The Science and Politics of I.Q.*, Harmondsworth, Penguin.

KAPO, R. (1981), *A Savage Culture*, London, Quartet Books.

KATZ, I., HENCHY, T. and ALLEN, H. (1968), 'Effects of the race tester, approval-disapproval, and need on negro children learning', *Journal of Personality and Social Psychology*, no. 8, January, pp. 38–42.

KATZ, P. and TAYLOR, D. (eds) (1988), *Eliminating Racism*, New York, Plenum.

KAZUKA, W. M. (1982), *Why So Few Black Businessmen?*, Hackney, Hackney Council for Racial Equality/Hackney Business Promotion Centre/Commission for Racial Equality.

KERNER, O. *et al.* (1968), *Report of the National Advisory Commission on Civil Disorders*, Washington, US Government Printing Office.

KETTLE, M. (1981), 'The evolution of an official explanation', *New Society*, 3 December 1981, pp. 404–5.

KIERNAN, V. G. (1978), 'Britons old and new', in C. Holmes (ed.), *Immigrants and Minorities in British Society*, London, Allen & Unwin, pp. 23–59.

KILLIAN, L. (1979), 'School busing in Britain: policies and perceptions', *Harvard Educational Review*, vol. 49, no. 2, pp. 185–206.

KIRP, D. (1979), *Doing Good By Doing Little*, London, University of California Press.

KLUG, F. (1982), *Racist Attacks*, London, Runnymede Trust.

KNOPF, T. A. (1970), 'Media myths on violence', *New Society*, 12 November, pp. 856–9.

KUSHNER, T. and LUNN, K. (eds) (1989), *Traditions of Intolerance*, Manchester, Manchester University Press.

LABOV, W. (1973), 'The logic of nonstandard English', in N. Keddie, (ed.) *Tinker, Tailor... The Myth of Cultural Deprivation*, Harmondsworth, Penguin.

LAWRENCE, D. (1974), *Black Migrants, White Natives*, Cambridge University Press.

LAWRENCE, E. (1982), 'Just plain common sense: the "roots" of racism', in CCCS, *The Empire Strikes Back*, London, Hutchinson, pp. 47–94.

LAYTON-HENRY, Z. (1984), *The Politics of Race in Britain*, London, Allen & Unwin.

LEAB, E. J. (1975), *From Sambo to Superspade*, London, Secker & Warburg.

LEBZELTER, G. (1980), 'Henry Hamilton Beamish and the Britons: champions of anti-semitism', in K. Lunn and R. Thurlow (eds), *British Fascism*, London, Croom Helm, pp. 41–56.

LEE, G. and WRENCH, J. (1981), *In Search of a Skill: Ethnic Minority Youth and Apprenticeships*, London, CRE.

LEE, T. R. (1977), *Race and Residence: The Concentration and Dispersal of Immigrants in London*, Oxford, Clarendon Press.

LEVITAS, R. (ed.) (1986), *The Ideology of the New Right*, Cambridge, Polity Press.

LEWIS, O. (1967), *La Vida*, London, Secker & Warburg.

LITTLE, A. (1975a), 'Performance of children from ethnic minority backgrounds in primary schools', *Oxford Review of Education*, vol. 1, no. 2, pp. 117–35.

LITTLE, A. (1975b), 'The educational achievement of ethnic minority children in London schools', in G. K. Verma and C. Bagley (eds), *Race and Education Across Cultures*, London, Heinemann Educational Books.

LITTLE, A. and WILLEY, R. (1981), *Multi-Ethnic Education: The Way Forward, (Schools Council Pamphlet, 18)*, London, Schools Council.

LONDON RACE AND HOUSING FORUM (1981), *Racial Harassment on Local Authority Housing Estates*, London, Commission for Racial Equality.

LORIMER, D. (1978), *Colour, Class and the Victorians*, Leicester University Press.

LOWE, S. (1986), *Urban Social Movements*, London, Macmillan.

LUNN, K. and THURLOW, R. (eds) (1980) *British Fascism*, London, Croom Helm.

LYNCH, J. (1987), *Prejudice Reduction and the Schools*, London, Cassell.

MCINTOSH, N. and SMITH, D. (1974), *The Extent of Racial Disadvantage*, PEP, vol. 40, no. 547.

MCLAUGHLIN, J. E. (1988), 'Ireland and Colonialism', in E. Cashmore (ed.) *Dictionary of Race and Ethnic Relations*, 2nd edition, London, Routledge, pp. 153–155.

MCQUAIL, D. (1977), 'The influence and effects of mass media', in J. Curran, M. Gurevitch and J. Woollacott (eds), *Mass Communication and Society*, London, Edward Arnold, pp. 70–95.

MACDOUGALL, C. (1968), *Interpretive Reporting*, New York, Macmillan.

MERCER, J. R. (1972), 'IQ: the lethal label', *Psychology Today*, September, pp. 44–7; 95–7.

MERTON, R. K. (1948), 'The self-fulfilling prophecy', *Antioch Review*, vol. 8, summer, pp. 193—210.

MIAH, M. (1976), *Busing and the Black Struggle*, New York, Pathfinder Press.

MILES, R. (1982), *Racism and Migrant Labour*, London, Routledge & Kegan Paul.

MILES, R. (1987), 'Recent Marxist theories of nationalism and the issue of racism', *British Journal of Sociology*, vol. 38, no. 1, pp. 24–43.

MILES, R. (1989), *Racism*, London, Routledge.

MILES, R. and PHIZACKLEA, A. (1977), 'Class, race, ethnicity and political action', *Political Studies*, vol. 15, no. 4, pp. 491–507.

MILES, R. and PHIZACKLEA, A. (1981), 'The TUC and black workers 1974–1976', in P. Braham *et al.*, *Discrimination and Disadvantage in Employment*, pp. 246–65.

MILNER, D. (1975), *Children and Race*, Harmondsworth, Penguin.

MOONMAN, E. (1981), 'Copycat hooligans', *Contemporary Affairs Briefing*, vol. 9, no. 1, pp. 1–9.

MOORE, R. and WALLACE, T. (1975), *Slamming the Door*, Oxford, Martin Robertson.

MORELL, J. (1980), 'Arnold Leese and the Imperial Fascist League: the impact of racial fascism', in K. Lunn and R. Thurlow (eds), *British Fascism*, London, Croom Helm, pp. 57–75.

MORRISON, L. (1975), 'A black journalist's experience of British journalism', in C. Husband (ed.), *White Media and Black Britain*, London, Arrow Books, pp. 165–79.

MORTIMORE, J. and BLACKSTONE, T. (1982), *Disadvantage and Education*, London, Heinemann Educational Books.

MORTIMORE, P. and MORTIMORE, J. (1981), *Achievement in Schools III, Ethnic Minorities*, London, ILEA Research and Statistics Report.

MOSLEY, O. (1968), *My Life*, London, Nelson Books.

MOYNAHAN, B. (1976), 'The divided city', *Sunday Times Supplement*, 12 December, pp. 47–56.

MURDOCK, G. and McCRON, R. (1979), 'The television and delinquency debate', *Screen Education*, no. 30, spring, pp. 51–67.

MURDOCK, G. and TROYNA, B. (1981), 'Recruiting racists', *Youth in Society*, no. 60, November, pp. 13–15.

MYRDAL, G. (1964), *The American Dilemma*, New York, McGraw-Hill.

NASH, M. (1972), 'Race and the ideology of race', in P. Baxter and B. Sansom (eds), *Race and Social Difference*, Harmondsworth, Penguin, pp. 111–22.

NATIONAL UNION OF TEACHERS (1978), *Race, Intelligence and Education: A Teachers' Guide to Facts and the Issues*, London, National Union of Teachers.

NEUMANN, F. (1967), *Behemoth: The Structure and Practice of National Socialism*, London, Frank Cass.

NEWMAN, O. (1972), *Defensible Space*, London Architectural Press.

NEW SOCIETY (1982), *Race and Riots '81*, (New Society Social Studies Reader), London, IPC.

NEWSOM, J. *et al.*, (1963), *Half Our Future*, London, HMSO.

NICHOLSON, C. (1974), *Strangers to England: Immigration to England 1100–1945*, London, Leyland.

NORTHAM, G. (1988), *Shooting in the Dark*, London, Faber & Faber.

NORTHRUP, H. (1944), *Organized Labour and the Negro*, New York, Harper & Row.

NUGENT, N. (1980), 'Post-war fascism?', in K. Lunn and R. Thurlow (eds), *British Fascism*, London, Croom Helm, pp. 205–23.

OGBU, J. (1978), *Minority Education and Caste*, London, Academic Press.

PARK, R. E. (1952), *Human Communities*, New York, Free Press.

PARK, R. E., BURGESS, E. and MACKENZIE, R. (1923), *The City*, University of Chicago Press.

PARKER, J. and DUGMORE, K. (1976), *Colour and the Allocation of GLC Housing*, London, GLC.

PARKIN, F. (1979), *Marxism and Class Theory*, London, Tavistock.

PATTERSON, S. (1968), *Immigrants in Industry*, London, Oxford University Press.

PEACH, C. (1968), *West Indian Migration to Britain*, IRR/Oxford University Press.

PEACH, C. and SHAH, S. (1980), 'The contribution of council house allocation to West Indian desegregation in London, 1961–1971', *Urban Studies*, vol. 17, no. 3, pp. 334–41.

PEACH, C. and SMITH, S. (1981), 'Introduction' in C. Peach, V. Robinson and S. Smith (eds), *Ethnic Segregation in Cities*, London, Croom Helm, pp. 9–22.

PEACH, C., ROBINSON, V. and SMITH, S. (eds) (1981), *Ethnic Segregation in Cities*, London, Croom Helm.

PEARSON, D. G. (1981), *Race, Class and Political Activism*, Farnborough, Gower Press.

PETTIGREW, T. (1958), 'Personality and sociocultural factors and intergroup attitudes', *Journal of Conflict Resolution*, 2, pp. 29–42.

PETTIGREW, T. (1959), 'Regional differences in anti-negro prejudice', *Journal of Abnormal and Social Psychology*, 59, pp. 28–36.

PETTIGREW, T. (1964), *A Profile of the Negro American*, New York, Van Nostrand.

PHILLIPS, M. (1978), 'West Indian Businessmen', *New Society*, 18 May, pp. 354–6.

PHILPOTT, S. (1973), *West Indian Migrants: The Montserrat Case*, London, Athlone Press.

PHIZACKLEA, A. (ed.) (1983), *One-way ticket: Migration and female labour*, London, Routledge & Kegan Paul.

PHIZACKLEA, A. and MILES, R., (1980), *Labour and Racism*, London, Routledge & Kegan Paul.

PHIZACKLEA, A. and MILES, R., (1981), 'The strike at Grunwick', in P. Braham *et al.*, *Discrimination and Disadvantage in Employment*, pp. 266–74.

PHOENIX, A. (1988), 'The Afro-Caribbean myth', *New Society*, 4 March, pp. 10–13.

PLANT, M. (1970), 'The attitudes of coloured immigrants in two areas of Birmingham to the concept of dispersal', *Race*, vol. 12, no. 3, pp. 323–8.

PLOWDEN, B., *et al.*, (1967), *Children and their Primary Schools, vol. 1*, London, HMSO.

POLLACK, L. (1974), *Discrimination in Employment, the American response*, London, Runnymede Trust.

PRYCE, K. (1979), *Endless Pressure*, Harmondsworth, Penguin.

RAINWATER, L. (1966), 'Fear and the house-as-haven in the lower class', *AIP Journal*, 32, January.

RAINWATER, L. (1973), *Behind Ghetto Walls*, Harmondsworth, Penguin.

RAINWATER, L. and YANCEY, W. L. (1967), *The Moynihan Report and the Politics of Controversy (including D. P. Moynihan's The Negro Family: The Case for National Action)*, Massachusetts, MIT Press.

RAMDIN, R. (1987), *The Making of the Black Working Class in Britain*, Aldershot, Gower.

RANDEL, W. P. (1965), *The Ku Klux Klan*, London, Hamish Hamilton.

RATCLIFFE, P. (1981), *Racism and Reaction*, London, Routledge & Kegan Paul.

REES, T. (1982), 'Immigration Policies in the United Kingdom', in C. Husband (ed.) *'Race' in Britain: Continuity and Change*, London, Hutchinson/Open University, pp. 75–96.

REEVES, F. and CHEVANNES, M. (1981), 'The underachievement of Rampton', *Multiracial Education*, vol. 10, no. 1, pp. 35–42.

Report of the National Advisory Commission on Civil Disorders (1968), New York, Bantam Books.

REX, J. (1970, 2nd ed. 1982), *Race Relations in Sociological Theory*, London, Weidenfeld & Nicolson.

REX, J. (1973), *Race, Colonialism and the City*, London, Routledge & Kegan Paul.

REX, J. (1979), 'Black militancy and class conflict', in R. Miles and A. Phizacklea (eds), *Racism and Political Action in Britain*, London, Routledge & Kegan Paul, pp. 79–92.

REX, J. (1981), *Social Conflict*, London, Longman.

REX, J. (1982), 'West Indian and Asian youth', in E. Cashmore and B. Troyna, (eds), *Black Youth in Crisis*, London, Allen & Unwin, pp. 53–71.

REX, J. and MASON, D. (eds) (1986), *Theories of Race and Ethnic Relations*, Cambridge, Cambridge University Press.

REX, J. and TOMLINSON, S. (1979), *Colonial Immigrants in a British City*, London, Routledge & Kegan Paul.

REX, J. and MOORE, R. (1981), *Race, Community and Conflict*, London, Oxford University Press.

RICHARDSON, K. and SPEARS, D. (1972), *Race, Culture and Intelligence*, Harmondsworth, Penguin.

ROBBINS, D. (1981), '"Affirmative action" in the USA: a lost opportunity?', *New Community*, vol. 9, no. 3, pp. 399–406.

ROBERTS, B. (1982), 'The debate on "Sus" ', in E. Cashmore and B. Troyna (eds), *Black Youth in Crisis*, London, Allen & Unwin, pp. 100–28.

ROBINSON, V. (1980), 'Correlates of Asian Immigration: 1959–1974', *New Community*, vol. 8, no. 2, pp. 115–23.

ROBINSON, V. (1981), 'The development of South Asian settlement in Britain and the myth of return', in C. Peach, V. Robinson and S. Smith (eds), *Ethnic Segregation in Cities*, London, Croom Helm, pp. 149–69.

RODNEY, W. (1972), *How Europe Underdeveloped Africa*, London, Bogle L'Ouverture Publications.

RODRIGUEZ, C. (1989), *The Puerto Ricans: Born in the USA*, London, Unwin Hyman.

ROSE, E. J. B. *et al.* (1969), *Colour and Citizenship*, London, Institute of Race Relations/Oxford University Press.

ROSE, S. P. R. (1970), 'The environmental determinants of brain function', *Cambridge Society for Social Responsibility in Science Bulletin*, July Special Issue.

ROSENFELD, G. (1971), *'Shut Those Thick Lips'*, New York, Holt, Rinehart & Winston.

ROY, A. (1978), 'Amin's Asian Refugees Back in Business', *The Daily Telegraph*, 5 July, p. 2.

RUBINSTEIN, D. and STONEMAN, C. (eds) (1972), *Education for Democracy*, Harmondsworth, Penguin.

RUNNYMEDE TRUST and RADICAL RACE STATISTICS GROUP (1980), *Britain's Black Population*, London, Heinemann Educational Books.

RUTTER, M. and MADGE, N. (1976), *Cycles of Disadvantage*, London, Heinemann Educational Books.

SAIFULLAH KHAN, V. (1976), 'Pakistanis in Britain: perceptions of a population', *New Community*, vol. 5, no. 3, pp. 222–9.

SAIFULLAH KHAN, V. (1977), 'The Pakistanis', in J. L. Watson (ed.) *Between Two Cultures*, Oxford, Basil Blackwell, pp. 57–89.

SAMPSON, A. (1982), *The Changing Anatomy of Britain*, London, Hodder and Stoughton.

SAMUEL, R. (ed.) (1989), *Minorities and Outsiders*, London, Routledge.

SARRE, P., PHILLIPS, D. and SKELLINGTON, R. (1989), *Ethnic Minority Housing: Explanations and Policies*, Aldershot, Gower.

SARUP, M. (1982), *Education, State and Crisis: A Marxist Perspective*, London, Routledge & Kegan Paul.

SAUNDERS, P. (1981), *Sociological Theory and the Urban Question*, London, Hutchinson.

SCARMAN, THE RT HON, LORD, (1981), *The Brixton Disorders, 10–12 April 1981*, Cmnd, 8427, London, HMSO.

SCARR, S. and WEINBERG, R. A. (1976), 'IQ test performance of black children adopted by white families', *American Psychologist*, vol. 31, pp. 726–39.

SCHOEN, D. (1977), *Enoch Powell and the Powellites*, London, Macmillan.

SEIDEL, G. (1986), 'Culture, nation and "race" in the British and French New Right' in R. Levitas (ed.) *The Ideology of the New Right*, Cambridge, Polity Press, pp. 107–35.

SELECT COMMITTEE ON RACE RELATIONS AND IMMIGRATION (1975), *Employment Vol. II*, London, HMSO.

SEYMOUR-URE, C. (1974), *The Political Impact of Mass Media*, London, Constable.

SHAW, A. (1988), *A Pakistani Community in Britain*, Oxford, Basil Blackwell.

SHAW, J., NORDLIE, P. and SHAPIRO, R. (eds) (1987), *Strategies for Improving Race Relations*, Manchester, Manchester University Press.

SHULMAN, M. (1981) 'Programming of the petrol bombers', *New Standard*, 16 July, p. 7.

SILLS, A., TARPEY, M. and GOLDING, P. (1982), *Asians in the Inner City*, Centre for Mass Communication Research, Leicester University.

SIMONS, H. J. and SIMONS, R. E. (1969), *Class and Colour in South Africa, 1850–1950*, Harmondsworth, Penguin.

SINGER, A. (1978), 'The little Bengal in Brick Lane', *The Guardian*, 5 June, p. 17.

SINGH TATLA, D. and SINGH, E. (1989), 'The Punjabi Press', *New Community*, vol. 15, no. 2, pp. 171–84.

SITKOFF, H. (1981), *The Struggle for Black Equality, 1954–1980*, New York, Hill & Wang.

SIVANANDAN, A. (1981/2), 'From resistance to rebellion: Asian and Afro-Caribbean struggles in Britain', *Race and Class*, vol. 23, nos 2/3, pp. 111–52.

SIVANANDAN, A. (1982), 'Race, class and the state', in *A Different Hunger: Writings on Black Resistance*, London, Pluto Press.

SKIDELSKY, R. (1981), *Oswald Mosley*, London, Macmillan.

SMITH, D. (1977), *Racial Disadvantage in Britain*, Harmondsworth, Penguin.

SMITH, D. (1981), *Unemployment and Racial Minorities* (PSI No. 594), London, Policy Studies Institute.

SMITH, D. J. and GRAY, J. (1985), *Police and People in London: the PSI Report*, Aldershot, Gower.

SMITH, S. J. (1989), *The Politics of 'Race' and Residence*, Cambridge, Polity Press.

SMITH, T. E. (1981), *Commonwealth Migration: Flows and Policies*, London, Macmillan.

SMITHIES, B. and FIDDICK, P. (1969), *Enoch Powell on Immigration*, London, Sphere Books.

SOLOMOS, J. (1988), *Black Youth, Racism and the State*, Cambridge, Cambridge University Press.

SOUTHGATE, P. (1982), 'The disturbances of July 1981 in Handsworth, Birmingham: a survey of the views and experiences of male residents' in S. Field and P. Southgage, *Public Disorders*, London, Home Office Research Study No. 72, pp. 41–73.

SREBRNIK, H. (1978), 'Star Wars: Racism as science fiction?', *Canadian Jewish Outlook*, May, pp. 10–11.

STONE, M. (1981), *The Education of the Black Child in Britain: The Myth of Multiracial Education*, London, Fontana.

SUMMERS, A. and WOLFE, B. (1977), 'Do schools make a difference?' *American Economic Review*, vol. 67, September, pp. 639–52.

SYER, M. (1982), 'Racism, ways of thinking and school', in J. Tierney, (ed.) *Race, Migration and Schooling*, London, Holt Education, pp. 86–107.

TAYLOR, F. (1974), *Race, School and Community*, Berkshire, NFER.

TAYLOR, M. (1981), *Caught Between: A Review of Research into the Education of Pupils of West Indian Origin*, Berkshire, NFER-Nelson.

TAYLOR, S. (1978), 'Racism and youth', *New Society*, 3 August, p. 249.

TAYLOR, S. (1981a), 'Riots: Some explanations', *New Community*, vol. 9, no. 2, pp. 167–72.

TAYLOR, S. (1981b), 'The far right fragments', *New Society*, 28 March 1981, pp. 538–9.

TAYLOR, S. (1982), *The National Front in English Politics*, London, Macmillan.

THACKARA, J. (1979), 'The mass media and racism', in C. Gardner (ed.) *Media, Politics and Culture*, London, Macmillan.

THAYER, G. (1965), *The British Political Fringe*, London, Blond.

THERNSTROM, S., ORLOV, A. and HANDLIN, O. (eds) (1980), *Harvard Encyclopedia of American Ethnic Groups*, Cambridge, Mass., Harvard University Press.

THOMPSON, K. (1988), *Under Siege: Racial Violence in Britain Today*, Harmondsworth, Penguin.

THURLOW, R. C. (1980), 'The return of Jeremiah: the rejected knowledge of Sir Oswald Mosley in the 1930s', in K. Lunn and R. Thurlow (eds), *British Fascism*, London, Croom Helm, pp. 100–13.

TIERNEY, J. (ed.) (1982), *Race, Migration and Schooling*, London, Holt, Rinehart & Winston.

TIGER, L. (1969), *Men in Groups*, New York, Random House.

TOBIAS, P. V. (1972), 'The meaning of race', in P. Baxter and B. Sansom (eds), *Race and Social Difference*, Harmondsworth, Penguin, pp. 19–43.

TOMLINSON, J. (1981), *Left, Right: The March of Political Extremism in Britain*, London, John Calder.

TOMLINSON, S. (1980), 'The educational performance of ethnic minority children', *New Community*, vol. 8, no. 3, pp. 213–34.

TOWNSEND, H. E. R. and BRITTAN, E. (1973), *Multiracial Education: Need and Innovation*, (Schools Council Working Paper 50), London, Schools Council.

TRACEY, M. and TROYNA, B. (1979), 'What could the BBC do about the NF?', *Broadcast*, 30 April, pp. 12–14.

TRADES UNION CONGRESS (1981), 'Race relations at work', in P. Braham *et al.* *Discrimination and Disadvantage in Employment*, London, Harper & Row, pp. 275–9.

TRADES UNION CONGRESS (1989), *Tackling Racism*, London, TUC.

TROYNA, B. (1980), 'The media and the electoral decline of the National Front', *Patterns of Prejudice*, vol. 14, no. 3, pp. 25–30.

TROYNA, B. (1981), *Public Awareness and the Media: A Study of Reporting on Race*, London, Commission for Racial Equality.

TROYNA, B. (1982a), 'The ideological and policy response to black pupils in British Schools', in A. Hartnett (ed.), *The Social Sciences in Educational Studies*, London, Heinemann Educational Books, pp. 127–43.

TROYNA, B. (1982b), 'Reporting the National Front: British values observed', in C. Husband (ed.), *'Race' in Britain: Continuity and Change*, London, Hutchinson, pp. 259–78.

TROYNA, B. (1988), 'Paradigm regained: A critique of "cultural deficit" perspectives in contemporary educational research', *Comparative Education*, vol. 24, no. 3, pp. 273–283.

TROYNA, B. and SMITH, D. (eds) (1983), *Racism, School and the Labour Market*, Leicester, National Youth Bureau.

TROYNA, B. and CARRINGTON, B. (1990), *Education, Racism and Reform*, London, Routledge.

TUMBER, H. (1982), *Television and the Riots*, London, British Film Institute.

TWITCHIN, J. (ed.) (1988), *The Black and White Media Show Book*, Stoke, Trentham Books.

TYLER, W. (1977), *The Sociology of Educational Inequality*, London, Methuen.

US BUREAU OF THE CENSUS (1980), *Statistical Abstract of the United States*, Washington, DC, Government Printing Office.

US COMMISSION ON CIVIL RIGHTS (1967), *Racial Isolation in the Public Schools*, Washington, DC, Government Printing Office.

VAN DEN BERGH, P. (1978), *Race and Racism*, New York, John Wiley.

VAN DIJK, T. A. (1987), *News Analysis*, Hove, Lawrence Erlbaum.

VAN DIJK, T. A. (1989), *Communicating Racism*, Newbury Park, Ca., Sage.

VERMA, G. K. (ed.) (1989), *Education for All: A Landmark in Pluralism*, Lewes, The Falmer Press.

VERMA, G. K. and BAGLEY, C. (1975), *Race and Education Across Cultures*, London, Heinemann Educational Books.

WAGLEY, C. and HARRIS, M. (1958), *Minorities in the New World*, New York, Columbia University Press.

WAIND, A. (1981), 'Asian girls: a shelter from fear', *New Society*, 3 December, pp. 418–19.

WALKER, M. (1977), *The National Front*, London, Fontana.

WALVIN, J. (1971), *The Black Presence*, London, Orback & Chambers.

WARD, R. (1977/78), 'The American experience: parallels and development' (Book Review), *New Community*, vol. 6, nos 1 & 2, pp. 170–1.

WARD, R. and JENKINS, R. (eds) (1984), *Ethinic Communities in Business*, Cambridge, Cambridge University Press.

WARD, R. and REEVES, F. (1980), *West Indians in Business in Britain: Submission to Home Affairs Committee Race Relations and Immigration Sub-Committee (Racial Disadvantage)*, London, HMSO, 15 December.

WATSON, J. L. (ed.) (1977), *Between Two Cultures*, Oxford, Basil Blackwell.

WATSON, P. (1972), 'Can racial discrimination affect IQ?', in K. Richardson *et al.* (eds), *Race, Culture and Intelligence*, Harmondsworth, Penguin.

WATSON, P. (ed.) (1973a), *Psychology and Race*, Harmondsworth, Penguin.

WATSON, P. (1973b), 'Race and intelligence through the looking glass', in P. Watson (ed.), *Psychology and Race*, Harmondsworth, Penguin, pp. 260–76.

WEIR, S. (1978), 'Youngsters in the Front line', *New Society*, 27 April, pp. 189–93.

WELLS, B. W. P. (1980), *Personality and Heredity*, London, Longman.

WHALE, J. (1970), 'News', *The Listener*, 15 October, p. 510.

WILLIAMS, F. (1989), *Social Policy: A critical introduction*, Cambridge, Polity Press.

WILLIAMS, J. (1967), 'The younger generation', in J. Rex and R. Moore, *Race, Community and Conflict*, London, Oxford University Press.

WILLIAMS, J. (1979), 'Perspectives on the multicultrual curriculum', *The Social Science Teacher*, vol. 8, no. 4, pp. 126–33.

WILLIAMS, J. (1985), 'Redefining institutional racism', *Ethnic and Racial Studies*, vol. 8, no. 3, pp. 323–348.

WILKINSON, P. (1981), *The New Fascists*, London, Grant-McIntyre.

WILSON, E. O. (1975), *Sociobiology: The New Synthesis,* Cambridge, Mass., Harvard University Press.

WILSON, W. J. (1976), *Power, Racism and Privilege,* New York, Free Press.

WILSON, W. J. (1987), *The Truly Disadvantaged: The inner city, the underclass and public policy*, Chicago, University of Chicago Press.

WIRTH, L. (1938), 'Urbanism as a way of life', *American Journal of Sociology*, vol. 44, July, pp. 1–24.

WIRTH, L. (10th ed., 1969), *The Ghetto*, The University of Chicago Press.

WRIGHT, P. (1968), *The Coloured Worker in British Industry*, London, Oxford University Press.

YEBOAH, S. K. (1988), *The Ideology of Racism*, London, Hansib.

YOUNG, M. (1965), *The Rise of Meritocracy 1870–2033*, Harmondsworth, Penguin.

ZANDEN, W. V. (1960), 'The Klan revival', *American Journal of Sociology*, vol. 65, no. 5, March, pp. 456–62.

ZUBRZYCKI, J. (1956), *Polish Immigrants in Britain*, The Hague, Nijhoff.

Other Books by the Same Authors

Cashmore

Making Sense of Sport

United Kingdom? Class, Race and Gender since the War

Dictionary of Race and Ethnic Relations

The Logic of Racism

Having to: The World of One Parent Families

No Future: Youth and Society

Approaching Social Theory (with Bob Mullan)

Black Sportsmen

Rastaman

Troyna

Education, Racism and Reform (with Bruce Carrington)

Children and Controversial Issues (with Bruce Carrington)

Racial Inequality in Education

Racism, Education and the State (with Jenny Williams)

Racism, School and the Labour Market (with Douglas Smith)

Public Awareness and the Media: A Study of Reporting on Race

Cashmore and Troyna are the editors of Black Youth in Crisis

Name Index

Subject Index

Title Index